Paths of Revolution

Paths of Revolution

Selected Essays

Adolfo Gilly

Edited with an Introduction by Tony Wood
Translated by Lorna Scott Fox

VERSO

London • New York

First published by Verso 2022
Translation of Chapter 1 © Félix Gutiérrez 2022
Translation of Chapter 3 © Bobbye Ortiz 2022
Translation of Chapter 4 © Tony Wood 2022
Translation © Lorna Scott Fox 2022
Introduction © Tony Wood 2022
Most of these essays appear here in English for the first time.
Details of earlier publication can be found in the acknowledgments.

1 3 5 7 9 10 8 6 4 2

Verso
UK: 6 Meard Street, London W1F 0EG
US: 388 Atlantic Avenue, Brooklyn, NY 11217
versobooks.com

Verso is the imprint of New Left Books

ISBN-13: 978-1-83976-500-1
ISBN-13: 978-1-83976-507-0 (US EBK)
ISBN-13: 978-1-83976-506-3 (UK EBK)

British Library Cataloguing in Publication Data
A catalogue record for this book is available from the British Library

Library of Congress Cataloging-in-Publication Data

Names: Gilly, Adolfo, author. | Wood, Tony, editor. | Fox, Lorna Scott,
    translator.
Title: Paths of revolution : selected essays / Adolfo Gilly ; edited with
    an introduction by Tony Wood ; translated by Lorna Scott Fox.
Description: London ; New York : Verso Books, 2022. | Includes
    bibliographical references and index.
Identifiers: LCCN 2022025064 (print) | LCCN 2022025065 (ebook) | ISBN
    9781839765001 (paperback) | ISBN 9781839765070 (ebk)
Subjects: LCSH: Latin America—Politics and government—1948- |
    Insurgency—Latin America—History—20th century.
Classification: LCC F1406.8 .G55 2022 (print) | LCC F1406.8 (ebook) | DDC
    980.03/3—dc23/eng/20220527
LC record available at https://lccn.loc.gov/2022025064
LC ebook record available at https://lccn.loc.gov/2022025065

Typeset in Minion Pro by MJ & N Gavan, Truro, Cornwall
Printed in the UK by CPI Group (UK) Ltd, Croydon, CR0 4YY

Contents

Introduction

Tony Wood

Adolfo Gilly has lived many lives: leftist militant, journalist, political prisoner, public intellectual, historian. At times, these roles have overlapped; at others, remained distinct. But in each of them, he has been a direct observer of key events in Latin American history, from the Cuban Missile Crisis to Central America's guerrilla movements of the 1960s, and from Mexico's Zapatista uprising of 1994 to the indigenous and popular mobilizations that swept Evo Morales into power in Bolivia in the early 2000s. In that sense, Gilly provides a living link—across the tumult of several decades—between the postwar generations of the Latin American left and the radical upsurges accompanying the "Pink Tide."

More than simply testifying to these developments, he has been among the Latin American left's sharpest analysts of them, producing a body of work that spans the realms of reportage, commentary, historical scholarship, and the literary essay. Yet to date, only two of Gilly's books and a scattering of essays have been published in English. In the Anglophone world, he is perhaps best known for his landmark history of the Mexican Revolution, *La revolución interrumpida* (The Interrupted Revolution, 1971)—written in a jail cell in Mexico City's Lecumberri Prison, where Gilly was confined from 1966 to 1972.[1]

This volume presents Gilly to English-language readers in his full breadth for the first time. Drawing from across his oeuvre, it showcases

---

1   Published in English as *The Mexican Revolution* (London: New Left Books, 1983; rev. ed. New York: New Press, 2005).

his remarkable range: it includes close-quarters reportage from Cuba, Chile, and Guatemala; historical syntheses on the long trajectories of insurgency in Mexico and Bolivia; sharp political analyses of the global fate of revolution in the twentieth century; and literary essays and theoretical reflections.

Though the subjects and forms of these texts vary considerably, there are some threads that remain present throughout. First, Gilly consistently emphasizes the active, shaping role played by mass action from below—whether by urban workers in La Paz, peasant armies in Morelos, or indigenous movements in Chiapas. He is always attentive to popular political consciousness in moments of revolt, emphasizing the moral rage against injustice that often drives mobilizations more than any pre-formed ideological program. Second, Gilly analyzes closely the regime of domination against which popular forces are rebelling. In Latin America, these have historically combined capitalist exploitation with colonial forms of social and racial oppression, a palimpsest of indignities that Gilly foregrounds in his historical work in particular. Third, while the earlier texts in this selection were written by Gilly in his role as a militant, overall, his work displays a remarkable capacity for self-critical reflection, soberly assessing the strengths and weaknesses of the left at a given moment. Finally, the essays bring out his broad culture, his ready curiosity and constant openness to influences and ideas. Scattered throughout them, too, are grace notes of his characteristic humor and self-deprecating irony.

Born Adolfo Malvagni Gilly in Buenos Aires in 1928, he would eventually adopt his mother's surname as his nom de plume.[2] His father, Atilio Malvagni, was a former lieutenant in the Argentine navy and a lawyer who drafted the country's maritime navigation law in the 1950s. His mother, Delfa Esther Gilly, was from a family of French-descended landowners (Gilly is one of the names inscribed on the Arc de Triomphe). Both parents transmitted a love of culture to Adolfo and his two sisters, Delfa and Graciela, taking them to operas and concerts at the Teatro Colón and encouraging them to read widely; Gilly recalls devouring works by Cervantes, Dante, Alexandre Dumas, and Jules Verne in his father's library. Fittingly, one of his earliest jobs kept him close to the world of print: working at a printshop, he corrected proofs and set type with a Linotype press.

---

2   Biographical data in this paragraph and the following are derived from conversations between the author and Gilly; this includes an interview published as "'What Exists Cannot Be True,'" *New Left Review* 64, July–August 2010, pp. 29–46.

Gilly came to political consciousness in the 1940s. In 1946, the same year Juan Domingo Perón rose to power on the back of mass support from the Argentine working classes, Gilly joined the Juventud Socialista, the youth wing of the Argentine Socialist Party. But the following year, he left the party after the leadership shut down the student newspaper *Rebeldía* for its "leftism." He and others formed a short-lived Workers' Revolutionary Movement (Movimiento Obrero Revolucionario, MOR) before gravitating, at the end of the 1940s, toward the Trotskyist Fourth International (FI).

Gilly's militancy in the ranks of the Fourth International—his nom de guerre was "Lucero"—would shape the rest of his personal and political trajectory, sending him from Buenos Aires to the Bolivian altiplano and from revolutionary Havana to the jungles of Guatemala. He aligned himself with the current within the FI led by Homero Cristalli, better known under his pseudonym "J. Posadas." Posadas later gained notoriety for his domineering manner, his sectarian maneuvering, and his eccentric views (for example, on UFOs). But it was Posadas's reading of Latin American realities and his view of the revolutionary potential of anti-imperialist movements that appealed to Gilly. Reflecting on his reasons for joining the FI, Gilly recalled that in the late 1940s, other parts of the Argentine left tended to see Perón either as an agent of British imperialism or as "some sort of snake charmer with a flute" who had bewitched the masses. Posadas, by contrast, had argued that "Peronism was the specific form that the organization of the working class took in our country, and we had to understand it . . . the workers may have been following a charismatic leader, but they did so for their own reasons."[3] This early impulse to interpret popular politics on its own terms would recur throughout Gilly's work.

It was the Latin America Bureau of the FI, controlled by Posadas, that sent Gilly to Bolivia in 1956, in the heady period after the country's National Revolution of 1952. Trotskyism occupied an unusually prominent place in the Bolivian political landscape compared to the rest of Latin America, with the Revolutionary Workers' Party (Partido Obrero Revolucionario, POR) acquiring a mass working-class following and exerting a strong influence on the powerful miners' unions. The four years Gilly spent there, as he recounts in the 2003 interview that appears as Chapter 12 of this volume, introduced him to a world of Andean indigenous traditions and peasant politics that was entirely new to him. It was

---

3   Ibid., pp. 30–1.

also in Bolivia that he began writing for the Uruguayan leftist weekly *Marcha*, for whom he would continue to produce reportage thereafter, including the account of a day spent with Salvador Allende in 1964 reproduced here as Chapter 2.

Gilly spent the years 1960–62 in Europe, working as a representative of the FI's secretariat and based mostly in Italy. This was a time of significant shifts in the nature of industrial labor; as he later put it: "More important than the political questions which preoccupied the main currents of the left were the very real changes that were taking place in the factories."[4] The "hot autumn" of 1969 was still a few years off, but Gilly recalls seeing the beginnings of the workers' councils and the autonomist movement. It was also a contentious time within the FI, as strategic differences over the relative importance of proletarian revolution in Europe versus national and anticolonial revolutions in the "Third World" led to an internal split. The two currents were led, respectively, by Ernest Mandel and Michel Pablo; Gilly movingly recalls what divided and united the two in a remembrance of Mandel included here as Chapter 14. Mandel ultimately remained at the head of the FI, but Gilly's sympathies with the "Pabloite" view clearly informed much of his later work: "As I see it now," he observed in 2010, "it is the revolt of the colonial world that gives the twentieth century its meaning."[5]

The Cuban Revolution was a transformative event for the Latin American left as a whole, seeming to provide a new model for a radical convergence between anti-imperialism and socialism. Sent to the island by the FI in 1962, Gilly liaised there between the Latin America Bureau and Cuba's Trotskyist currents, a marginal but vocal presence within the broader Cuban revolutionary coalition—nestling awkwardly alongside Stalinists and Fidel Castro's 26 July Movement. Gilly's reports from the island—extracts appear here in Chapter 1—convey his enthusiasm for the revolution's early radical thrust and its capacity to mobilize the populace. But he also draws attention to the growing strength of bureaucratic tendencies. Trotskyist criticisms along these lines drew the anger of Fidel Castro, and in October 1963, amid a wider crackdown on leftist dissenters, Gilly was arrested and expelled from Cuba. The quarrel between the Cuban government and the Trotskyist movement would have lingering repercussions. In October 1965, Gilly analyzed Che Guevara's resignation of his government posts as a defeat for the Cuban Revolution's left

4   Ibid., p. 36.
5   Ibid., p. 39.

wing.[6] This view was angrily rejected by Fidel Castro, who made a point of denouncing Gilly by name when he attacked left critics of the Revolution in his speech at the end of the Tricontinental Conference in February 1966.

Between 1964 and 1966, Gilly was integrally involved in one of Latin American Trotskyism's closest engagements with a guerrilla movement, the Guatemalan Revolutionary Movement of November 13 (Movimiento Revolucionario 13 de Noviembre, MR-13). Formed in 1960 by progressive Guatemalan army officers who opposed the dictatorship of Miguel Ydígoras—most notably its decision to allow the US to train anti-Castro fighters on Guatemalan soil—the MR-13 took a decisive leftward turn in late 1963, adopting socialism as its formal goal and aligning itself with the Fourth International. For the next two years, militants of the Mexican Revolutionary Workers Party (Trotskyist) (Partido Obrero Revolucionario [Trotskista], POR[T]), would be incorporated into its ranks.[7]

Gilly served as the liaison between the guerrillas and the FI while also writing for *Marcha*, moving between Guatemala, Mexico, and other Latin American countries. On one such trip in May 1965 he traveled to Colombia, where he met the radical priest Camilo Torres Restrepo. Gilly recollects their meeting in Chapter 4, which includes extracts from the profile of the priest he published in *Marcha* in early 1966, after Torres was killed in a clash with the Colombian armed forces.

Gilly also produced reportage on the MR-13's struggle. Written in early 1965, the extracts reproduced in Chapter 3 depict the MR-13 as a highly committed and politicized force, as well as memorably evoking the everyday realities of the guerrillas' lives. But the note of optimism running through Gilly's account would soon prove tragically unfounded: in April 1966, the MR-13—partly under pressure from Cuba—expelled the Trotskyists even as it came under sustained assault from Guatemalan

6   Gilly, "La renuncia del Che" [1965], in *La senda de la guerrilla* (Mexico City: Editorial Nueva Imagen 1986), pp. 41–9.

7   Partido Obrero Revolucionario (Trotskista), POR(T): formed in 1959 by the majority who split from the student group Juventud Socialista; accepted as the Mexican section of the Fourth International in 1961; integrally involved in the 1968 student strike in Mexico; active until the late 1970s. On the alliance between the POR(T) and the MR-13, including some discussion of Gilly's role, see Verónika Oikión Solano, "Un encuentro decisivo en la encrucijada revolucionaria: La influencia del PORT en el MR-13," in Alberto Martín Alvarez, ed., *La izquierda revolucionaria latinoamericana* (Colima: Universidad de Colima, 2010), pp. 51–89. See also Carlos Mignon, "Adolfo Gilly, el movimiento trotskista y la revolución socialista en América Latina," in Daniel Gaido et al., eds., *Historia del Socialismo Internacional: Ensayos marxistas* (Santiago: Ariadna Ediciones, 2020).

government forces. Several of Gilly's comrades were killed or disappeared in the harsh repression that followed. A decade later, Gilly would write an unsparing critical analysis of the Guatemalan experience, pointing to failings shared with other guerrilla movements in Latin America in the 1960s—above all, a marked voluntarism and "lack of knowledge, theoretical or practical, of the role of the working class."[8] But the main weight of his criticism was directed at the Trotskyist movement rather than the guerrillas of the MR-13, whose commitment and dedication he continued to uphold.

Gilly fled Guatemala for Mexico in April 1966. Barely two weeks after his arrival, he was arrested and jailed along with several comrades. He spent the next six years in Lecumberri Prison, the "Black Palace" that now serves as Mexico's national archive. (Back in the late 1960s, Gilly mischievously noted, "It was me who had been archived."[9]) In the wake of Mexico's 1968, when government forces gunned down protestors in Tlatelolco, many more political prisoners joined Gilly and his comrades in Lecumberri. Chapter 5 reproduces extracts from his unsuccessful appeal hearing in 1969, where he denounced the repressive rule of the Partido Revolucionario Institucional (Institutional Revolutionary Party, PRI).[10] He recalled the atmosphere among the "politicals" in N-Block as being "almost like a monastery," and he read widely and voraciously: the entire Marx–Engels correspondence, Hegel, the poetry of Octavio Paz, among countless others. But the project that consumed much of his time was his landmark history of the Mexican Revolution, *La revolución interrumpida*.

Inspired by the example of Trotsky's *History of the Russian Revolution*, which he reread in prison, Gilly sought to establish "the inner impetus behind the movements of the masses—not who won which battle but what the hell all these people wanted."[11] Gilly also sought to establish the "curve of the revolution": its internal evolution across a convulsive decade, from the disintegration of the ancien régime of Porfirio Díaz in 1910–11 to the ascendancy in 1914 of the peasant armies of Emiliano Zapata in the south and Pancho Villa in the north, followed by the gradual

8   Adolfo Gilly, "Guerrilla, programa y partido en Guatemala (crítica retrospectiva de una derrota)," *Coyoacán*, no. 3, April–June 1978; also in *La senda de la guerrilla*, pp. 109–30.

9   Gilly, "'What Exists Cannot Be True,'" p. 39.

10   In 1929, Mexico's post-revolutionary rulers established the political party that would govern Mexico for the rest of the century; it adopted the name Partido Revolucionario Institucional in 1946.

11   Gilly, "'What Exists Cannot Be True,'" p. 41.

defeat of those popular insurgencies; Zapata was eventually assassinated in 1919, Villa in 1923. Gilly lucidly represented the maelstrom of Mexico's revolutionary years as a clash between contending social forces, driven by conflicting aspirations and visions of the country's future—a set of contradictions crystallized in the Constitution of 1917.

Published in 1971, while Gilly was still in Lecumberri, *La revolución interrumpida* remains unrivaled as a single-volume social history of the Mexican Revolution. It offered a counter to official narratives, in which, as Gilly put it, "Everyone was a good guy, and it was totally unclear why they all ended up killing each other."[12] At the same time, it ran against the tide of revisionist studies that had begun to appear in the wake of 1968, and that sought to undermine the revolution as the founding myth of PRI rule. Gilly recuperated the original social impetus behind the Revolution, the popular struggles that had been "interrupted" as per the book's title, without thereby legitimating the one-party state that had been its outcome.

Released from prison in March 1972, he spent four years in Europe, again working for the FI but growing increasingly disillusioned with the Posadists. "The atmosphere was conspiratorial, sectarian and rigid," he recalled: "I had felt much freer in prison."[13] He returned to Mexico in 1976 and settled there for good, gaining Mexican citizenship in 1982. From 1979 onwards he taught in the Department of Political and Social Sciences at the Universidad Nacional Autónoma de México (UNAM), and established himself as a prominent voice on the country's left, intervening in debates as a scholar and public intellectual. The scale and scope of Gilly's work increased as he addressed an ever-wider variety of themes and ranged further back into Mexico's past to explain its present; hence the bulk of the essays in this volume date from after the 1990s.

At the end of the 1980s, with the PRI's legitimacy ebbing after years of debt crises and corruption, a broad social and political coalition emerged in support of the 1988 presidential campaign of Cuauhtémoc Cárdenas, son of former president Lázaro Cárdenas. Running against the PRI's Carlos Salinas, Cárdenas was robbed of victory only by blatant fraud. Gilly had been among the first on the left to back Cárdenas's campaign, and in 1989 took part in the foundation of the Party of the Democratic Revolution (Partido de la Revolución Democrática, PRD). He was also an advisor to Cárdenas when the latter was elected governor of Mexico

12   Ibid.
13   Ibid., p. 42.

City in 1997, though he took his distance from the PRD as it veered increasingly toward the center.

Fittingly, it was during this interval that Gilly produced his book on the presidency of Lázaro Cárdenas.[14] Published in 1994, it depicted *cardenismo* as a final attempt to fulfill the promises of the Mexican Revolution, emphasizing the motivations that drove ordinary Mexicans to invest their hopes in the left-populist president. (Chapter 8 of this volume gives a capsule version of his arguments.) In a sense, Gilly was also returning to the concerns of his youth: it was his reading of Trotsky's analyses of Cárdenas, written during the Bolshevik leader's Mexican exile in 1938, that had helped draw the eighteen-year-old Gilly to the Fourth International.[15]

In the Mexico of the 1990s, it was not neo-*cardenismo* that revived the buried energies of the Mexican Revolution but the rebellion of the Zapatistas in Chiapas. On 1 January 1994—the day the North American Free Trade Agreement negotiated by Salinas and Clinton came into force—the predominantly indigenous troops of the Zapatista Army of National Liberation (Ejército Zapatista de Liberación Nacional, EZLN) seized the city of San Cristóbal and launched an insurgency that would electrify Mexican politics. Gilly was again a prominent early supporter, meeting with the EZLN in May 1994 and writing a study of the Chiapas rebellion; excerpts from it appear here as Chapter 9.

In his work on the Zapatistas, Gilly sought to bring out the deep legacies of indigenous oppression that gave rise to the rebellion. His engagement with that longer history was informed not only by the work of Mexican historians and anthropologists such as Guillermo Bonfil Batalla, but also by lessons drawn from a broader historiography, especially work by the Subaltern Studies school on resistance to British colonial rule in India. Chapter 7, depicting Mexico as a "Subaltern Civilization," reflects these twin influences. The same combination of historical depth and comparative sweep also informed his assessment of the indigenous and popular revolts in Bolivia in the early 2000s. As Chapters 10 and 11 show, the mobilizations that eventually took Evo Morales to power were propelled both by immediate reactions against neoliberal rule and by longer traditions of collective resistance.

Much of Gilly's work in recent decades has been historical in nature, the product of a distinguished scholarly career that has seen him invited

---

14   Adolfo Gilly, *El cardenismo. Una utopía mexicana* (Mexico City: Ediciones Era, 1994).

15   Gilly, "'What Exists Cannot Be True,'" p. 32.

for stints as visiting professor at Chicago, Columbia, NYU, Stanford, Yale, and the National Humanities Center (twice). As well as the books on the Mexican Revolution and *cardenismo* noted above, he has also written a monograph on the "Ten Tragic Days" of February 1913, which culminated in the deposition and killing of the Mexican president, Francisco Madero, by US-supported military dictator Victoriano Huerta.[16] In 2019, Gilly's magisterial biographical study of the Mexican revolutionary general Felipe Ángeles was published to widespread acclaim.[17] He has also engaged with thinkers from a range of times and places, producing a suite of essays in 2006 that drew on the historical ideas of Antonio Gramsci, Walter Benjamin, Karl Polanyi, E. P. Thompson, Guillermo Bonfil Batalla, and Ranajit Guha as keys for understanding the history of Mexico and of Latin America more broadly.[18]

Yet historical scholarship represents only one facet of Gilly's activities. Chapters 13 to 17 comprise essays in which he reflects on the broader fate of the left in the twentieth century, and on the global transformations wrought by the neoliberal turn. Moreover, no selection from Gilly's oeuvre would be complete without drawing attention to his literary and artistic interests, which have been a constant feature since his teenage encounters with the work of the Surrealist André Breton and the novels of Herman Melville, among many others. In numerous essays, he has written about an array of figures whose work has impacted upon him, from Argentine poets Alejandra Pizarnik and Juan Gelman to the eighteenth-century Italian artist Giovanni Battista Piranesi.[19] Part IV of this selection includes four essays that highlight this dimension of Gilly's writing. In Chapter 18 we see Gilly trace the interconnections between André Breton and Octavio Paz, while in Chapter 19 he offers a thoughtful engagement with Peruvian novelist and anthropologist José María Arguedas. Chapter 20 addresses the work on race and modernity of Ecuadorean-born philosopher Bolívar Echeverría, a longtime colleague of Gilly's at UNAM, while the final chapter contains Gilly's reflections on

---

16 Adolfo Gilly, *Cada quien morirá por su lado. Una historia militar de la Decena Trágica* (Mexico City: Ediciones Era, 2013).

17 Adolfo Gilly, *Felipe Ángeles, el estratega* (Mexico City: Ediciones Era, 2019).

18 Adolfo Gilly, *Historia a contrapelo. Una constelación* (Mexico City: Ediciones Era, 2006).

19 Among Gilly's numerous essay collections, see in particular *Nuestra caída en la modernidad* (Mexico City: Boldó i Climent, 1988); *Pasiones cardinales* (Mexico City: Cal y Arena, 2001); *El Siglo del relámpago. Siete ensayos sobre el siglo XX* (Mexico City: Editorial Itaca, 2002); *Historia a contrapelo* (2006); *Historias clandestinas* (Mexico City: Editorial Itaca, 2009); and with Rhina Roux, *El tiempo del despojo* (Mexico City: Editorial Itaca, 2015).

the historian's craft, in dialogue with Marc Bloch and Walter Benjamin. As well as demonstrating Gilly's broad range of interests, the essays in this final section also bring to the fore his capacity to put ideas into dialogue across time and space—to form, as the subtitle of one of his books puts it, a constellation.[20]

The present volume can do no more than offer a sample of Gilly's considerable output. The goal has been to provide a selection that is representative of his thought and his experiences, across a series of very different phases in Latin America's political development and in Gilly's individual trajectory. An observer of radical mobilizations from the 1950s to the present, in his writings he has sought to trace their lineages back through decades or even centuries, identifying what is genuinely new while at the same time pointing to deep continuities—and always with an eye on the substance of popular politics, on what drives people to action under different forms of domination. As well as testifying to Gilly's singular personality and lifelong political and intellectual engagement, then, the essays gathered here also hope to convey a sense of the integrity—in both senses of the word—of Latin America's revolutionary traditions.

---

20   Gilly, *Historia a contrapelo.*

Part I

Witnessing Revolution

1

Cuba in October

(1964)

Gilly lived in Cuba from mid-1962 to late 1963, representing the Fourth International's Latin American Bureau. His nuanced view of the island in the early 1960s—celebrating the role of mass popular mobilization but with a wary eye on conservative tendencies within the Revolution—is evident in the following edited extracts from his reports on the Revolution's early years, first published in English as a special issue of the New York–based Marxist journal Monthly Review *in October 1964.*

"To Arms!" A red poster showing a civilian holding a machine gun on high and three words in large white letters, "¡A Las Armas!," appeared on all the streets of Havana on Tuesday, October 23, 1962. For eighteen hours, Cuba had been on a war footing. Kennedy had issued his threat of invasion and Fidel Castro had called a general mobilization.

The poster—one color, three words, one gesture—summed up the instantaneous reaction of the Cuban people. From that moment until the end of the October crisis, these people were the protagonists of one of the great moments of this century.

It was as if a long-contained tension relaxed, as if the whole country had said as one: "At last!" The long wait for invasion, the war of nerves, the sneak attacks, the landing of spies, the blockade—all this was past. Now was the hour of struggle and everyone threw themselves into it, body and soul.

It is difficult to imagine the harmony, the unanimity, the fervor that a people can reach in such moments. All of Cuba said: "To arms," and took them up. Journalism, propaganda, bureaucratic slowness, routine—all that was put aside. Cuba was one man and his rifle.

On the 23rd, the army and all the militia were mobilized. The combat companies of the militia started for the interior. The companies for popular defense spread out across Havana. Many thousands of men and women who until then had not been in the militia, volunteered and started training. Cuba was a military camp on a war footing.

For all of Cuba had a collective goal: to face the invasion and defend the Revolution that was in danger. And in those crucial days the Cuban people learned things about themselves that they had not known before.

There was not the slightest fear or alarm. Alarmism is an expression of insecurity and fright, and it shows itself in a thousand ways: one reaction, for example, is to rush to buy supplies for the family. But in Cuba there was none of this. It simply did not occur to anyone to think about himself or his family as something separate from the collective destiny. In the face of the direct, immediate threat of invasion by the most powerful military nation in the world only ninety miles away, who on this little island of seven million was going to dash for groceries?

All individualism, all family interests, all private solutions were annulled and absorbed by the magnitude of the approaching struggle. But it was more than that: in Cuba at that time, as at other great moments in history, the whole population had a common objective. They saw everything clearly; the struggle was defined and stripped to its essentials; petty politics were brushed aside, and all was clean and pure: our rifles against theirs. When a people sees the world at gunpoint, it looks clear and simple.

The Cuban Revolution is a daily fervor. Despite internal problems and privilege-seekers, despite those who try to set themselves over the workers, despite the counterrevolutionaries disguised as bureaucrats, revolutionary fervor still permeates life in Cuba and lends its tone and color to everything. Even after five years of revolution. But during the October days, that fervor attained a purity free of all dross. The best facets of the human soul—generosity, fraternity, equality—cast their undimmed light on the struggle and the Revolution, and the whole country, facing annihilation, put aside all that is limited, private, egoistical, and separate from the collective destinies of the country and all humanity. Cuba lived those days not as a country which defends its own existence but as a part of humanity fighting for its future. And it lived them to the full. No one ever will be able to erase that experience from the memory and soul of the Cuban people, nor from those of humanity.

On October 26 and 27, Havana reached its point of greatest tension. Several government leaders were with the army in the interior of the country. The attack was expected on the 27th; Havana calculated that the first bombardment was due on the afternoon of that day. It was remarkable to see the city, practically defenseless against a mass aerial attack, wait tensely yet calmly while going about its business. I walked around Havana that morning. Nowhere were there signs of alarm or fear. Paradoxically, only the supposed beneficiaries of the invasion, the counterrevolutionaries, had disappeared or were paralyzed: they had nothing to defend and no way to fight; they could only wait. At one of the more important ministries, I was able to talk to one of the few important functionaries who were there to attend to urgent matters. "We expect the attack this afternoon between three and four," he told me. It was eleven in the morning. In the elevator, one militiaman said to another that he had not shaved that morning. "It seems it may come at any moment. You won't shave now until after the war." That day the whole country lived in the same climate.

Only on the 29th did Cuba learn of the agreement between Kennedy and Khrushchev. The daily *Revolución* announced it with a headline on page one: "Khrushchev orders missiles withdrawn from Cuba." It also printed the text of the letters between Khrushchev and Kennedy, unknown until then in Cuba, and the cables of the news agencies from the start of the crisis until its denouement, which likewise had not been published by the Cuban press in the previous days. It was obvious that the publication was not done on the personal initiative of the paper's director, Carlos Franqui, but on that of the prime minister [Fidel Castro], who in this way defined for the people the degree of his responsibility for negotiations in which he had not participated.

The reaction was instantaneous. That morning, in every corner of Havana, groups commented indignantly on the withdrawal of the missiles. "Why didn't they consult us, since we were the ones who were going to die?" I heard one say. "They betrayed us, like in Spain," I heard another. Furious because Cuba had not been consulted and the missiles had been withdrawn without a fight, people everywhere protested. In Havana, popular opinion always expresses itself during crucial moments in similar, almost identical phrases and arguments: simultaneously, from one end of the city to the other, as if a conference had been held or a signal given. And yet neither the press, the radio, nor government leaders had uttered a word about this. They had limited themselves to telling the news and gauging the reaction.

At street corners, factories, the university, people analyzed the published cables line by line and Khrushchev's letters word by word. It was impressive to see such unanimity, without previous discussion or previous agreement; no one approved of Khrushchev's calling Kennedy "respected president," or his saying that "you and I well know what atomic war means." "Right, and we, we here staking our lives, we don't know it, and that's why they didn't consult us!" I heard this comment many times, similarly phrased.

All the tension, all the heroism displayed by the Cuban people in the previous days now turned into a solid wall of protest against the withdrawal of the missiles. There were meetings at the University of Havana and rallies on the university grounds. In trenches, factories, state farms, and cities, everyone waited for the official statement from Fidel Castro, announced for the first of November. Fidel Castro personally walked around the streets and meeting places of Havana on the 29th and 30th and visited groups in the trenches. The protests and pressures he heard firsthand were everywhere the same.

In a section committee of the Committees for the Defense of the Revolution (the neighborhood organizations of revolutionary citizens, organized by blocks and then by sections), I listened to the explanations offered by a government propaganda team to the section leaders. In summary, a man asserted that the agreement was a triumph, that Kennedy had been forced to promise that he would not invade Cuba, and that Khrushchev's position had saved the peace and inflicted a defeat on imperialism. Those present listened with faces full of skepticism. The speaker added that it was necessary to explain all this to the people and undo the disaster which *Revolución* had provoked by so bluntly publishing the news that Khrushchev had ordered the withdrawal of the missiles. That this information was true and that the paper had, for once, done no more than comply with an elementary duty toward the news did not seem to bother the speaker who, in the best manner of a functionary of any state anywhere, attributed the reaction of the masses to the "maneuvers" of a few "confusionists."

I remember that only one person stood up to support the speaker. He was an old man. "These are problems of high politics," he said, "that are beyond our comprehension. The explanation of this compañero is just, and we should accept it and transmit it. I remember very well that when the pact between Stalin and Hitler was signed, the same thing happened. Many compañeros did not understand and tore up their party cards. And, nevertheless, that was an act of high politics that enabled the Soviet Union to be better prepared for the Nazi attack." The old communist had just repeated with complete ingenuousness the old explanation abandoned long ago; in other words, he mentioned the rope in the home of the hanged. If others present did not seem to know a great deal about what lay behind the German–Soviet pact, their faces showed that in any case they were not much in agreement with the Kennedy–Khrushchev pact.

Thousands of meetings like this were held all over Cuba. The Cuban people were duly informed, and it was explained and illustrated how the withdrawal of the missiles was a correct and wise measure, and that only counterrevolutionaries, confusionists, and divisionists could be opposed to it. At many meetings, the audience listened in silence. At others, they asked questions that were highly embarrassing to the intermediaries sent to repeat the explanations that they themselves had been given, and of which, it must be said, many were not even half convinced themselves. Whenever they were stumped, the answer was: "Well, we'll have to wait and see what Fidel says."

The people waited to hear what Fidel would say. But it did not wait in a vacuum. It waited with an opinion already collectively formed, firm as a stone, with the conviction that Fidel had also come to the same opinion. A massive pressure—invisible but everywhere tremendously present—was exerted on the revolutionary government and Fidel Castro between October 29 and 31: there had to be protest over the withdrawal of the missiles.

When Fidel Castro spoke and said that there were differences with the Soviet government, there was no doubt that he could not have said anything less, and that this was the minimum statement he could make in response to popular pressure. All Cubans were glued to television sets in homes, public places, and in every headquarters of the Committees for Defense [of the Revolution]. Castro's statement provoked a unanimous outburst in front of those television sets. The same scene, repeated hundreds and thousands of times all over the island: "There it is! We said it ourselves!" The same faces that had listened silently to all the explanations for the withdrawal of the missiles and of Khrushchev's "wisdom," or that had simply expressed doubt, now lit up joyfully: "Fidel says we were right!" They felt they had defeated the whole apparatus and all the "explainers," all the intermediaries and leaders who had arrogated to themselves the right to represent them.

With the withdrawal of the missiles, Khrushchev's standing with the Cuban people fell sharply. They have no means of expressing this change of feeling and that is why the outer forms seem to be maintained. But not a single portrait of Khrushchev is hung anywhere in Cuba except on the initiative of the apparatus, and the portraits of Mao Tse-tung that have appeared everywhere were certainly not the apparatus's idea. It is a way of saying: Since I cannot remove Khrushchev's portrait, I will hang Mao Tse-tung's beside it. And whenever an excuse can be found, Khrushchev's disappears. What is more, from that moment of October 29, popular verses were born and circulated with dizzying speed across Havana and all over the island, all aggressively opposed to Khrushchev for withdrawing the missiles.

When, weeks later, the missiles finally left Cuba, and their long, unmistakable silhouettes passed by on trucks, there were places on the roads of Pinar del Río where the population turned out into the streets to stop the convoy. "*Tovarisch*," they said to the Soviet soldiers, "why are you taking them away? Why are you leaving? You have to stay and defend Cuba." The soldiers answered that these were their orders and tears ran down their faces.

Later, when trucks passed through Havana full of Soviet soldiers in civilian clothes who were departing for good with their suitcases, I saw women, men, and children in the street wave goodbye to them, at once surprised and moved, some with tears in their eyes.

When Fidel Castro, on November 15, 1962, spoke against the flight of North American planes over Cuba, he ended his speech with the statement that Cuba would never be defeated "so long as there remains a single man, woman, or child in this land." He was not expressing a mere personal conviction but a decision the Cuban people had collectively taken, in the deepest recesses of their minds and hearts, during the years of the Revolution, and irrevocably confirmed in those historic days of October.

It is not the relations between men and things (property) that have changed most in Cuba; it is the relations between men themselves. When private capital accumulation was abolished in Cuba, with it went property as a goal of human life, inheritance as its continuer, and family egoism as an exclusive sentiment opposed to social solidarity.

This did not happen all at once. Cuban men and women were born under capitalism. Yet you find that Cubans now frequently look at themselves and comment on how much their thoughts, their mutual relations, and their scale of social and individual values have changed.

It has not been four years since capitalism disappeared from Cuba. But already no Cuban—and I refer to the Cuban people, not to that tiny vestigial minority whose eyes are still on the capitalist past and its lost privileges, real or imaginary—even fleetingly thinks of a sugar cane plantation or a factory or a ship as something that can belong to one person or to a group of persons rather than to society. In Cuba, the very idea of this type of private property now appears illogical and unnatural.

For the maintenance and functioning of private property, more than those "detachments of armed men" that constitute the state are needed to defend it. Its defense, and indeed the very functioning of repressive groups, are based on the acceptance of private property by the majority. When the Revolution tore down the old state and nationalized the means of production, a new concept was formed and affirmed by all, for they have seen that the economy can still function, that private property is not necessary, and that the fruits of production are common property simply because of their social function. In turn, social life is now organized around collective property. The meaning of the state and of the people's relation to the state changes, for it now defends the property that belongs to all, instead of the property that formerly belonged only to some. Just as feudal servitude, which was once "the natural order of things," is today unacceptable to the human mind in capitalist countries, so private ownership of a factory or plantation is unacceptable, even unimaginable, to a contemporary Cuban.

At the same time, the newly conquered world is not stable. On Havana's horizon looms the permanent silhouette of a United States warship, watching the port, a reminder of the blockade and the constant threat of invasion, a reminder that what has been conquered is still in danger. The sense of defense, of being always on alert, the sense of living at war and defending one's life, is present in every minute of a Cuban's life, in each act of social life.

The warship is not the only hostile presence. Cuba must build and thrive. It must do business, export and import, and do it in a world where capitalism exists and is economically strong. Even in its commerce with the socialist countries, which are its major partners, Cuba must trade at world market prices and on the basis of exchange relations that are essentially capitalist relations. By this means, capitalism—the old regime—tries to penetrate and influence and modify the new life. That Cubans view the economy as a battleground is not just a propaganda slogan: it is part of the struggle to defend their new, social, regime.

Until now, the battle has apparently been a defensive one. But in the minds of the Cuban people, neither military defense nor the economy are separate from politics. In fact, politics dominates everything. And politics is first of all international. At that point, the battle stops being defensive. The intense feeling of involvement Cubans have with the revolutionary struggles of other countries arises from the feeling that they are defending their own revolution, as well as from their daily realization that the world is one, and that the Cuban Revolution can only survive by advancing abroad. Subject to commercial relations with the capitalist countries or with socialist countries fundamentally on the basis of world market prices, the Revolution is weak. Sustained by the extension of the Revolution to other countries, by the prospect of new socialist revolutions, the Revolution feels itself to be strong.

That is why, blockaded though it is, Cuba does not have the psychology of a blockaded or isolated country. There is no basis for comparison with the situation of the Soviet Union in the 1920s. Not only because a whole system of socialist countries now exists, but primarily because the forces that maintain the Cuban Revolution—the world revolution—are generally on the offensive. That is the other part of daily life in Cuba: on the one hand, there is no private property; on the other, Cuba forms part of a revolution that is ongoing and can only end by triumphing in the whole world.

As it happens, the Revolution has given only minor material advantages to a great part of the Cuban population. Conversely, it has brought them problems and difficulties that did not exist before. But that is not how revolutions are weighed. What matters is that the Revolution has given the people a new feeling, which can be summed up as equality. This sentiment is in part a confidence in their own security, now and in the future. Security is no longer identified with owning property or a savings account but with the existence and continuance of the socialist revolution, collective property, and social organization. The increase in the birth rate in the midst of the uncertainty that the blockade, rationing, and the threat of invasion and atomic bombing could be expected to inspire, is a reflection of this new feeling of security. Such a feeling springs also from the people's having seen their own forces in action; from their everyday, firsthand discovery of what millions all over Cuba are capable of, not only at Playa Girón [the Bay of Pigs] but in terms of daily organization and work. The new social relations also contribute to this new sense of security.

The Revolution and the workers' state unite the Cuban people. But within this unity the social revolution continues, not only with regard to the forms of conducting the Revolution but also concerning the social and political relations between the state and the Revolution. The attitude toward equality is one of the touchstones of this struggle.

The word *compañero*, for example, is an expression of social fraternity and of equality. This word sounds as fresh in Cuba as it might sound in a trade union in the middle of a great strike. In Cuba, however, it is everywhere: compañero [or compañera] is the official who greets you, the bus driver, the waitress at a coffee shop, the attendant at a retail store, or the man in the street whom you stop to ask the time. Everyone you talk to or who talks to you is a compañero.

The word is not a formality. It underlines the social fraternity, the common objective, the struggle, and the singular enemy that unites everyone. In Cuba, compañero and *camarada* (comrade) are currently used without any difference in meaning. But camarada has a more emphatic, warmer sound, depending on the case, and it gives a more intense accent to a relationship. It is not so much the old communist militants who have adopted the use of camarada as, in the main, the militant new youth of the Revolution.

The use of compañero stands for equality in dealing with one another and, above all, for fraternity and commonality of goals, and this equality is observed and held dear by the people in all social situations. More important than living better or eating better—there is no eating *more*—is this major victory of the Revolution, this feeling of being equal to everyone else. This defense of equality in behavior is one form of defense by the masses of their right to participate and decide in the Revolution: to decide their own destinies. This equality is not a concession from above; it is an imposition from below.

The aspiration toward equality as the basis for social functioning establishes a daily scale of values completely different from that of a capitalist country. The psychology of that comfortable middle class, who keep track of the latest automobile model or TV set purchased by the neighbors so as to buy a better one themselves, no longer exists, for the Revolution has swept it away. Social importance or social values in the community are no longer measured by property. On the contrary, many who do have such privileges try to disguise or conceal them. The individual and social preoccupation with such possessive competitiveness has been redirected toward collective revolutionary goals. This fountain of human energy is inexhaustible, and it is still far from being exploited to its fullest, even by the Cuban leadership. Yet it is on this energy that the strength and solidity of the leadership is based when it faces its enemies; and the leaders themselves demonstrate that they know and understand this, at least to some degree, when they defend egalitarian measures and attitudes.

For example, the disappearance of commercial advertising alone spares everyone an enormous amount of mental energy. No longer are any roads or streets or television screens or walls plastered with appeals to buy this or that product. The companies that once directed the attention and social preoccupations of the petty bourgeoisie or the labor aristocracy toward buying their products have disappeared. Should some hypothetical company wish to sell some hypothetical car, it would not, given the social psychology of present-day Cuba, base its advertising on the prestige and distinction of owning the latest luxury model, as the whole society is opposed to this.

It must be emphasized that this is not solely determined by collective property. The Revolution, alive and in motion, is also responsible. In Czechoslovakia, where only collective property exists, the effects of material incentives and the wide disparities of salary and social status show up, among some sectors of officialdom, in symbols of authority and prestige that are a direct reflection of capitalism—for example, in different models of automobiles. There, it is unnecessary to disguise or justify one's privileges; the state justifies them (although the Czech workers, for their part, hold the same opinion of privilege and equality as the Cubans). In Cuba, the living Revolution prevents this and enables the sentiment of the masses to impose its own scale of values; its pressure does not allow consolidation of, or lend official status to, forms of inequality as though they were normal, acceptable, or desirable.

The Revolution, with the austerity of an army in the field, continues to be the dominant line of Cuban society. This line is imposed from below against those privilege-seeking tendencies that try to find support in the Cuban state, in the influence of capitalism around the world, but above all, in the organization of the state in other socialist countries where a bureaucratic stratum, while defending the workers' regime, officially sanctions inequality within it.

By means of the blockade, the government of the United States has tried to keep the development of the Cuban economy from influencing Latin America and, at the same time, to bring about the downfall of Fidel Castro's government or encourage opposition to him. But the blockade has had two effects. On the one hand, it has set up a barrier to prevent some Cuban influences from seeping out. But this barrier works both ways, so that it has, on the other hand, stopped capitalism from establishing a more solid alliance with the conservative, bureaucratic sectors of the Revolution—as it has managed to do to some extent in Yugoslavia and Poland—and from making its influence felt inside the Revolution itself.

For this reason, numerous leading figures of North American imperialism recently recommended, in view of the failure of the economic blockade, establishing relations of "coexistence" with the island. This is not merely an acknowledgment of failure; it is also a search for more efficient methods of influencing the Revolution from inside.

Rationing and food shortages, for example, cause big daily problems for the Cuban people. But far from weakening the Revolution, in a certain sense this helps to fortify it internally. No one wants rationing or considers it desirable. Yet, once established as a necessity, rationing strengthens the most radical tendencies of the Revolution, the tendencies that want equality; and it weakens the tendencies that are sensitive to capitalist influence.

Equality in eating is one more form of militant egalitarianism. The awareness that what is on one's table each day is on everyone's table, that what is lacking for one is lacking for all, is a strong element in fostering internal unity. Only the Revolution has been able to achieve this result. It has achieved it at practically every level, for a top state functionary's meals are subject to the same rationing as those of a worker or an office employee. If this is not absolutely the case—there are also restaurants where you can pay to eat more than average—it is, at any rate, the dominant trend.

The ration card is not only a testimony to scarcity. The Revolution has converted it—something impossible with any other type of rationing—into a testament to equality in difficult times. The people defend it as a guarantee of equality in distribution. That is why a slogan as apparently elementary as "Everyone eats the same," launched by Fidel Castro when rationing was established, found an immediate echo among the people and was later adopted in many other situations in which privilege or inequality were being combated.

The word "bureaucrat" has become commonplace in Cuba. But not everyone ascribes the same meaning to it. The leaders of the Revolution —particularly Che Guevara—have conducted campaigns against bureaucracy and have criticized bureaucrats. They give the term an administrative meaning that refers to unnecessary paperwork and to the functionaries who delay work, needlessly prolong proceedings, and make the operation of the state machinery cumbersome. "Bureaucrat" in this context means much the same as it does in capitalist states.

Popular parlance, however, gives the words "bureaucrat" and "bureaucracy" a wider meaning. The "bureaucrat" is the functionary who takes advantage of his job to enjoy special privileges, who hangs on to his position with declarations of revolutionary fervor and uses intimidating methods to fend off criticism. This meaning, more precise from a Marxist point of view than the administrative sense, has not been taught in any school or in any Marxist manual circulating in Cuba (all translations of which are mass-produced in the Soviet Union), for in these schools and these manuals, "no such animal exists." But the people have learned from daily experience that bureaucracy and bureaucrats are not simply administrative facts but social and economic phenomena.

The term used is not always "bureaucrat." The workers also call them, for example, "the ones with the briefcases," because they always arrive in a great hurry with a briefcase under one arm, supposedly containing very important documents; they glance at the people working and leave again with the same haste. "The ones with the briefcases" is an allusion to an unproductive social group who, along with other special privileges, have that of deciding and leading in matters where the masses should be taking the initiative. The hostility of this and other such expressions is a form of social struggle inside the Revolution, a struggle for equality and for the right to decide.

The Cuban masses—at home, at work, in the street—criticize privilege, look for ways to combat it, maintain constant vigilance, and present an enduring obstacle to the consolidation of a privileged social stratum.

At the same time, they unanimously and violently reject all criticism from anyone who is outside the Revolution or against it. For equality and privilege are internal problems of the Revolution. They have nothing to do with, and cannot be compared to, what occurs in the capitalist world. Any attempt by opponents of the Revolution to make use of these [internal] criticisms is immediately repudiated. Thus, the people will staunchly defend against an enemy the same leader whom they criticize and spurn at home. Here is a traditional attitude of the working-class movement, applied at the level of a whole nation. That is why the counterrevolutionary radio stations in Miami have absolutely no echo in Cuba, not only because of the lies they broadcast but also because they come from the enemy.

But none of this denies the social struggle for equality inside Cuba. On the contrary, this struggle is one of the most vital elements of the Revolution and one of its domestic motors. Equality refers not only to standards of living or salaries. It also refers to the very essence of what a revolution is, in Cuba or anywhere else: the right of the people to decide their own destiny. The excessive influence of leaders, the impossibility of voicing criticisms in the press, the violent reaction of functionaries to revolutionary criticism, the lack of decisive elective bodies of the masses (committees, councils, soviets empowered to decide not just this or that limited aspect of municipal affairs but the basic issues of state policy)— all these are viewed as assaults on equality and on the equal right of all to give their opinions and to decide. And it is impossible to separate this concept of equality, equality in living conditions, from social behavior or any other aspect of social life.

The dialectic of equality is not confined to Cuba. In fact, it is interwoven with the same dialectic in other socialist countries. The conditions are not the same in all, but their interdependence is close. Those sectors protecting their privileges in the Soviet Union or in Poland are not at all keen to see socialist democracy or social equality exist so fully in Cuba today. This kind of an example would find fertile ground in the population of other socialist countries, whose enthusiasm for Cuba is based partly on the image the country offers of an extension of socialism, and partly on the degree to which there is a truly fresh and lively socialist democracy at work in the Cuban Revolution.

But nor are the enemies of the Cuban Revolution interested in seeing this regime succeed. The widest possible participation of simple workers and farmers in the leadership of the Cuban state, freedom of speech, equality throughout social life—all this would also have an enormous impact on the populations of capitalist countries. Even in the United States, it would disprove the many untruths and calumnies told about Cuba. On these issues, the interests of the North American government and the Soviet Union coincide, though for different reasons.

This is why, as we noted above, the advocacy of "coexistence" and trade with Cuba is not simply a confession of failure but also a search for new ways to influence the Revolution from inside. A leading sector of the capitalist world has reached the conclusion that the alternative is not to overthrow the government of Fidel Castro and re-establish capitalism but to neutralize the Revolution. And to do so before the blockade becomes totally futile, they have to lean on the conservative forces within the Revolution itself.

This basic struggle is present, tacitly or obliquely, in all internal discussions and disputes, and its outcome will be decisive for the future of the Revolution. Whoever denies this dialectic, to paint a picture of the Cuban Revolution without shading or lacunae, is providing cover for local conservative forces in allegiance with pro-capitalist forces, and holding back the development of the Revolution. That is why the propagandistic writings of many so-called friends of the Revolution, who refuse to discuss its truly rich dialectic or who deny it, are biased. Such writing works against the Cuban Revolution, for it prevents its partisans—the millions of workers, farmers, students, and intellectuals who stand up for it throughout the world—from learning and intervening with their opinions and their strength to give a boost to those sectors and trends that want to carry forward the Cuban Revolution, not to neutralize it or slow it down.

2

Chile: A Day with Allende

(1964)

Gilly was in Chile for much of 1964, reporting for Marcha *magazine in Montevideo. That July, he spent a day on the campaign trail with Salvador Allende, who was running for president in the elections due in September of that year. A Socialist senator at the time, Allende had been health minister in 1939–42 and had run unsuccessfully for president twice before, in 1952 and 1958. This third attempt, as the candidate of the Frente de Acción Popular (Popular Action Front, FRAP)—a coalition between Socialists, Communists, and centrists—would also end in defeat, but Allende's 39 percent of the vote provided a platform for his eventual victory in 1970.*

It is nine o'clock in the morning, and cold outside. Through the big glazed door giving onto the courtyard garden, the day looks gray. I'm in Salvador Allende's living room, waiting to accompany him on the day's scheduled visits to several factories and the Santiago market. Glass shelves mounted in the recess of a window display row upon row of translucid Chinese carvings in ivory, jade, and semi-precious stones. Under the glass lid of the table in the middle of the room are some books: an Italian edition of Neruda's *Twenty Poems*; modern painting books; copies of *Paris que j'aime* and *Versailles que j'aime*; a *Paris Match* with John XXIII on the cover. And an Italian edition, in Spanish, of Neruda's *Sumario*, crafted in the Piedmontese village of Alpignano by master printer A. Tallone and bearing a handwritten dedication from the author that ends, "To my chief and friend, with 1964 and victory."

Our departure being delayed, I wander from the Chi Pai-Shih on the wall to the empty bottle of Vino Gran Reserva still sitting on the dining room table, next to three coffee cups, vestiges of after-dinner conviviality. Then Allende appears and asks me to wait in the library, he won't be long. That's better: I leave off peering at the Andean pottery in the dining room and undertake a quick survey of the tall bookcases. The two LPs on top of the pile by the record player are a Juliette Gréco and an Edith Piaf.

But the most expressive faces are the eleven photos—not counting the one of Tencha de Allende, smiling on a pair of skis—that preside over the library side by side.[1] I note: Pedro Aguirre Cerda, president of Chile thanks to the mandate won by the Frente Popular in 1938, under whom Allende served as a minister; Arturo Alessandri, Aguirre Cerda's predecessor and father of the current incumbent; Che Guevara; Fidel Castro having lunch with Allende in his office, with a dedication and a date, February 1959; Francisco Julião and his family; Nicolás Guillén ("To Tencha, without Salvador, 1961"); Eleanor Roosevelt; Manuel Rojas.[2] Hung a little higher than the others, a picture of Raúl Castro with Allende. Beside it, but bigger, a portrait of Mao Tse-tung.

At ten o'clock the phone calls and the rapid morning visitors are done, and we set off in a truck driven by one of the campaign managers. Ahead of us goes a jeep equipped with loudspeakers. There are three of us in the vehicle, with no special escort. We're going to a shoe factory.

"They did it to Kennedy ..."

Julio Durán crops up in our conversation. The leader of the Radical Party made some comments a few days ago accusing President Alessandri and his ministers of favoring, through his passivity, the reinforcement of communism. He also charged [Eduardo] Frei with "injecting the body of the nation with morphine," lulling it with hopes of legal buffers against the communist threat embodied in the Frente de Acción Popular (FRAP).[3] Meanwhile, the communists were supposedly preparing a violent assault

1   [Hortensia Bussi de Allende (1914–2009): Allende's wife, known as "Tencha."]

2   [Francisco Julião (1915–99): Brazilian lawyer, closely involved with the Peasant Leagues in the late 1950s; state and federal deputy for the Brazilian Socialist Party from 1952 to 1964. Nicolás Guillén (1902–89): Cuban Communist poet, head of the Cuban National Writers' Union from 1961 until his death. Manuel Rojas (1896–1973): Chilean leftist writer and journalist.]

3   [Eduardo Frei (1911–82): Christian Democrat, winner of the 1964 election, serving as Chilean president until 1970.]

on power, involving the invasion and looting of Santiago by a "rabble" from the outer slums.

"Durán represents the ultras," Allende says. "His position is clearly pro-coup. He's a desperate man, making appeals the way Lacerda did before the coup against Goulart.[4] He wants to play the role of Lacerda in Brazil. But he's not bold enough to be a Lacerda."

"So, what does Durán plan to do?" I ask.

"Did you read Olivares's piece in last night's *Última Hora*? It's a good explanation."

Augusto Olivares, Allende's press secretary, observed with regard to Durán's statements: "The very same language was used in Brazil on the eve of the coup d'état that put an end to Goulart's constitutional path. The selfsame procedure was deployed in the Dominican Republic, enabling foreign interests, the military, the oligarchs, and the Catholic Church to overthrow President Juan Bosch. The same system worked in Honduras, Ecuador, and Argentina. It's a proven tactic, now coming to Chile via the oratory of Julio Durán." And Olivares notes something more than oratory in all this: "According to information from a reliable source, the members of a group called Chile Libre (Free Chile), the origin of whose funds is not known, has been infiltrating diverse social organizations with the aim of 'militarizing' them, turning them into shock brigades." He concludes that Durán's words contain "a veiled threat, and the warning of a coup d'état."

"Is there any connection between that and the rumors about your health?" I ask Allende.

The week before, Durán's press officer announced on the radio that Allende had suffered "a hemiplegic attack" and would have to withdraw from the race. Santiago was shaken by rumors for forty-eight hours after this allegation, whose only basis was a bout of laryngitis suffered by the FRAP candidate.

"The whole hoo-ha around my supposed illness was sinister. I was said to be disabled, or at death's door. Which also betrays certain desires. Don't you think there are people assessing the possibility of eliminating me? If they got rid of Kennedy, imagine over here . . . I can't go around with an armed guard, and I don't want to. Here we are, just the three of us, as you can see. Though it wouldn't be very difficult. On all these tours,

---

4 [Carlos Lacerda (1914–77): Brazilian right-wing politician, governor of Guanabara state, who had called for US intervention in Brazil prior to the April 1964 military coup. João Goulart (1919–76): Brazilian president from 1961 until his removal by the coup.]

they treat me to drinks, they press in from every side. A drop of poison
or a tiny needle, job done. There are modern methods now."

"Not that modern," I say. "Poison or stabbing have long traditions.
The Kennedy killing was newer."

"It was all they could do to reach a president of the United States, a
highly protected man. But I'm not going to have someone taste everything before I do."

"All the same, any attack on you at this moment would spark an uprising throughout the country. That acts as a restraint, as well."

"No doubt it does," says Allende. "But what would happen? The same
as happened to Gaitán in 1948: a *Bogotazo*.[5] Those behind the assassination can then aim their machine guns at the people to keep them down.
Of course, the aftermath is unpredictable, that's why they're afraid."

"The right talks up a crisis in the FRAP. Do you think there is a crisis
in the coalition that supports Frei?"

"Of course. The Conservatives and Liberals are furious at being sidelined by Frei, who never invites them to any political events or puts them
beside him on a podium. They are working for him halfheartedly. They
disagree on many topics, too, including Cuba. The Christian Democrats
are against intervention, whereas the Conservatives advocate sanctions.
There are Liberals who support me, now. 'Allende is a responsible man,'
they say. And some Conservatives have decided to leave their people
free to vote as they please. Besides, the situation in the countryside has
changed. The Curicó election showed that Conservatives and Liberals no
longer control the campesino vote, on which they think they can rely.[6]
It's no longer a matter of a landowner having this many campesinos on
his *fundo* and therefore this many votes in his pocket. Our strength in
the countryside is growing steadily."

It's not only the Conservative Party and the Christian Democrats who
are divided over the Cuban question. The day after this conversation
with Allende, Julio Durán's Radical Party, fiercely anti-Cuban though it
is, backed the principle of nonintervention.

5   [Jorge Eliécer Gaitán (1898–1948): Colombian left-populist politician whose
assassination in the country's capital triggered a wave of unrest known as the "Bogotazo."
The event marked the start of a decade-long civil conflict commonly referred to as "la
Violencia."]

6   [A reference to the March 1964 congressional by-election held in Curicó in
central Chile, which the FRAP candidate won with 39.5 percent of the vote.]

Shoe Factories

While we were talking, the truck crossed the Mapocho River and entered the first factory of the day, a shoe factory with 800 workers, whose trade-union leadership is largely Allendist.

Allende tours the various sections. He greets everyone, shakes hands and more hands. If someone looks at him unsmilingly, he puts out his hand and they shake it. ("See how I extracted the greetings, my journalist friend?" he said to me later, amused.) The walls and machines are plastered with Allende pictures, posters, and insignia. *Allendismo* is obviously on top. However, some Frei supporters have joined forces ahead of the FRAP candidate's visit by putting up a smattering of Frei posters and portraits on other walls and machines. Shortly after, under a light drizzle, the candidate begins his speech. The workers in their leather tanners' aprons stand in the courtyard, listening gravely. The female workers are clustered around Allende on the steps.

"In the people's government, the government will be you," Allende says. "You will govern through the parties that make up the Frente de Acción Popular and the Central Única de Trabajadores [Trade Union Federation, CUT]. In nationalized companies, the workers, along with the white-collar employees and technicians, will be represented on the management board. In private companies, like this one, they will form commissions to cooperate in management. This also suits the business owner: for example, it's in his interests for workers to be aware, in a given situation, that the company's economic condition does not allow for the presentation of too high a list of demands. The commissions will be useful there, too."

We leave for the next factory. I ask Allende: "Will your government implement workers' self-management in nationalized companies, as other campaign leaders have suggested?"

"It will be as I laid out in my speech. It's one form of self-management. But not in private companies."

"Will a proportion of the profits be shared among the workers? Will it be like self-management in Yugoslavia or Algeria?"

"We have to look into that. But it won't be like Yugoslavia. My government will not be socialist, but transitional. For instance, there's no reason to nationalize a shoe business like the one we just saw. What we need to do is create purchasing power and an internal market for it to develop. And tackle the dearth of foreign currency. Nationalizing resources now in the hands of foreign capital: copper, iron, saltpeter;

nationalizing credit, and carrying out agrarian reform, will bring in more foreign currency, expand the internal market, and give us the financial means to stimulate development."

The workforce is gathered in the yard of the second shoe factory. There are 300 workers here. The union president, greeting Allende from an improvised podium, explains the problems facing them: "We're only working three or four days a week. It's piecework, not a fixed wage, which makes for a very tough situation. We're fighting to resolve it in our list of demands." Other workers outline other issues.

"In this country," Allende responds, "seventy percent of rural children go barefoot. We have to raise purchasing power for a factory like this to run at full capacity and provide more jobs for everyone. This will be your task in government. The CUT will be represented in the National Economic Council, the government, the Central Planning Office, and the autonomous bodies."

In the Market

La Vega Central is Santiago's market, where farm produce arrives from all over to serve the city. As with every market, its resident characters are diverse, colorful, unruly, and exuberant: vendors, porters, hangers-on. Our welcome mirrors the market itself—unruly and exuberant, a wave of enthusiasm expressed in shouting, laughing, pushing, a mad crush as everyone tries to get closer to Allende.

When we reach the flower market, Allende pauses outside the door. The human tide at his heels, crying "Allende, Allende," might overturn all the displays. "Just a minute!" he announces through the megaphone. "We must look out for the stalls of our compañeras the florists. You all wait here. Nobody goes in! You stay there because I'm the boss!" Laughter, clapping, redoubled cries of "Allende! Allende!" Then Allende walks in. He is followed by everyone else, casually, but taking the utmost care not to damage the blooms. Such is the compromise solution that has been reached.

The flower sellers have set up a table with champagne. Allende is offered a glass; I am offered another. He sips. I wait a while, watching him. No visible effects. "Good," I think, "no deadly powders this time, either." I down mine without fear. Chile makes excellent champagne. Then we walk through the market, jostled and shoved all the way. In the center, Allende makes a speech to an approving, elated crowd that seems to be on holiday.

Pekingese Interlude

The tour will resume in the afternoon. We stop for lunch with four of Allende's entourage: two socialist men, one socialist woman, and the leader of the candidate's Women's Commando, married to a "Pekingese" (the local name for a pro-Chinese communist).

"There are three thousand CIA agents in Chile right now," one of the socialists tells me. "A Mormon mission has appeared in the Villa Alemana, near Valparaíso. Before they did any preaching, they installed a high-power transmitter."

"Why do you suppose they come?" I ask. "To encourage the use of peaceful means?"

"Here the peaceful means will only last until the election," he said. "The critical period comes after that, between victory at the polls and the handover on November 4. If not then, when the nationalization of natural resources begins. Sooner or later, they will resort to violence, and we'll have to respond. There can be no peaceful revolutionary change or peaceful revolution because the bourgeoisie won't accept it. Sooner or later, they'll react."

None of the four disagree. The socialist woman says to me: "You know there are two tendencies over here, those who believe in peaceful means and those, like me, who don't. Sometimes I get carried away on the podium, and I feel them tugging at the hem of my coat to tone it down."

"They tugged at the hem of Jaime Barros's coat, too . . ." I say with a grin.

Jaime Barros is the Communist senator who attacked the Church in the Senate on June 23, pulling no punches: "Why does the Church not declare its assets in terms of farms, coffee and hemp plantations, haciendas, whole swathes of urban property, blocks of rental homes in every plaza of every city and town in Latin America? Why does it not declare the fabulous fortune it hoards in the Grace Company, with its global imperialist ramifications, and distribute it equitably among the millions of poor, instead of profiting from their ignorance and hunger?[7] Do you not consider that all this is the property of the people who produced it with their labor, and that if you fail to return it, the people may hold you accountable?" The next day, Barros was disavowed by his party and read out a retraction of his words in the Senate.

---

7   [A reference to W. R. Grace and Company, an American shipping, mining, and transport conglomerate, which at the time had vast holdings in South America.]

"But Jaime Barros was perfectly right! Instead of forcing him to retract they should have backed him up. He might have lost us the vote of a few Catholics, but he won us most of the Radicals," says one of the four.

That evening the papers had run a letter addressed to Barros by an old Liberal militant, supporting the senator against the onslaught of the right and pointing out: "Nobody protested when the Christian Democrats assaulted the Casa Masónica, nor when the pope blessed the soldiers and weapons that would destroy Ethiopia; and nobody protests against the cruel clerical tyranny of Franco's Spain."

Goldwater, Fidel Castro, and Brizola

By four o'clock we're on the road again, with Salvador Allende in the pickup truck. We are heading for the Philips plant, which has 370 workers and 330 white-collar employees.

"What's the significance of the Goldwater candidacy in the United States?" I ask.

"It's a serious misstep by the Republican Party, that will lose it a lot of support. Goldwater will not be accepted by the people of the United States. The election will demonstrate their rejection of figures like him, who turn their backs on the historical process."

"What do you make of Fidel Castro's declarations to the *New York Times*?"

"Fidel Castro repeated what he's always said: that he's prepared to negotiate on reasonable terms. It is a sensible and responsible position for a ruler to take."

"And what do you think of the movement represented by Brizola in Brazil?"[8]

"I'd rather speak of the movement of the Brazilian people. Its task is to restore democracy in the country. Brizola is part of that movement. As for the man himself, he is a true Latin American of the left."

"What about the danger of a Brazilian-style coup that people keep talking about?"

"Our movement is an authentically revolutionary process, within legal parameters. We will pass new laws in accordance with current laws,

8   [Leonel Brizola (1922–2004): left-populist politician, prominent in the Brazilian Labor Party founded in 1945 by supporters of President Getúlio Vargas; briefly tried to rally popular resistance after the 1964 military coup.]

and a new constitution in accordance with the existing one. We don't need violence. But, as I've said before, we will not tolerate the violence of others. Chile will not be another Brazil."

We go inside the Philips building. It is the opposite of this morning's market: orderly, spotless, and quiet. Allende meets with the executives. Later, in the canteen, he addresses the workers and white-collar employees. A considerable number of them have assembled, testifying to the strength of *allendismo* even in a firm with higher-than-average wages and conditions.

Allende says: "Nobody denies the need for change in this country, and nobody can deny that if change does not occur, Chile will be exposed to a violent breakdown of the democratic and juridical order.

"If there are two hundred thousand Chileans in Argentina, it's because over here there is no work. We have people with no jobs and children with no schools. Of every hundred university students, only two are workers' children. And there is not a single child of campesinos in the university.

"A campesino in Curicó earns 500 pesos a day. Your average salary is 450 pesos an hour. Any of you blow the campesino's daily wage on a day's smokes. I, who don't smoke, drink it away in wine. A liter of red costs more than 500 pesos.

"Who can guarantee that this apparent peace and quiet will go on indefinitely? There's a germ of revolt here, of justified revolt, and we want it to be expressed through elections, for change to be achieved through legal means. That is the intention of the popular government that will triumph on September 4th."

Night is falling as we depart. We go on to the Zig Zag printing press, employer of 1,200 people. Allende tours the premises. More greetings, more handshakes. I hang back in the workshop, running my finger over the lead lines, breathing in the smell of ink, fresh galleys, newly printed paper, a smell that's closer to me, more intense and expressive, than that of the flower market. When I emerge from a small forest of Linotypes, the retinue has moved away into the courtyard where the event is about to start. I wave goodbye from a distance and leave. The candidate can look forward to a cup of tea with the *allendista* ladies of the barrio and then to a street rally. Not me: I am once more crossing the Mapocho, on foot this time and with my hands in my coat pockets.

Postscript: A Shorter, Clean-Shaven, and Better-Dressed Fidel

At the time I was interviewing him, Allende was going around different neighborhoods in Santiago. With a third of the country's electorate, the capital is "difficult terrain" for Allendism, according to the experts working on his campaign. And yet his popularity is growing. On the evening of the day after I accompanied him to the factories, I went to the Almacenes París, a department store on the corner of Alameda and Ahumada, right in the center of town. People milled at the door, shouting "Allende! Allende!" Inside, the FRAP candidate was talking to the department store staff. Passersby found out he was there and joined the crowd, shouting along in a spontaneous demonstration. I managed to get in, and heard Allende's response to a question from an employee:

"They say I'm Fidel Castro in a shorter, clean-shaven, more elegant version. Much of the national and international press attacks me ruthlessly. It's not true. I am not planning on a socialist government. It will be a government of transition toward socialism. Chile will attain socialism, but when? In five, ten, thirty years' time? Only an irresponsible demagogue would venture any such predictions now.

"But we are clear about one thing: ours will be a government of transition away from capitalism, which has failed in Chile, and toward socialism, which is the future of humanity. Some say we need to replace capitalism with a communitarian regime. So far, I haven't met anyone among my adversaries who upholds that position, or can define what a communitarian regime might be, or where such a thing exists. On the other hand, 1.2 billion people currently live under socialism.

"We will nationalize our natural resources and trade with every country in the world. We will nationalize public services and the electricity and telephone companies. I was recently talking to the chief executive of the telephone company, who is a friend of mine, and told him: 'I'll be round on September 5th to ask you to prepare to hand over the keys, even if you don't like it.'

"We will not nationalize distribution, or businesses like this one. It would be a mistake for the people's government to tackle that now. On the contrary, we want businesses to have more to sell. I'm not saying that merely because I am here; if we did intend to nationalize these stores, I would have no problem in informing the managers as calmly as I informed the telephone company boss. But we don't.

"You sell fabrics. Mr. Yarur (a leading textile industrialist) tells me he produces about five hundred different prints. Excellent: may he continue to do so under the people's government. Well-dressed women are a joy to see. However, we will be setting Mr. Yarur a quota of everyday textile production to satisfy the basic needs of the population, as assessed by our planners. First the quota, then the fancy prints. And we will set price controls. In short, private manufacturing will carry on as it does now; it will not be nationalized, but we will implement planning, and take control of output and prices.

"That's why we say that, while not a socialist government, ours will still be an authentically revolutionary one, leaving this failed capitalism behind and paving the way for the coming move to socialism."

3

The Guerrilla Movement in Guatemala

(1965)

After his stint in Chile, Gilly coordinated relations between the Fourth International's Latin American Bureau and affiliated organizations across the region. This included overseeing its links with guerrilla movements such as Guatemala's Revolutionary Movement of November 13 (MR-13), which formally aligned itself with the Fourth International in 1964. Gilly was among the Trotskyist militants who spent time with the MR-13, combining political work with reportage. The following are edited extracts from reports published in Monthly Review *in May and June 1965. A year later, the Guatemalan government unleashed a harsh counterinsurgent campaign in which scores of militants were killed or disappeared. Gilly was among those who managed to escape to Mexico.*

With a Guerrilla Patrol

As dusk fell, the guerrilla patrol halted its march over the mountains. We removed our shoulder packs and put up hammocks. We opened some cans of food, while tortillas were heated over the open fire. A compañero tuned in to Radio Havana. It was 6 p.m. Maybe there was still daylight beyond the thickly wooded slope where we had pitched our camp, but all we could see were each other's faces in the glow of the fire. After the newscast, as on every other night, there was a political discussion in which the entire patrol took part.

Was it true that in 1954 workers and peasants throughout Guatemala called for arms with which to defend the Árbenz government against the "liberationist" coup organized by the State Department?[1] Or did they simply wait for the army to smash the coup? And to what extent did Árbenz institute agrarian reforms? Was good land distributed? Did the entire peasantry benefit, or only a sector of it?

One of the *guerrilleros* asked the questions that night, and each of the others gave his answer and related his own experience or that of his family during the period in question. The patrol, led by Commander Marco Antonio Yon Sosa, national director of the Revolutionary Movement of November 13 (MR-13), consisted of campesinos alongside men of urban or military background. Each one gave an answer that flowed from his own experience: some insisted that the people had demanded weapons; others reported the reactions of the military group that had been close to Árbenz at the time of the crisis.

The following afternoon, the patrol encamped near a peasant's hut, and that night we had freshly made tortillas, hot coffee, and roast bananas. In his or her own way, each member of the family welcomed the guerrilleros, one of whom outlined the program of the Movement to them, telling of its most recent struggles and perspectives, and explaining how all campesinos could participate in this struggle, not only by collaborating with the guerrilla groups but by organizing among themselves. The conversation, as usually happens in political discussions with Guatemalan peasants, turned to the experiences of the Árbenz era.

"The land over there," said the peasant, pointing, "was distributed. Then came the 'liberation' and it was taken away from us. The land over there"—he pointed in another direction—"was not distributed. It's the best land, belonging to rich people, so it wasn't touched."

In the days to come, conversations with other campesinos during the guerrilla march or in the evening camp fleshed out answers to all the questions.

That evening, another peasant told us: "In my village we got together and demanded arms from the government. They promised to give them to us, but they gave us nothing." Someone else said: "I was working in Tiquisate at the time. Government representatives came to us at the time of the Castillo Armas uprising [against Árbenz] and asked our leaders if, between the six *fincas* [farms] we were working on, we could raise three

---

1 [Jacobo Árbenz (1913–71): president of Guatemala democratically elected in 1950; toppled in 1954 by a CIA-engineered coup.]

hundred men, who would then be armed. We told them we could. We returned to our fincas, and when we called for fifty volunteers from each, the peasants got angry and said that they were all volunteers; the next day, instead of three hundred there were three thousand men assembled, waiting to be armed. But the government representatives never returned, and the Árbenz government collapsed."

A peasant stopped his work in a field as he watched our column approach. "I'd heard that you people were in the area, but I've never actually seen any guerrillas before," he said cheerfully. "You're armed, that's good. You can't fight with nothing but machetes for weapons. In the days of Don Jacobo [Árbenz], we all got together and asked for arms, but they didn't give us any and that finished him off. If the peasants had been armed, no one could have overthrown him." As he said goodbye he added: "One of these days I might pick up my gun and join you in the mountains. Take care of yourselves." And he went on plowing his land, a small and rocky plot of ground on the mountainside, which he had cleared—*descombrado*, as they say in Guatemala—with his own hands.

A formal roundtable discussion, taking place somewhere far from the struggle, on the question of whether or not the people had demanded arms in 1954, might go unresolved for weeks; but up here in the sierra, the peasants answered the question without the slightest hesitation—the same way as the Guatemalan workers, along with hundreds of students and white-collar workers, flocked in buses and trucks to the barracks in those crucial June days of 1954, calling for arms with which to defend the Guatemalan Revolution, would have solved the question in reality.

Today, the Guatemalan guerrilleros of MR-13 are fighting for the socialist revolution and for a government of workers and peasants. Neither the method nor the program was drawn up by a group of pure theoreticians, as a kind of parlor game. If, for the first time in Latin America, a guerrilla movement has sprung up in Guatemala that openly declares its socialist objectives, this is without doubt due to the influence of the world revolutionary process and the Cuban socialist revolution. But it is also—or, above all—due to the deep collective experience of the Guatemalan people, to the defeat suffered in 1954, and to the fact that, since then, workers and peasants, instead of lapsing into resignation or retreat, have gone on fighting as best they can. They have maintained a permanent state of unrest under the subsequent dictatorships, and they have drawn a series of conclusions from the 1954 defeat at the hands of the counterrevolution.

The first of these conclusions is that the counterrevolution triumphed because the people were unarmed. The second, that the government did not arm the people because it was relying on the military to defend the Revolution. "It wasn't us who were in the government; it was Colonel Árbenz, who was merely a friend of ours," a peasant told us. An armed people, and power directly exercised by the masses: out of the Árbenz experience the Guatemalan masses have drawn up this essential program for the socialist revolution, though they may not use those words.

The peasant who had said to us, "You're armed, that's good," expressed a common conviction and a growing decision: "One of these days I might pick up my gun and join you in the mountains."

The electoral path is barred in Guatemala, not only because the bourgeoisie cannot hold democratic elections and still remain in power. It is also barred because the workers and peasants do not believe in elections; they have no illusions about elections. The electoral experience was thoroughly explored with Árbenz, and it failed. For this reason, armed revolution has won support. An additional and important reason is that the peasants, after thinking through the Árbenz fiasco, have become firmly convinced that it is not enough to have the land; it is also necessary to have a government and weapons with which to defend it. It is not enough simply to ask for arms; they must first possess them and organize themselves, gun in hand. Peasant organization and arms, arms and peasant organization are for them two inseparable and equally indispensable elements. In Guatemala, there is no need to convince the campesinos of these facts; all that is required is to propose forms and methods for putting them into practice. It is to fulfill this task that the guerrilla forces of MR-13 are marching through the mountains, fighting and organizing.

Armed Propaganda

"Our struggle is not primarily military but social," Commander Yon Sosa told me in one of our conversations in the sierra. "It's not our intention to destroy the government by military means; we intend to dissolve it through social action. This means that at the same time we must be organizing the bases of the government that will replace the old one, a government of workers and peasants. Our guerrilla force organizes on the social level. Sure, we fight weapons in hand, but we also organize the campesino masses and the city workers. They are the ones who'll topple the capitalist dictatorship."

The chief task of the Guatemalan guerrilla force today is peasant organization; all military actions are subordinate to that. When a guerrilla squad goes marching through the mountains, its machine guns, rifles, and grenades are not the principal weapons of struggle; these are necessary, indispensable, providing the basis of security. But the principal weapon is the word—written and spoken, especially spoken.

During the weeks we spent in the mountains, the guerrilla patrol I was with—one of several, covering various zones of Northeast Guatemala —had no encounter with the army. Such was not the intention; it didn't enter into our plans. The patrol always knew where the army was, which mountain passes and trails it used and when it used them. This information was volunteered by the local campesinos, meaning the guerrillas were always able to avoid a clash if they so wished.

At the same time, their lengthy talks with the peasants enabled them to confirm the organizational progress made in zones where guerrilla forces had passed through weeks or months earlier. In other areas they spoke with peasants who were seeing guerrilleros for the first time. And everywhere, they heard denunciations of repressive acts committed by landowners and the military. Wherever they were, the guerrilleros constantly spread their revolutionary message; its keyword was "organize."

Such were the tasks of the guerrilla patrols. The number of their members varied according to need and the likelihood of armed clashes. A large number was necessary only in cases of planned military actions.

The patrol would approach a village, knowing in advance whether the army had been there recently and if and when it had departed. This knowledge was provided not only by the peasants themselves but also by unmistakable clues left by the army itself. Our patrol sometimes spent several days following the trail of an army detachment, verifying its route, where it had halted and where it had altered course. Each detail deduced from physical evidence would later be confirmed and elaborated upon by the local peasants.

Once the patrol entered the village, it would assemble the inhabitants. On a first visit, the patrol would explain what it was fighting for. After several years of guerrilla activity, most peasants would already be aware, at least, of their existence and would have heard more about them from other peasants. But they often don't know what exactly it is the guerrillas want or are attempting to do. The army and the government have put out extensive propaganda that portrays the guerrillas as bandits, cattle thieves, and highway robbers. The first encounter between a guerrilla group and a campesino village will often bring to the surface the peasant's deep-rooted suspicion, a defense mechanism of people to whom the outside world has brought nothing but the exaction of tribute, exploitation, and repression. But as guerrilla influence spreads, these same peasants undertake to spread the truth from village to village about the guerrillas and their objectives.

The Legend of the Guerrilla Force

Legend converted into news and news converted into legend have spread all over the highland region. As in the Algerian and Congolese revolutions—as in all revolutions and especially in peasant wars—news and legend become weapons of struggle. They strengthen the will to fight, to resist pressures and attacks, to lend support in adverse circumstances. They also serve to deceive, intimidate, demoralize, and undermine the army. There is no barrier between peasant and soldier; the soldier is really just a peasant in uniform, subject to military discipline. When the news-legend reaches him via the peasants, it spreads through the ranks, inducing the troops to see invincible guerrillas everywhere.

The peasants believe that the men of the guerrilla force cannot be injured, for they are always accompanied by a "sage"—a wizard—who protects them from bullets. Others say that they have "chemistry"—that is, magic—and that is why the army cannot kill them.

They also say that Commander Yon Sosa, if he finds himself surrounded by the enemy, can adopt another shape and thus escape. When the situation is really critical, the legend has it that he turns into a bunch of bananas; the army marches past him and he overhears everything they say. One afternoon we returned to our encampment, dog-tired. We'd been on short rations for two days, and food supplies were not expected until the next day. That morning we'd eaten the last of our provisions; all there was for supper, before bedding down, were two tortillas apiece and some coffee. One of the guerrilleros said to Yon Sosa: "Look here, Commander, couldn't you turn into a bunch of bananas for a little while?"

A police sergeant told an imprisoned MR-13 member:

> It's impossible to nab that Yon Sosa. Just imagine, once we had him surrounded, him and all his men, in a house. There was a gun battle that lasted an hour. Suddenly, he and his men stopped firing. We waited. Silence. About half an hour went by. Then the door opened, and a little

black dog trotted out. You won't believe me but it was Yon Sosa himself, escaping disguised as a dog!

Legend is fused with religion and witchcraft with the Bible. In a village the guerrilleros had entered for the first time, an old evangelist doggedly followed them around, clutching a Bible, attempting to convert them. Meanwhile, one of the guerrilleros explained the movement's program to him. They had a long conversation on politics and religion, and the old man's parting words were: "You have right on your side. You fight for justice and that is in the Bible. And the Bible has guerrilleros, too; the Maccabees were guerrilleros, just like you."

Later, Commander Turcios told me that there are many evangelists in the villages, and they always cite the Maccabees to explain their support for the guerrilleros. "Those Maccabees!" he said. "After all these centuries, they've turned out to be magnificent allies for us!"

These are not mere anecdotes; they are proof that the guerrilla force has sunk deep roots into the consciousness of the peasantry, for whom it is a symbol of hope. There is no power that can destroy these roots.

Daily Life in a Guerrilla Camp

Equality is the keystone of guerrilla life. Duties such as carrying equipment and preparing food are equitably shared. Anything that threatens equality, anything that might imply privilege for one group or another, immediately weakens the spirit and internal unity of the guerrilla force. Equality becomes the guerrillero's second nature. One night, one of the commanders distributed, among the twelve of us present, the last piece of bean cake, of which there was scarcely enough for one. To divide it equally demanded the precision of a surgeon's scalpel. The slices were minute; chewing and swallowing them scarcely gave the illusion of eating. But at least they were equal.

Equality plus the discussion of all problems—from the most fundamental political issues to the slightest friction among the guerrilleros themselves—unite the guerrilla force, as does collectively facing danger. In this way, the guerrilla force can resist, develop greater strength, and snatch victories from the very hardships and perils of the struggle; and it can unite with the campesino masses in whose midst it exists and struggles.

The guerrilla force engages in continual political discussion. Its principal medium is the newspaper *Revolución Socialista*. Each issue that reaches a guerrilla camp is read and discussed by the entire group. The paper assists the guerrilleros in their organizational work among the peasants by providing them with explanations of political issues; furthermore, it gives cohesion to the internal life of the guerrilla unit itself, without which it would be impossible to undertake the organization of external groups.

Revolución Socialista is not written only for the peasants and workers who are sympathetic to the guerrilla movement and for the population at large; perusal of the paper makes clear that it is largely addressed to the movement itself and to its closest collaborators. In this regard, it follows Lenin's conception of the newspaper as a collective political instrument of organization. The validity of this conception is borne out by the ways in which the guerrilla force utilizes it: articles are discussed at marching halts and their central points will subsequently reappear in conversations with peasants; when time and circumstances permit, the paper is read aloud to them and analyzed. Indigenous members of a guerrilla unit, when they have a free moment, get together to read *Revolución Socialista*, *Pekín Informa* (Peking Review), and other documents and discuss them in their own language.

The international situation occupies an important place in the political discussions of the guerrilleros: Latin America, the Congo, Vietnam. They live the news from Vietnam almost as if it were a neighboring village. One night, two guerrilleros and I listened to a United States broadcast on South Vietnam; it described, in dramatic language, the vicissitudes of the war against the Vietnamese guerrillas—the ambushes and surprise attacks of the guerrillas and their allies among the population, carried out against the United States and the South Vietnamese government forces. We talked spiritedly and long that night. One of the men, who had been asleep in his hammock, woke up and joined the discussion.

The Guatemalan guerrilla force envisions its own socialist objective with great clarity and feels, therefore, all the more strongly linked to the fate of the socialist countries—Cuba, China, the Soviet Union. It observes the revolutionary advances in Vietnam and the Congo, the socialist and revolutionary struggles in Europe, Asia, and the entire world—and feels them to be part of its own strength, sees their participants as its allies. Every guerrillero understands that such struggles contribute to the weakening of the Guatemalan dictatorship and its backers in Washington and the Pentagon; it senses that the Vietnamese guerrilleros are, in their fashion, striking at [Enrique] Peralta Azurdia, the Guatemalan dictator.

Some of the guerrilleros are unmarried. Others have wives and families whom they have left behind in villages and towns; they speak infrequently of their families, but when they do mention them, one realizes that their silence does not signify indifference but the contrary. War is war and has its own laws. As the words of a song of the International Brigades in Spain had it: "We have come from all corners of the Earth. / We are here and ready for the struggle. / If we have left our homes to do battle it is because the International is our home."

The Guatemalan guerrilleros also sing, needless to say. New words have been set to the tune of "El Grito," a popular Guatemalan song: "If you're a good Guatemalan and a real man, pick up your rifle and go to the mountains, where dignity awaits you." But when the singing begins, Mexican songs are the most often heard, perhaps because of the gaiety of their melodies and because their lyrics—from which bullets are never absent—reflect the combative guerrilla spirit.

"In the villages, after we've held a political discussion, we usually have a singalong with the peasants, especially in indigenous communities," I was told. "They perform their songs for us, and we reciprocate. And do you know which one they always ask for? 'The Tomb of Pancho Villa'!" For the Guatemalan peasant, the Mexican guerrillero Villa lives on, at least in music.

Interview with the Commander of the Guerrilla Forces

It rained and rained. We had been marching all day in the rain; night had fallen, and it was still raining. That's how it is in the Sierra de las Minas once it begins raining. With a machete as their only tool, the guerrilleros had put up a *champa*—a makeshift hut of turf slabs and tree branches, lashed together with lianas.

Most of the men were asleep in their hammocks, which were strung up between the trees, each one protected from the rain by a sheet of waterproof nylon stretched overhead. There was no one left in the *champa* but the guerrillero on guard duty, Commander Yon Sosa and me—and a monkey, our next morning's breakfast, caught earlier that day and now skinned and roasting over a fire. Yon Sosa and I talked, not for the first time, about the Guatemalan Revolution. That night I decided to take notes. I dug in my pocket, removing a comb, a handkerchief, a bottle of pills, and a can of sardines until, at the bottom, I found my notebook—somewhat damp—and a pencil. I transcribe my jottings here, now that I have been able to dry out my notebook in the sun and decipher its contents. Yon Sosa began our discussion by commenting:

You can't imagine the progress we've made since a year ago. Now we are able to see our goals much more clearly, and our confidence in ourselves has grown markedly.

Have your forces increased?
Yes. But it's not only a matter of material strength. The decisive turn occurred when we adopted a program of socialist revolution. True, we were fighting even before, but we suffered from confusion in many areas. However, in the process of fighting, living with the peasants, and encountering many frustrations, we reached the conclusion that in Guatemala the only real revolution of the masses that can be made is a socialist revolution. And how we've advanced since reaching that conclusion! A multitude of things that formerly seemed confusing have been clarified. There were compañeros who agreed in theory with the need for socialism but who feared the peasants would not understand the socialist program and would be frightened off by the prospect of such a drastic step. It was they who didn't understand the campesinos! To those peasant community leaders, the idea of socialist revolution appears so simple and logical that they are impatient with anyone who attempts to propose some other solution. This is our strength, and it constitutes not only material strength but also the strength of the program.

And did no one tell you that with such a program you would antagonize the bourgeoisie?
Of course, we were warned of that eventuality. They tried everything to make us hesitate, to intimidate us. But what convinced us was observing how the peasants responded to our program. The program passed the test of the masses, and from that point on we were adamant. Anyhow, what does it matter what the bourgeoisie says? They're already against us. Have you found a single bourgeois who supports the guerrilleros or the militant peasant leaders? And what clout does the national bourgeoisie have, anyhow? In Guatemala, none. Furthermore, ever since we took up arms and went to the Sierra, they have grown more closely linked than ever to imperialism and more vehemently opposed to us.

And do your differences with the Communists stem from this matter of attitude toward the national bourgeoisie?
That seems to me to be the main difference, though there are others. We have discussed many problems with them and, frankly, I fail to understand the reasoning of the compañeros in the PGT.[2] On the one hand, they ask why we attack the national bourgeoisie so sharply, since in Guatemala it is virtually nonexistent. Yet on the other hand, they say it is necessary to unite the greatest possible number of forces against the principal enemy, which is imperialism, and therefore to win the support of, or at least to neutralize, the national bourgeoisie. In other words, when we attack the bourgeoisie, they say it doesn't exist, it vanishes. But when it's a question of enlisting it as an ally, it seems that it does exist. The peasants are much more down-to-earth: "The rich are all the same, and we must be rid of the lot of them," they say.

Yon Sosa took out his machete and cut a slice of monkey meat, now cooked to perfection. He divided it and handed me a piece. "Taste it. But tomorrow you'd better not mention that we started nibbling at the monkey meat because the others will put us on trial and likely shoot us for violating equality!" He continued:

Look, I don't know much theory, but I'm studying and learning in the struggle. Experience has already taught me that there is a basic difference between these compañeros and us: whenever a situation gets difficult, we try to resolve it through struggle, we try to advance; but *they* are inclined to resolve it through negotiations and agreements. Maybe it's because I come from a *chafa* background [*chafa* comes from *chafarote*, a nickname given to soldiers by Guatemalans], but I believe that things will be resolved by force of arms or not at all. This is not only true now, under the Peralta Azurdia dictatorship; it was true in the time of Árbenz, who ought to have armed the people.

2   [The Partido Guatemalteco del Trabajo (Guatemalan Labor Party) was the name of the country's Communist Party; founded in 1949, it supported the governments of Juan José Arévalo and Jacobo Árbenz in the late 1940s and early 1950s, notably supplying key personnel and ideas for Árbenz's agrarian reform. In 1962 the PGT joined the Fuerzas Armadas Rebeldes (Rebel Armed Forces), an alliance that included the MR-13 until the MR-13 broke with it in 1964.]

How did you all become socialists?
While we were dodging bullets. It's impossible to fight for very long side by side with peasants and not become a socialist. An armed revolution must become a socialist revolution. Which countries similar to ours have been able to emerge from backwardness? Cuba, China, North Vietnam, North Korea—they all took the socialist path. A backward country cannot advance along the capitalist path, and there is no third alternative. All you have to do is look around and see what's going on in the world. How could we not be for socialism?

But it's not enough to be for the socialist revolution, you have to say so. There are compañeros who think that while they themselves can understand it, the masses can't and therefore it must not be mentioned. This shows lack of trust in the masses. These compañeros think that the peasants care only about their crops, whereas peasants today are interested in Cuba, China, the Congo, and everything that's happening in the world. You need only talk to them to find out. But you must talk to them in simple language, not in abstract formulas; and there's nothing simpler than the idea of a government of workers and peasants.

What do you think about Vietnam?
But why do you ask? You heard the discussion last night with the other guerrilleros; you even added your two centavos' worth! But, if you like, I'll answer you as a guerrilla commander to a journalist. I think the imperialists are a bunch of bastards: you can only get rid of them with guns, and that's what the Vietnamese guerrilleros are doing. In doing so, they're helping us, however far away they are. We are supporting them, as much as we are able, by attempting to overthrow capitalism in Guatemala and by combating imperialism— not with declarations but with guns. The Congolese guerrilleros are doing the same. When we have a workers' state in Guatemala, you can be sure that we won't equivocate—we shall extend the revolution, helping all the other countries of Latin America to accomplish theirs, if they haven't already done it.

But won't this bring you into conflict with imperialism?
Do you really want me to answer that question?

You don't think I want the monkey to answer it.
Then I'll answer with some questions of my own. Do you think we're not going to tangle with the imperialists anyhow, not just after our victory but also before? And do you suppose that if they're intervening in Vietnam and in the Congo they won't intervene here in Guatemala, whenever they decide that the dictatorship is not doing a good enough job of holding back the revolution? And aren't they intervening already? And didn't they intervene, when Árbenz was removed? And are we going to fool them by pretending to be moderates? If they don't finish us off now it's because they're unable to; and if they don't liquidate us when we're on the verge of winning power or already in power, it will also be because they're unable. And the more support we have from the peoples of Latin America, the less able they'll be. And the more we support the struggles of other Latin Americans, the more they'll support ours. Conflict with imperialism? We're under no illusions: they'll intervene as much as they can, more than in Cuba, as much as in Vietnam. But, as in Vietnam, things will go badly for them. We must spell out our ideas on this subject; we must not be evasive or sow illusions among the masses, for this would destroy their trust in us.

What is the position of MR-13 on the guerrilla movements of Latin America?
At the national meeting of our Movement, held recently in the mountains, we approved the Declaration of the Sierra de las Minas, in which we invited the guerrilla movements of Venezuela and Colombia to a joint conference, to be held in any of our three countries, in guerrilla-held territory. It would be good if guerrillero representatives could come from Vietnam, the Congo, "Portuguese" Guinea, from all the countries where armed struggle is taking place. And we could issue a joint declaration addressed to all the revolutionary peoples of the world, appealing for their support for the guerrilla movements of our countries and for a great Latin American front against imperialism.

And what else?
If you're going to write all that, please add this at the end: we don't just seek support from our Cuban, Venezuelan, and Colombian compañeros. We also ask it of the Socialist and Communist compañeros in Chile; the nationalist compañeros in Brazil; the Uruguayans; the Peronist compañeros in Argentina; the miners' unions and the

peasants of Bolivia; the revolutionaries of Peru, Ecuador, Mexico, all Central America.

Our country is small and our movement is young, but a country is no longer small once it is fighting, weapons in hand, for its liberation. Write that the Guatemalan Revolution did not end in 1954; it survives in the underground struggles in the towns and in the mountain villages; write that we send our greetings and offer our solidarity to all the Latin American masses who are struggling for the same goals as us; and write that Guatemala is moving toward socialism and Guatemala will not falter.

The fire was flickering, the rain was still falling. The compañero on guard duty reminded us that we would have to be up at dawn, ready to continue our march. A few minutes later I was stretched out in my hammock, asleep, as the rain pelted down on the waterproof nylon sheet.[3]

---

3   [In the late 1970s, Gilly wrote an unsparing, self-critical analysis of the Trotsky-ists' engagement with the MR-13, highlighting their inability to connect revolutionary theory to practice, program to reality. See "Guerrilla, programa y partido en Guatemala (crítica retrospectiva de una derrota)," *Coyoacán*, no. 3, April–June 1978.]

4

Camilo Torres, the Forerunner

(2016)

Camilo Torres Restrepo, the Colombian priest who took the side of the world's poor and risked everything with them until the last day of his life, died on February 15, 1966, fifty years ago today.

I met Camilo in Bogotá in May 1965. I was on my way to Montevideo after doing an extensive report on the Revolutionary Movement of November 13 (MR-13) in the mountains of Guatemala. The text later appeared in *Monthly Review*, an independent socialist and Marxist journal published in New York and Buenos Aires.

I stopped over in Bogotá. I was carrying a letter from the Buenos Aires publisher of the magazine addressed to Camilo Torres Restrepo, dean of the School of Public Administration in Bogotá, and no sooner had I arrived than I went looking for the addressee. I went up to the fourteenth floor of a building where his office was, asked for Dr Camilo Torres, and to my surprise as an unrepentant Marxist, a priest came out. I told him I had a message for Professor Camilo Torres. The man who had appeared gave me an amused look and said: "Yes, I'm Camilo Torres." Who knows what bewildered expression crossed my face, but Camilo acted casually, smiled, and we went into his office and began to talk.

The dialogue, unexpected for both of us, lasted the several days I stayed in Bogotá: with Camilo, with Monsignor Germán Guzmán,[1] with

---

1 [Germán Guzmán Campos (1912–88): sociologist and priest, granted the honorific title of Monsignor by Pope John XXIII in 1960; published a biography of Camilo Torres in 1967, and later settled in Mexico.]

Guitemie Olivieri[2] and the team of assistants Camilo had at the university; and also, one afternoon, with Camilo's mother in her house, a sweet woman of whom I still, half a century and many adventures later, retain unforgettable memories.

Camilo took me in his car around what were the rich neighborhoods at the time. This was where his family were from, and he pointed out their homes. Then he took me to the poor neighborhoods of Bogotá. In the course of long conversations, I told him and Monsignor Guzmán about the experiences of the MR-13 in Guatemala, led by three soldiers: Colonel Augusto Vicente Loarca and the lieutenants Marco Antonio Yon Sosa and Luis Turcios Lima. The bishop listened and eagerly took notes; only later did I understand why.

Months later, when I was in Montevideo, I had lengthy discussions with the editor of *Marcha*, the unforgettable Carlos Quijano, and with Eduardo Galeano, then a young and brilliant 25-year-old assistant editor. They published a long report I wrote on Camilo Torres. It was February 1966. By that time Camilo had already gone into the mountains and my piece was titled "Camilo, guerrillero". The following are some passages from it.

Last May I spoke with Camilo in Bogotá. Camilo Torres is a young man, and he looks young. Tall, he has a lively manner. And while he shows such passion for ideas while talking, he tends to turn these ideas toward practical conclusions and organizational measures. He is not an ordinary priest: he has a political and intellectual formation, combined with an interest in knowing and understanding what people think. He was eager to hear about the experiences of the Guatemalan guerrillas. In his approach to problems and his way of understanding the feelings of ordinary people there are certain similarities with Frantz Fanon's form of analysis, though at that time Torres had not read the works of the theorist of the Algerian Revolution's insurrectionary phase. This is what the Colombian priest wrote around that time, when he was a sociologist, in a study on "the violence":[3]

---

2   [Marguerite-Marie Olivieri (1933–2009): French Catholic, originally an anticolonial activist in Paris, then worked alongside Torres in Colombia; later exiled to Mexico before returning to France.]

3   ["La Violencia" is the term given to Colombia's decade-long civil war, notionally lasting from the assassination of Liberal leader Jorge Eliécer Gaitán in 1948 until the late 1950s.]

The guerrillas have imposed the discipline that the campesinos themselves were asking for; they have made authority more democratic; and
they have given confidence and security to our rural communities. We
mention this in discussing how the feeling of inferiority has disappeared
from peasant areas where the phenomenon of violence has occurred.
Despite everything, the violence has set in motion a social process
that the ruling classes did not foresee. It has awoken the peasants' consciousness; it has given them group solidarity, a feeling of superiority
and security in their actions that has opened up possibilities for social
advance and has institutionalized aggressivity, with the result that the
Colombian campesino has begun to prefer the interests of the peasantry
over those of the traditional parties. As a result of this, a political and
socioeconomic pressure group will form that can produce structural
changes of a kind the ruling classes least desire and expect. We can say
that for Colombia, "the violence" has been the most important socio-
cultural change in peasant areas since the time of the Spanish conquest.

I asked Camilo if he thought that Christians needed to take a clear stance
on these questions. He answered:

> But of course. Christians, if they want to be real Christians and not just
> in words, have to participate actively in social changes. Passive faith
> is not enough to get closer to God. You must also have charity. And
> charity means, concretely, living the feeling of human fraternity. That
> feeling is manifested today in the popular revolutionary movements, in
> the need for weak and oppressed countries to unite in order to put an
> end to exploitation. Christians need to side with the oppressed, not the
> oppressors.

Camilo Torres was then thirty-seven years old. The son of an aristo-
cratic Colombian family, until May 1965 he was dean of the School of
Public Administration. In 1964 he had been removed from a chair at
the National University in Bogotá for supporting a student strike. As a
professor of sociology, together with Monsignor Guzmán he carried out
research into the situation of the Colombian peasantry. Up to the age of
eighteen, when he went to the seminary, he was raised on his family's
lands, riding with the proud cowboys of the eastern plains of Colombia.

At the university in Bogotá, he was shaken and carried along by the
student movements, and he was not only a teacher for the students but
also a leader. His renewed contact with the peasants came later, when

he had already lived and taken part in the student struggles. No doubt the two experiences joined together in his mind. And Camilo, who until shortly beforehand had tried to explain to the ruling classes that they had to put an end to the exploitation, misery, and oppression of the peasantry if they wanted to avoid a very violent social explosion, drew the conclusion that only a revolution that changed the entire economic and social structure of the country could improve the situation of the peasantry. He also saw that such a transformation would be resisted by those ruling classes with all the means at their disposal. The sociologist had given way to the revolutionary, and the student leader was internally preparing himself to become a peasant leader.

By May 1965, Camilo Torres was already making regular visits to peasant villages, playing a part in organizing them around their needs and the demands of their communities. In April, the Colombian Curia had decided that Camilo had to leave to study in Belgium. He spoke to me about this crucial dilemma in his life. If he didn't go, they would transfer him to lay status and he would have to give up his priestly attire, the cassock.

"But are you really and truly Catholic?" I asked him.

"Of course," he replied. "I believe in Christ and when I speak with him in my prayers I call him '*patrón*', because he is my chief, my boss."

"In that case," I said, "why does it matter to you whether you wear the cassock or not?"

"Look," he said, "I believe in Christ, and my relationship with him has nothing to do with the garments I wear. But for my people, for the campesinos who trust in me, the cassock is symbolic and very important. I have to respect that feeling. The [church] hierarchy knows it and for that reason, if I don't go, they want to demote me to lay status."

"Well," I said, "I think you have no choice but to explain the situation and the dilemma to the peasant communities who listen to you and trust you."

In my notes, I registered that Camilo was experiencing an inner conflict: to go, in order to keep his position in the Church and then return, or to stay and have to face an immediate rupture? Going might mean that the students and peasants who supported him would see him as a deserter. Staying would mean breaking with the institutional Church of which he felt himself to be an integral part. All the indications are that the pressure from his own people resolved the conflict. Camilo refused to obey the Curia's orders and asked to be reduced to lay status, without thereby renouncing the priesthood.

From then on, all his activity was concentrated on the campaign for the People's United Front,[4] on public rallies and above all on the publication of the weekly *Frente Unido*, edited by Camilo Torres himself. In its first issue, dated August 26, 1965, in Bogotá, he published a manifesto titled "Message to the Christians." In it he defined his beliefs, his ideas, his commitments, and his life.

On February 15, 1966, Camilo died in a clash with the military. To this day the Colombian army has not said where his remains lie. The day will come . . .

To my immense surprise, one Sunday in August or September 1971, Guitemie Olivieri came to see me in Lecumberri Prison's N-Block. She spoke to me at length about Camilo and about our earlier meeting in Bogotá. But that's another story, and it's not my place to tell it to you, nor yours to hear it.

---

4   [Frente Unido del Pueblo: a broad coalition Torres sought to assemble, bringing together social democrats, Christian Democrats, dissident Liberals, Communists and others, against the ruling National Front of Liberals and Conservatives.]

5

A Political Defense

(1969)

Gilly was arrested in April 1966, barely two weeks after arriving in Mexico from Guatemala. Tortured by the Mexican police in their attempt to extract a confession, he was then imprisoned in the capital's Lecumberri Prison, where he remained until March 1972. What follows is an edited extract from the text Gilly read at his appeal hearing on October 7, 1969— three years into his imprisonment, and one year after Mexican government forces killed hundreds of demonstrators in the Mexico City neighborhood of Tlatelolco.

The brief submitted by our accuser should suffice for us to immediately —right now—walk out of that door that opens onto the street, rather than the one behind us that leads back into the prison. However, let me add a few arguments to those which the Prosecutor's Office has, despite itself, made in our defense.

We said in our political defense at the first hearing that this trial was a juridical farce. This so displeased the Prosecutor's Office that they requested our sentences be increased for having made such a statement (which proves once again that they have a real mania for persecuting opinions and punishing ideas.)

Yes, this trial is a farce, a piece of theater. Even the room we're in looks like a theater, with the audience in the stalls and the stage where we, the accused, sit with the judge, his clerks, and the public prosecutors, all very formal and democratic in appearance. But, as at the theater, we all know this is pure fiction. Because the reality lies behind the stage, outside this room. And that reality, where these proceedings are concerned, consists of the days and nights of torture inflicted on us by the Federal Security Directorate, and the marks left by those blows, which were still visible when we appeared before the lower court and which that judge saw but ignored, just as the man sitting over there, representing the Prosecutor's Office, also saw them at the time. The reality consists of three years spent in prison without trial, when the Constitution sets a compulsory maximum of one year. The reality is that monstrous judgment, handed down not by the judge but by the government whose orders he obeys. A ruling which, for example, condemned this speaker—imprisoned two weeks after arriving in the country—to more than six years behind bars because, according to the judgment, he attended a political meeting and championed Trotskyist ideas in foreign magazines and publications. It condemned our comrade Oscar Fernández Bruno to eight and a half years in prison for being a member of the Workers' Revolutionary Party (Trotskyist) [POR (T)] and on top of that declared him to be a "forger of seals"; his wife, our comrade Teresa Confreta, got more than five years for belonging to the Trotskyist party and for having attended various political meetings, where they discussed a student strike and the country's situation; and so on for the rest of the defendants, today free on bail after spending two years in prison.

But the reality is not only that; it's much worse. It's the oppression and repression unleashed by the government against the Mexican people, it's the persecution of ideas, of revolutionary or simply democratic organizations, it's the daily denial of the Mexican people's right to organize, their right to freedom of speech, of the press, and of assembly; it's the hundreds of political prisoners, trade unionists, and peasants locked up in the jails of Mexico City and the provinces. It's the oppression and repression meted out to the masses in order to defend the interests of the big imperialist and capitalist enterprises, the banks, the landowners—whether publicly declared or disguised—and the political bosses, the interests of all those who live off the exploitation of Mexican workers from the country and the city, to defend, in a word, the capitalist system.

The reality is Tlatelolco, the most brutal and visible image of that repression. But it is also the daily Tlatelolco perpetrated by the capitalist regime against the Mexican people, the thousands who die every day from lack of food, lack of medical attention, the shortage of housing and poor sanitary conditions, from super-exploitation in wretched workplaces, or from childhood illnesses caused by poverty and unemployment and by the insalubriousness of peasants' and workers' housing.

There are thousands of statistics like those we presented in our defense at the initial trial that show how the capitalist regime prevents the Mexican people from eating meat, eggs, milk, bread, fruit; from having housing, sewerage, electricity, potable water; from enjoying medical and sanitary attention, adequate primary education, the minimum wage, rest and recreation. It is a daily Tlatelolco, a massacre the capitalist system carries out day after day. And to bolster that system, farces such as this one are mounted against revolutionary socialists, the army is sent onto the streets every week and the most basic democratic rights of the people are denied, the right of the masses to organize and struggle for the country's advancement and for their own living and working conditions.

This trial is occurring in a climate of intimidation. In this very courtroom, plainclothes policemen are taking note of everyone in the public gallery. In prison, we were constantly threatened with being machine-gunned or with other kinds of reprisal. The latest was this anonymous photocopied communication received by some comrades who are political prisoners, warning that if a supposed threat against the president and his associates (made in a clumsy, unsigned note, clearly the handiwork of the police) is carried out, then corresponding reprisals would be suffered not only by the prisoners, but also by any family and friends who visit them, and the families of those friends. The anonymous note came with a list of the family and friends who had visited each prisoner, with their respective home addresses—a list to which only the Ministry of the Interior and some other government departments have access. The envelopes containing these notes and lists were hand-delivered to these comrades by personnel associated with the management of the prison, so that there could be no doubt as to the origin of these threats. The name of our lawyer here present, Carlos Fernández del Real, appears on one of those lists.

Those envelopes were, in a word, official notification from the government that as well as being political prisoners, it now considers us political hostages. It's in this climate of repression, terrorism, and intimidation, which includes everyone present, that this trial is being conducted. That is the reality behind this juridical theater.

We made it clear in our first defense, and our present attorneys have reaffirmed it: there is no conspiracy here, no crime to prosecute.

We invite you to read our defense statement. We repeat what we said there: "Our accusers have been unable to cite *a single illegal act*, to provide *a single example of a crime*, to present *a single witness* that would entitle them to jail, try, and sentence us according to the very Penal Code you invoke. Nothing, not a single deed: the only thing on trial here is ideas—the articulation and discussion of ideas and the organization of the struggle for socialism. In other words, this is a trial against the most basic democratic rights consecrated by the Mexican Constitution."

The judgment equates "struggling to establish a socialist regime" with "overthrowing the established government." That is a trap! They are two different things, which don't necessarily follow one from the other, as the police and the lower-court judge assert. We Trotskyists do struggle for a socialist government, a government of workers and peasants. But we did not propose to "overthrow the established government," that is, the one that currently exists. Not because we support the government that carried out the Tlatelolco massacre but because it would be absurd to call for the overthrow of any government before the masses possess the organizations, the independent revolutionary working-class party, the leadership, and the organizational means required for the struggle. Revolutions are made by the masses, not by conspirators.

What the Workers' Revolutionary Party (Trotskyist) proposed and proposes, what it fought for and still does, is to drive forward the independent organization of the masses, to develop their class, union, and political organisms—mass trade unions by branch of industry, peasant unions, a central worker and peasant union, a mass workers' party rooted in these unions—in accordance with an anti-imperialist and anti-capitalist program. Such are the instruments that will allow the masses to establish their own government of workers and peasants. That is not a conspiracy: those are public goals, ideas set out in all our newspapers and writings. That struggle is perfectly legal, just as it is legal to publish fliers and newspapers, to support strikes with the goal of improvements for workers or students, to participate in meetings, to argue for one's ideas—the sum total of "crimes" for which the original judge sentenced us to so many years in prison.

That judge may well think that, according to his prehistoric criteria, we have the worst intentions imaginable for the future. But he can't condemn us for that. No penal code punishes intentions—that is to say, ideas. He can criticize us for contending that the socialist revolution will be violent. Yes, revolution is always violent, and nothing proves this better than Mexico's own history. No class surrenders power without fighting tooth and nail to preserve it. But anticipating the fact, and stating it, is neither a crime nor a conspiracy; nor is it punishable under Mexican law.

The prosecutor demands increased sentences for our "dissolvent ideas." It seems beyond belief that this gentleman should call the idea of struggling for socialist revolution "dissolvent"—in Mexico, a country forged by the hammer-blows of revolution! As has been recalled here, and as we said in our defense statement, the Constituent Congress in Querétaro had a socialist wing, led by Francisco J. Múgica.[1] Under [President Lázaro] Cárdenas, socialist schools and universities were set up, socialist education was established, "The Internationale" and other socialist anthems were officially sung at trade-union meetings and in schools. What is more, Cárdenas granted asylum to Trotsky, thereby enabling him to continue propagating his ideas, fighting for them, and laying the foundations for the Fourth International—the organization which you now seek to prosecute and condemn for being "dissolvent." It's you who are the dissolvent ones, trying to dissolve Mexico's revolutionary and democratic tradition! And it won't be long before the Mexican people "dissolve" you completely, removing you as an obstacle on the path of their historic progress.

There is no conspiracy here. There is no concrete agreement to carry out any of the actions listed in the relevant section of the Penal Code. To conspire is to reach agreement on the means, methods, date, and location of an action. It's a very concrete and precise activity, which by definition shuns vagueness and imprecision. Just consult the history of conspiracies, starting with the one that gave rise to Mexican independence, led by Miguel Hidalgo, whom a tribunal as legal as this one sentenced to execution by firing squad. Those were conspiracies. Here, there was nothing of the kind. And if it were true that a small party like the POR(T), with its limited material means and scarce numbers, was conspiring with the intention of "overthrowing the established government" of the United States of Mexico—if that ludicrous, stupid, nonsensical idea were true, then it would mean that these supposed "conspirators" were crazy: they were planning an impossible crime, for which they lacked even the most remotely adequate means. In which case, there would be incontestable grounds for acquittal: insanity.

But none of us is insane. We Trotskyists are fighting for the independent, political and trade-union organization of the country's masses, with

---

1 [Francisco Múgica (1884–1954): prominent Revolutionary general; subsequently represented the left wing of the post-revolutionary regime and served as ideological mentor to President Lázaro Cárdenas.]

an anti-imperialist and anti-capitalist program: nationalization, without compensation, of imperialist enterprises and major national enterprises; transfer of all land to the peasantry, to be collectively cultivated; planning of the economy by, and at the service of, mass organizations; workers' control of production; pay increases and a sliding pay-scale; full employment; democratic rights; education in service of the people and its needs; the expulsion of imperialism and its agents from the country; a government of workers and peasants; and socialism. The government seeks to impede that fight, along with the efforts of any tendency or party engaged in impelling the revolutionary struggle for socialism. The government represses these because it is afraid of the emergence of any organization independent of the state, owing to its own weakness and lack of social support. As a result, it throws us in jail, just as it jails other revolutionaries or simple democratic activists and accuses us of conspiracy.

Such is the aim of this judgment against us: to intimidate and terrorize the masses, to hamper their struggles and organization. The judgment achieves this by legal means. The army that is occupying the streets and squares achieves it by military means. The mobsters in the official unions, which support the government, achieve it by gangster methods. The local political bosses achieve it through the police and paramilitaries. But all these techniques of intimidation, from the legal to the military, from jail sentences to tanks, have failed. They have not impeded the struggle. They have not succeeded in blocking the development of revolutionary tendencies in the workers' and peasants' movements. They could not prevent thousands of demonstrators taking over the streets and squares in 1968, demanding democratic rights and freedoms, nor can they hold back the series of worker and peasant actions now unfolding. These will far exceed the already impressive strength of last year's student mobilization.

No, we Trotskyists do not conspire. But we do prepare for such revolutionary struggles. We have been and will be involved in them, as an inseparable and conscious part of Mexico's great masses. And one way in which we prepare ourselves, and make ready for those struggles, is precisely to reject this trumped-up trial, not submitting to its treacherous rules, and denouncing this legal farce and its counterrevolutionary goals.

This judgment has another objective: to condemn, in the form of our persons, the Fourth International and the international organization of the struggle for socialism. That is why, as our attorneys have shown, it invents a new "crime": that of being foreign. So, we are condemned three times over for a single alleged act: first, for conspiracy; second, invoking the same textual bases, for violating the Population Law, i.e., for being foreign; and, finally, the ruling construes this last fact as proof of dangerousness and thus increases the length of our sentences. To round it off, now the Prosecutor's Office insists that once again our sentences must be increased for that same "crime": that of being foreigners.

Well, we have two things to say about this: first, that this criterion is a juridical aberration, against the spirit and the letter of Mexico's Constitution and its laws; second, that even though three of us were born in another country, for the Mexican people we are not foreigners, just as Javier Mina was not a foreigner, and as Che Guevara was never a foreigner in Cuba.[2]

We declare here and now that we have the joy, pride, and satisfaction of living and struggling in Mexico. In that sense, we are completely Mexican. We are part of Mexico and its history. And even if it be in prison, we are glad, very glad, to be living in Mexico, to form part of the Mexican people, to participate in its struggles, even from prison. If we are condemned, we will stay in Mexico and you won't be able to get us out of the country; it'll be the revolution that gets us out of jail. And if we are killed, as has been threatened time and again in prison, then we will be in Mexico for good, and we will carry on existing in the immortal life of the Mexican people. But even though we are already an inseparable part of Mexico, we are proletarian internationalists, like all Marxists, and our homeland is among all the peoples of Latin America and the world, not only the place where we were born.

That's how it was in the War of Independence, when in the far south, in Argentina, there were Mexicans fighting, just as there were Argentines who made it here, too, to fight for the independence of the Americas; and likewise, later, Italian workers who drove the first workers' organizations in Argentina, bringing to bear the experience of the European proletariat. That's how it has been in all the great revolutions that have brought progress to the countries of this world. That's how it is today, when for revolutionaries there are no national borders but only opposed classes, the exploiters and the exploited. That's how it was for the Mexicans who went to fight for the Spanish Revolution, and that's how it was for our Mexican comrades, David Aguilar and his compañera Eunice Campirán, who nearly four years ago were murdered by the Guatemalan

---

2   [Javier Mina (1789–1817): Spanish lawyer, leader of guerrilla forces against Napoleon's occupation of Spain, later died fighting for Mexican independence.]

dictatorship as fighters and militants for the Guatemalan socialist revolution.³ They were Guatemalan, just as we are Mexican.

This country, like all countries but more than many others, was made by the masses, by revolutions and revolutionaries. This country was formed by the mass wars of Independence and Reform, and by the immense popular insurrections of the Revolution of 1910.⁴ Mexico was created by those great organized forces of the people in arms that were the Northern Division and the Southern Army of Liberation, and their chiefs, Pancho Villa and Emiliano Zapata, who were murdered by you, the same people now running this trial. Mexico was built—and to build it they had to take up arms, seize land, organize strikes, reclaim the squares and the streets—by all those who labor and make decisions in production: oil, railway, and textile workers, miners and metal workers, electricians, and the rest, in all sectors; campesinos across the country; the nationalist and revolutionary petty bourgeoisie, from whose ranks sprang revolutionary intellectuals and anti-imperialist soldiers. Those are the builders of Mexico, with their labor and their battles. They never asked anyone what country they were born in before welcoming them into the struggle for national progress. No one asked for anyone's birth certificate in the revolutionary armies of Independence, the Reform, or the Revolution.

We are in Mexico, and we live in Mexico—albeit in prison, by your good offices—and as proletarian revolutionaries, we take part in the Mexican people's struggles. It is our duty and our pride to do so, and we would do the same in any other country. We are not here to invest our capital, demand protection from our embassies, or extract profits from Mexican workers and move the product of their labor to other metropoles. We are here with everything we possess, our ideas and our lives, nothing more, as part of the Mexican people. And the Mexican people has accepted us fraternally and unreservedly. In all the years we have spent in this country, no one—absolutely no one—has held it against us that we were born elsewhere, except this government that is judging us, represented by the gentleman over there from the Prosecutor's Office who is hanging his head.

3   [David Aguilar Mora (1939–65) and Eunice Campirán Villicaña (1943–66): Mexican members of the POR(T) working clandestinely with the MR-13; both tortured and killed by Guatemalan security forces.]
4   [The Reform: period of liberal, secular modernization in Mexico, embodied in the Constitution of 1857 and in the "War of Reform" of 1857–60, won by Liberals led by Benito Juárez.]

That man must know that his country had the historic courage to give asylum to Leon Trotsky when all the world's countries had closed their doors to him, allowing him to continue uninterrupted his work as a theorist and organizer of world revolution. And the Mexican people immediately accepted him as one of their own, and hundreds of thousands marched in a final homage to Leon Trotsky when he was assassinated.

That man, who invokes Article 33 of the Constitution against us after he and the government he represents have trampled all over the Constitution in this and every other political trial, must know perfectly well that Article 33 was not promulgated against revolutionaries but against imperialists—against the Yankee, French, or English invaders who had come to Mexico to subjugate it economically or militarily or to steal half its territory, and whom more than once the Mexican people have had to chase out in a hail of bullets.[5] He must also know that one of the revolutionaries who inspired the most progressive aspects of that Constitution, General Francisco J. Múgica, proposed and defended at the Constituent Congress in Querétaro the inclusion of an article declaring that all Latin Americans are also Mexican citizens, no matter which Latin American country they were born in.[6]

He must know besides, should his police duties have left him the time and ability to study the nation's history, that General Obregón himself—whose thinking we do not share—has a chapter in his book *Ocho mil kilómetros en campaña* entitled "Hostility of the Clergy, Large-scale Commerce, the Banks, Wealthy Industrialists and the Majority of Foreigners" to the forces of the revolution. In it, after condemning the attitude of those sectors and foreigners, he writes verbatim: "As a clarification to the preceding paragraph, as far as foreigners are concerned, I should say that *I have never counted Latin Americans among them*, for they have always come to our country to share our griefs and misfortunes, without any claims to superiority and without ever being a problem for us." It is not we who say so; it is a nationalist officer, founder of the modern Mexican Army and one of the figures who inspired the Constitution you claim to be defending. There you will find the sources to interpret the Article 33 you now cite, having ignored the thirty-two preceding articles as well as most of the others.

5   [Article 33 of the 1917 Mexican Constitution states, "Foreigners may not in any way participate in the political affairs of the country."]

6   [This article was not approved, but as a result of Múgica's intervention, the 1917 Constitution did provide for an expedited naturalization process for citizens of "Indolatino" states—two years' residency instead of five.]

Mexico will once more be invaded by the United States. We have said so at this trial, and the mouthpieces of imperialism have themselves announced it several times. When, encircled by the world revolution, imperialism unleashes the nuclear war it is planning against the workers' states and the peoples of the world—in which it will be definitively defeated and liquidated—one of its first military moves will be to invade Mexico's territory once again, to protect its southern border against the revolution. The Mexican people will resist; they will struggle and prevail by resorting to all revolutionary methods; they will turn to guerrilla warfare, as they did during the independence struggle against the Spanish, during the Juárez era against the French, and during the revolution of 1910 against the Yankee invaders. We Trotskyists, those who were born here and those whom you brand as foreigners, will then take up arms as part of the Mexican people. We have already said so in this trial, to that man from the Prosecutor's Office who has lowered his head and is avoiding our eyes—as though it were him and not us who are sitting in what is known as the dock. When the day comes, that man, and those he represents, may well find themselves in the position of their predecessors in Maximilian's "established government," Miramón and Mejía, where their colleague, CIA agent Humberto Carrillo Colón, finds himself now.[7] They will meet the same dismal end.

Having expressed its satisfaction with the terms of the monstrous sentence we are fighting against, the Prosecutor's Office, as an argument for even harsher sentences, adds the following to the "reasons" already presented: that our conduct during this trial proves we have not mended our ways, that we are irredeemable "delinquents" who have declared their resolve to keep on committing the same "crimes." Yes, we will continue to commit those "crimes"—the capital "crime" of upholding and fighting for the principles, the program, the goals, the methods, and the organization of Marxism and of the Fourth International.

---

7   [Generals Miguel Miramón and Tomás Mejía fought on the conservative side in the War of Reform and served with the French army in 1867; both were executed alongside the deposed Emperor Maximilian. Humberto Carrillo Colón: Mexican diplomat stationed in Havana, revealed in 1969 to be a CIA agent.]

6

Nicaragua and Bolivia: Two Paths

(1980)

Twenty-four years ago, having just arrived in La Paz, I saw the Bolivian miners', workers', and peasants' militias. It was my first sight of figures who up to that point had been mythical as far as I was concerned: workers and campesinos, armed and organized in their unions. A knot of emotion formed in my throat. The revolution of April 1952 was still fresh, the revolution that broke out in order to carry into power Víctor Paz Estenssoro and Hernán Siles Zuazo—elected president and vice president in 1951 but prevented from taking office by a military coup. Insurrections in La Paz, Oruro, and Potosí defeated and dissolved an army formerly at the service of mining tycoons and imperialist powers, which the people had called "the massacring army." Its weapons were transferred into the hands of trade-union militias.

In 1952 the mines were nationalized, and in 1953 the agrarian reform was launched (when peasants had already occupied many haciendas). After that, the revolution stalled; the militias' weapons began to age and they ran short of ammunition. The professional army was patiently reorganized, first by Paz Estenssoro and then by Siles Zuazo, and equipped with high-caliber modern weapons supplied by the US. At the same time, the state began to promote capitalist accumulation, private enterprise, and imperialist investments. The new army and new bourgeoisie developed side by side until, with the coup of 1964, that army once again seized power, resuming its murderous history. Everyone remembers one of the most notorious massacres, which took place on the feast of St. John in 1967, only months before the killing of Che Guevara.[1]

Bolivia has one of the strongest and most politically conscious mass organizations in Latin America: the mining unions and the Central Obrera Boliviana as a whole.[2] But in the absence of a political party to counter the national bourgeoisie and lacking weapons against the massacring army, consciousness, combativeness, and organization may suffice for heroic resistance—with dynamite and last stands on the barricades —but not for victory. It was Juan Lechín, one of the prime movers of the policy that led to disarming the militias, who affirmed that a military coup would be resisted by means of a general strike and some roadblocks.[3] In Argentina in 1955 and 1976, in Chile in 1973, and in other countries at other times, that old formula encouraged the most fateful of delusions: the idea that the workers might resist, after the fact and empty-handed, a military coup that has been technically and scientifically designed to slaughter them. Via the same disastrously passive policy, the Peronist union bureaucrats paved the way for the military dictatorship established in their country in 1976. And it was the Argentine military that provided advice and guidance for the [July 1980] Bolivian coup, with its methodical project of mass murder, according to denunciations recently made in Managua by Jaime Paz Zamora, the vice president-elect of Bolivia.[4]

A few days ago, watching the Sandinista militias in Estelí, I recalled the Bolivian campesinos parading by just as these were doing, a quarter of a century ago, confident of their revolution and marching with the very same gait.

I saw the Sandinista army, and the militias, too, in Managua on July 19th. The old army has been destroyed right down to the roots, and, unlike in Bolivia, the leadership of the revolution has no intention of rebuilding it; only the counterrevolutionaries dare suggest such a thing. I observed the discipline, the supple, easy stride, the modern weaponry of the Sandinista armed forces. I recalled the Bolivians once again, presently

1   [On the night of June 24, 1967, during the festival of San Juan, the Bolivian army surrounded and captured the mining camps of Siglo XX and Llallagua, killing eighty-seven men, women, and children.]

2   [Central Obrera Boliviana (Bolivian Workers' Central, COB): main trade union confederation in Bolivia, founded in 1952, with the Union Federation of Bolivian Mine Workers (FSTMB) its most prominent and militant component.]

3   [Juan Lechín (1914–2001): head of the Bolivian mineworkers' union from 1944 and, from 1952, also of the COB until 1987.]

4   [Hernán Siles Zuazo had won a plurality but not a majority in the June 1980 elections; the July coup by General Luis García Meza blocked Siles's impending election as president by the Bolivian congress.]

being slaughtered by another coup, despite the indescribable heroism with which they have resisted and even dismantled so many others. And I not only saw but keenly felt the radical difference between the two. It's right that the army should be Sandinista, despite the objections of [Alfonso] Robelo, the Consejo Superior de la Empresa Privada (Private Enterprise Council), conservatives, and others; it's right for troops to train intensively; it's right that this army should act as the shield of this revolution, until other, neighboring ones come to lighten its load and make the road ahead less arduous.[5]

Those who prioritize democracy over class can say what they like: the unending martyrdom of Bolivia is their answer, the unfailing result of what they propose. The Bolivian Revolution was only able to hold out for so many years because it formed militias, implemented an agrarian reform, nationalized the mines, and was sustained by unions with a combativeness and a tradition of struggle beyond compare. If it was unable to hold out longer, it's because all of this was interrupted halfway through, and the regrouping of capitalism and its army did the rest.

The Sandinista government has just announced the promulgation of an agrarian reform law targeting the high-quality lands which the *latifundistas* refuse to cultivate, because they balk at the reduction of rents. ("There still hasn't been an agrarian reform here," said Sergio Ramírez.[6] "The present initiative will be the first stage. Then there will be a second.") If the announced measure penetrates deeply enough, it will affect one of the most solid bases of the counterrevolution while amplifying the already extensive support of the revolutionary process. If the battle-hardened Sandinista army can be combined with advances in mass organization that allow full expression of the initiative, the brainpower, and the spontaneous aspirations of Nicaraguan workers—even without reaching the level attained by Bolivia's miners after decade upon decade of struggle—this country may still, like any other nation including the US, be open to attack or even devastation by a stronger power. But it will be, definitively, unconquerable.

Bolivia's miners are resisting and striving once again, as they have always done, to reorganize their ranks from below, patiently repairing

5   [Alfonso Robelo (1939–): cofounder in 1978 of the Movimiento Democrático Nicaragüense (Nicaraguan Democratic Movement, MDN), part of the moderate opposition to the Somoza regime; initially part of the government after Somoza's fall, he resigned in 1980 in protest at the Sandinistas' Marxist tendencies.]

6   [Sergio Ramírez (1942–): Nicaraguan politician and writer; a member of the first Sandinista government, he was elected vice president in 1984, serving a five-year term alongside Daniel Ortega. Now a prominent critic of the Ortega government.]

the organizational fabric destroyed by the killers. Now they can look to Managua and no doubt also to the general strike currently being prepared in El Salvador. Hence the importance of the fact that Managua's Casa de Gobierno served as the tribune for Bolivia's vice president to denounce the coup before the world.

At the same time, we Latin Americans need to find something more than a stimulus in the consolidation of the Nicaraguan Revolution and the advances of the Salvadoran Revolution; we must also extract the theoretical lessons and political experiences that will help in the reorganization, in each country and throughout the continent, of the projects, programs, and forces of the revolution. This latest military coup in Bolivia, once more overturning by fire and sword the result of democratic elections, at a time when that result is not backed up by a revolutionary force organized at every level, reminds us that no task is more urgent.

Managua, July 21, 1980

Part II

Clandestine Histories

7

Mexico: Subaltern Civilization

(2003)

1.

The country now called Mexico has experienced its history as a whirl-pool of antinomies. For the Spanish Empire, the landing of Hernán Cortés in 1519, the fall of Tenochtitlan in 1521, and the long war of the Conquest constituted a tale of redemption. In these new American lands, the Spanish Crown was carrying on from its expulsion of Moors and Jews and the unification of the Peninsula through religion and violence, bringing the Christian faith to boundless territories and unknown peoples.[1]

"In Spain, moreover, the Reconquest and unification provided recent evidence to strengthen the conviction that the new state had been assigned a redemptive mission, reserved for chosen, and hence superior, peoples," wrote Guillermo Bonfil Batalla around 1980.[2]

This imaginary construct of superiority/inferiority as a fact of nature, rather than of society, materialized in the deeds and behaviors of the Conquest, henceforth marked the Colony's relations of dominion and subordination, command and obedience, and prevailed until the

---

1 The beginning of this essay draws on passages from the Prologue to my book *Nuestra caída en la modernidad* (Mexico City: Joan Boldó i Climent, 1988).

2 Guillermo Bonfil Batalla, "Historias que no son todavía historia," in Carlos Pereyra et al., *Historia ¿para qué?* (Mexico City: Siglo XXI, 1980), p. 230.

oligarchical republics that succeeded the wars of independence of the nineteenth century.

The same colonial, and thus racial, matrix gave rise to the forms that would be taken by subalternity in the Mexican Republic.

The wealth of New Spain was destined for the Crown and its European wars; the souls of the indigenous people who extracted it were destined for the Christian heaven. The redemption, then, of precious buried metals through their incorporation into the market, and the redemption of an idolatrous people through their incorporation into the one true faith. Like any other conquering enterprise, this one had its own solid ideological justification and founded a new lineage of subalterns, distinct from those that existed in the metropole and, it might be said, subordinate to them, too.

The early modernity of the Age of Discovery dealt a catastrophic blow to the inhabitants of those lands and their ancient civilizations and cultures. Despite offering stubborn resistance, the indigenous world was annihilated. Its societies' trust in life, their internal relationships, their gods, their interaction with sky and earth, water and fire, all were destroyed.

In the version relayed by Miguel León-Portilla in his *The Broken Spears*, a Nahua poet says this about the fall of Tenochtitlan:

> We have pounded our hands in despair
> against the adobe walls,
> for our inheritance, our city, is lost and dead.
> The shields of our warriors were its defense,
> but they could not save it.[3]

Bernal Díaz del Castillo, in his *Conquest of New Spain*, describes the moment of the fall of Tenochtitlan with his Spaniard's words and peerless chronicler's art:

> During the whole ninety-three days of our siege of the capital, Mexican captains were yelling and shouting night and day, mustering the bands of warriors who were to fight on the causeway . . . Then there was the unceasing sound of their accursed drums and trumpets, and their

3 Miguel León-Portilla, ed., *The Broken Spears: The Aztec Account of the Conquest of Mexico*, trans. Angel María Garibay and Lysander Kemp (Boston: Beacon Press, [1959] 2006), p. 138.

melancholy kettledrums in the shrines and on their temple towers. Both day and night the din was so great that we could hardly hear one another speak. But after Guatemoc's capture, all the shouting and the other noises ceased.[4]

Then silence.

After Guatemoc's capture, all we soldiers became as deaf as if all the bells in a belfry had been ringing and had then suddenly stopped.[5]

The deafening silence of defeat hangs over the bloody scene:

I solemnly swear that all the houses and stockades in the lake were full of heads and corpses. I do not know how to describe it, but it was the same in the streets and courts of Tlatelolco. We could not walk without treading on the bodies and heads of dead Indians.[6]

This is mourned from the other side in the Nahua voice of the anonymous manuscript:

> Broken spears lie in the roads;
> we have torn our hair in our grief.
> The houses are roofless now, and their walls
> are red with blood.[7]

At the start of the century following that of the Conquest, the indigenous population of Mesoamerica had fallen to less than 10 percent of their numbers at the time of the European invasion. It had been devastated by disease, war, displacement, exploitation in the mines, and, above all, the shattering destruction of their world, the loss of their lives' meaning, solitude, humiliation, and grief. An indigenous document [purportedly] from 1531 evokes these feelings:

Thus, it is said . . . that secretly the lord Marqués [Cortés] will come to take our lands, take possession of ourselves, and establish new towns.

---

4   Bernal Díaz del Castillo, *The Conquest of New Spain*, trans. J. M. Cohen (London: Penguin, 1963), pp. 404–5.
5   Díaz del Castillo, *The Conquest of New Spain*, p. 404.
6   Ibid., p. 405.
7   León-Portilla, *The Broken Spears*, p. 137.

And where will they throw us? Where will they place us? A very great sadness afflicts us.[8]

2.

Redemption and fall: this strange Marriage of Heaven and Hell led to the birth of what would eventually be Mexico. At that period, the disputes of early modernity had only just begun in Europe, with the Italian Renaissance, the Protestant Reformation, and the discovery across the seas of lands and peoples beyond Europe's ken. This was the time of, as Edmundo O'Gorman called it, "the invention of America."[9]

In Iberian America, this modernity took the form of feudalism. And yet exchange value already lay at its heart, in the hunt for gold and other metals. "Gold is most excellent; gold constitutes treasure and anyone who has it can do whatever he likes in this world. With it, he can succeed in bringing souls to Paradise," wrote Christopher Columbus, the admiral of the high seas.[10] The nascent capitalist world, still wrapped in the political and cultural garb of feudal society; the view of gold as a universal commodity rather than a symbolic incarnation of religion, power, and riches are what brought down the old civilizations and cultures of Mesoamerica and the Andes.[11] The Nahua manuscript depicts this with strange and moving precision:

> They put a price on us: on the young men, the priests, the boys and girls . . .
>   Gold, jade, rich cloths, quetzal feathers—everything that was once precious was now considered worthless.[12]

But the great treasure of the Indies was not so much precious metals as the labor power of its natives. "The great prize in this scramble for riches," notes David Brading, "was an *encomienda*, the grant of a number of Indians who were henceforth obliged to offer free labor and tribute to

---

8   Cited in ibid., p. 160.
9   Edmundo O'Gorman, *México: el trauma de su historia* (Mexico City: Consejo Nacional para la Cultura y las Artes, 1999), p. 15.
10   David A. Brading, *The First America: The Spanish Monarchy, Creole Patriotism and the Liberal State 1492–1867* (New York: Cambridge University Press, 1991), p. 14.
11   Gilly, *Nuestra caída en la modernidad*.
12   León-Portilla, *The Broken Spears*, p. 138.

their Spanish master."[13] This was the specific form of slavery that underlay the dominance of the invaders and the fabled riches of their European empire.

Their world was incomprehensible to the native mind, quite meaningless, nothing but sound and fury. That mind never adapted to subjugation altogether. The old world of Mesoamerica appeared to vanish—from a figure between fifteen and twenty million souls in the first decades of the sixteenth century, they numbered scarcely 1,600,000 a short century later. Over time and successive generations, the remnant became bearers of the seed of the originary civilization, denied by the dominance of the invaders but persisting as a subaltern civilization within the hidden discourses and symbolic practices of the dominated.

It appeared to vanish, but it did not. Over the bodies and works of these native actors, both colonizers and colonized began weaving new networks, new ties of personal dependence and of deference toward hitherto nonexistent characters: the master, the owner of the encomienda and the hacienda, the soldier, the priest, the administrator, the Spaniard, the *criollo*, the white person.

Within that society, the indigenous worldview translated such relations into their own terms and their own imaginary. The forms taken by their obedience and deference to the overlords came from ancient times. Although the bearded white dominators did not know it, those native forms of deference would gradually bind with imperceptible ties and subtly alter those in charge of this strange, impenetrable human world, far from the metropolitan version of agrarian society and feudal command. The resulting command–obedience relation was an original creation, just as indigenous Catholicism and its rituals were.

In the new structure of domination, their way of worshipping the new gods reproduced their ancestral ways of communicating with the old ones. After all, the gods had changed but not the human beings who lodged their hopes, desires, and fears in them. Furthermore, their way of obeying their new masters was imbued from below by their way of obeying the old, since the masters had changed but not the labor force from which they extracted their wealth and power. Obedience has a language more enduring than words. As Steve Stern writes,

The natives played on the terrain of their colonizers in an unexpected way, inventing new rules as they went along. They didn't come in through the official door of paternalism, asking for the permission and kindness of an Indian protector, sticking to the rules and the corner to which they were relegated. Instead, they looked for another door, and in the process invaded and colonized the terrain, changing the dynamics of society and power.[14]

Over the centuries, these relations modified the cultures of both civilizations, the dominant and the subaltern. But they did not fuse them into one: the racial, colonial matrix of domination preserved and reproduced the division because, as Bonfil Batalla observes, "the colonial order perpetuates the difference between colonizers and colonized as an indispensable distinction for organizing and justifying colonial domination."[15] Enrique Florescano likewise underscores the persistence of that dividing line: "As soon as Hernán Cortés and his armies had achieved the conquest of Tenochtitlan, a dichotomy was put in place that still divides the country." The long history of skirmishes and wars between the sides, he goes on, "shows the inability of the invading culture to make the traditional culture disappear." That same history, however, "describes the inevitable transformation of native culture due to changes induced by European culture."[16]

To put it another way: as the social, cultural, and imaginary fabric born of the first violent antinomies gradually reformed and solidified, the customs, beliefs, and ways of life of the indigenous world—the ancient patterns of civilization denied by the institutions of power—began to permeate the relations of obedience and command of the new dispensation, mingling with Spanish ways and vice versa, until ultimately they configured a completely novel form of relation, distinct from any found in the metropole from which the rulers, priests, and laws had come.[17]

14   Steve Stern, "La contracorriente histórica: Los indígenas como colonizadores del Estado, siglos XVI a XX," in Leticia Reina, ed., *Los retos de la etnicidad en los estados-nación del siglo XXI,* (Mexico City: Centro de Investigaciones y Estudios Superiores en Antropología Social, 2000), pp. 73–91.
15   Guillermo Bonfil Batalla, *Pensar nuestra cultura* (Mexico City: Alianza, 1991), p. 64.
16   Enrique Florescano, *Etnia, Estado y nación. Ensayo sobre las identidades colectivas en México* (Mexico City: Aguilar, 1997), p. 502.
17   Without looking beyond the second half of the twentieth century, there are countless historians and writers, Mexican and foreign, who have dwelled on this fascinating process: Octavio Paz and Carlos Fuentes, Serge Gruzinski and Jacques Lafaye, Edmundo O'Gorman and Miguel León-Portilla, John Tutino and Eric van Young, Enrique Florescano and Alejandra Moreno Toscano, Alfredo López Austin and David Brading, François Chevalier and Inga Clendìnnen, Friedrich Katz and Alan Knight, Antonio García de León, Gilbert Joseph, Jan de Vos, Juan Pedro Viqueira, Jan Rus, James

The density of this original creation was not primarily owed to the upper and ruling classes. The authority these sectors exerted was molded from below by the vast subaltern world—by its forms of obeying, of demanding reciprocity, of resisting authority, of constantly rebelling against it and bargaining with it. The subaltern world, negated in terms of its history and originary identity, never ceased to define the overall tenor of social relations in those territories, a tonality determined by the subaltern's own past history and customs rather than by the European culture of the conquerors.[18]

3.

The ideological construction of colonial domination had to deny this real history. Despite their notoriously diverse cultures and languages, the native peoples were lumped together under the single name of "Indians," as Guillermo Bonfil points out in his 1980 essay "Historias que no son todavía historia" (Histories That Are Not Yet History), a work that already contained the germ of his later *México Profundo*. To such multiple histories, a single meaning was ascribed: to serve as the prolegomena of those peoples' entrance into proper history, the only universal history, the history of Europe. Their redemption by the Conquest was not the culmination of a past but the negation of it: "Indian history ended with the European invasion. That chapter was definitively closed. A new and different history began."[19]

Bonfil challenges this relegation of indigenous peoples' histories. In the first place, these histories were written as a "discourse of power from the viewpoint of the colonizers"; second, they have not yet concluded, being "open-ended histories, in progress, insisting on a future of their own."[20]

Lockhart, Stuart B. Schwartz, William Taylor, and many, many more. We could never list them all because this is the theme par excellence of Mexican history and is one source of the great Mexican passion for that discipline.

18   "In all forms of society there is one specific kind of production which predominates over the rest, whose relations thus assign rank and influence to the others. It is a general illumination which bathes all the other colours and modifies their particularity. It is a particular ether which determines the specific gravity of every being which has materialized within it," Marx writes in the *Grundrisse* (Cited in E. P. Thompson, *Making History: Writings on History and Culture* [New York: The New Press, 1994], pp. 218–19).

19   Bonfil Batalla, "Historias que no son todavía historia," pp. 227–45.

20   Resonance and consonance: "The multiplicity of histories resembles the multiplicity of languages. Universal history in the present-day sense can never be more than a

Bonfil's thinking converges here with that of a distant predecessor of the second half of the eighteenth century, the German philosopher Johann Gottfried Herder. In his *Ideas on the Philosophy of the History of Mankind* (1784–91), Herder contests the notion that, within the unfolding of supposed universal history, "civilization" or "*Kultur*" was a unilinear process destined to lead to the high and dominant level of European culture. He attacks Europe's subjugation of the peoples and civilizations of the whole planet:

> Men of all the quarters of the globe, who have perished over the ages, you have not lived solely to manure the earth with your ashes, so that at the end of time your posterity should be made happy by European culture. The very thought of a superior European culture is a blatant insult to the majesty of Nature.[21]

Guillermo Bonfil Batalla had many other illustrious forerunners and contemporaries. Born in 1935, he was an anthropologist, a prolific writer and polemicist, and a champion of indigenous peoples and their past and future histories. In 1972 he wrote an essay called "El concepto de indio en América: una categoría de la situación colonial" (The Concept of Indian in America: a Category of the Colonial Situation), which prefigured the development of his oeuvre and activities.[22] In 1987 he published *México Profundo*, and in 1991, shortly before his death, brought out a long essay whose title and content present a reasoned conclusion to the central proposal of his written work: to reach a pact among civilizations.[23]

In 1978, writing about his colleague Darcy Ribeiro, Bonfil expressed insights that surely apply to his own approach:

> Darcy . . . has always been essentially a politician, a political being. His fundamental and primary vocation is to participate, to be instrumental in the transformation of the social order. Not just by putting forward ideas, but by fighting directly and personally for their implementation . . .

kind of Esperanto. The idea of universal history is a messianic idea." (Walter Benjamin, "Paralipomena to 'On the Concept of History,'" in *Selected Writings, Vol. 4: 1938–1940*, trans. Edmund Jephcott et al. (Cambridge, MA: Belknap Press, 1996), p. 405).

   21   Quoted by Raymond Williams, *Keywords: A Vocabulary of Culture and Society*, (London: Fontana [1976] 1988), p. 89.

   22   Guillermo Bonfil Batalla, *Obras escogidas*, vol. 4 (Mexico City: Instituto Nacional Indigenista, 1995), pp. 337–57.

   23   Bonfil Batalla, "Quinientos años después: ¿llegaremos finalmente a un pacto de civilizaciones?" in ibid., vol. 4, pp. 425–54.

A wish to realize utopia and to embed himself in it—not as a spectator, but as a doer.[24]

This relationship of the subject, or researcher, with the subject (not only the object) of study; this reversible relation of subjectivities between the two terms (no matter how distant in time or space); this position as *doer* rather than *spectator* when it comes to investigative inquiry—a position also adopted by other great artisans in the trade such as Marc Bloch, author of both *The Royal Touch* and *Strange Defeat*—these elements are what situate Guillermo Bonfil in this peculiar constellation of "history against the grain."[25]

4.

The thread of racially based subalternity runs through all the transformations and configurations of the relation of dominance, serving as constitutive form from colonial times up to the Mexican Republic of today. This fact does nothing to dilute the specific character of each one of these forms, rural or urban, but it has acted consistently as an insuperable limit on republican life.

The liberal republic asserted the importance of indigenous histories as if they were its own: its ancestor was Cuauhtémoc, not Cortés. But, as ever, it inscribed them as antecedents coming to fruition in a republic that dissolved the Indians and their pasts and remade them as part of a single category of citizens, within a universal history that came from Europe, no longer religious and colonial in character but enlightened and republican. In the mid-1820s, José María Luis Mora could insist that legally speaking, "Indians no longer exist," even if the term nevertheless cropped up regularly in the debates of the period in attenuated form as "the so-called Indians."[26]

This abolition of a prior history by making it a tributary of the dominant history affirmed the original and consubstantial subalternity of

24 Ibid., vol. 1, p. 386.
25 [A reference to the title and subtitle of the book from which this essay is drawn: *Historia a contrapelo: Una constelación* (History Against the Grain: A Constellation) (Mexico City: Ediciones Era, 2006). The constellation in question is the series of critical left thinkers—Antonio Gramsci, Walter Benjamin, Karl Polanyi, E. P. Thompson, Ranajit Guha—with whom Gilly engages across the six essays in the book.]
26 Charles A. Hale, *Mexican Liberalism in the Age of Mora, 1821–53* (New Haven: Yale University Press, 1968), p. 218.

the indigenous population. As Bonfil reminds us in *México Profundo*: "Again, it was the colonial experience that organized society on the basis of hierarchical divisions. Physical features were used as social principles for ordering groups and individuals."[27]

That era spawned a constant in the kind of domination exercised by ruling republican elites: racial distinction, always denied and always present as the ultimate rationale for the right of command and as the deep root of the massive inequalities and violent conflicts of Mexican history.

That original line of fracture constitutes the foundation of a specific subalternity conceived of as the congenital inequality of different beings, in which the subaltern are not regarded as equals, nor as brothers, nor as free, because they only exist to take orders. This subalternity is based not on any wage differential but on the racial and colonial matrix, characterizing a Republic that lives up to its name in laws that are sometimes radical in their secularism and egalitarianism but not in everyday reality. For, as anyone can see for themselves, the line dividing the rich from those who live by manual labor tends to coincide with differences in skin color.

When this division is racially based and not merely between modern social classes united by the market—including the wage market—then the commands flow from one level of understanding, of notions of life and world, of civilization (because every colonial order entails a subordinated civilization) to another. In the process, these commands need to be translated, reinterpreted, and revalidated by the value system of the subaltern culture. That which in a commercially homogeneous society is assumed to be culturally horizontal becomes, in a society molded by colonialism, vertical, graded between dissimilar cultures and life-worlds. Racial subalternity imbues even the modern wage relation and shapes it in specific ways.

Bonfil himself acknowledges this contradiction when he reflects on the existence throughout history of a subordinated—and negated from above—culture of Indian origin:

> The Indian peoples are dominated peoples. But being dominated, in their case, involves very different characteristics and effects than the dominion exercised over the subaltern sectors of a monocultural society . . . In

---

27   Guillermo Bonfil Batalla, *México Profundo: Reclaiming a Civilization*, trans. Philip A. Dennis (Austin: University of Texas Press, 2010), p. 18.

the case of groups of different cultures, the culture of the subordinated peoples forms the backbone of resistance. By contrast, the dominated groups within a monoculture are not defending their own culture but rather struggling for equal access to a culture that also belongs to the dominant groups.[28]

5.

The agrarian and communitarian, and not republican, roots of the organizational forms of Mexican subalternity are extremely ancient. They persist today just beneath the surface: 4,000 years on this territory and 200 generations, who became majority urbanized only in the second half of the twentieth century and whose barrios and popular spaces host the rituals and customs of a recent agrarian past that is hardly past at all.

Mesoamerican civilization, Bonfil maintains, "is still alive in Mexican society, and its principles govern the profound cultural orientation of millions of Mexicans, far more than those who are identified or who identify themselves as 'Indian.'"[29] This applies to Indian pueblos, to traditional rural communities that call themselves "mestizo," and to ample swathes of the urban working class. These social sectors, he writes at the beginning of *México Profundo*, make up most of the population: "What unifies them and distinguishes them from the rest of Mexican society is that they are bearers of ways of understanding the world and of organizing human life that have their origins in Mesoamerican civilization and that have been forged here in Mexico through a long and complicated historical process."[30]

"From the European invasion onward," he also writes, "a structure was established in which Western civilization dominated that of Mesoamerica . . . The colonial order denied Mesoamerican civilization and justified, on grounds of its non-existence, the subjection and exploitation of Indian peoples."[31]

The old civilization, dominated and steadily modified by the new authorities, was not abolished, absorbed, or erased. Its negation was, for the dominators, as necessary as its persistence. This perennial contradiction was paramount in the unwritten definition of the rules

28 Bonfil Batalla, *Pensar nuestra cultura*, pp. 62–3.
29 Ibid., pp. 91–2.
30 Bonfil Batalla, *México Profundo*, p. 1.
31 Bonfil Batalla, *Pensar nuestra cultura*, pp. 91–2.

of command–obedience within the racial matrix of dominion over a civilization that had been rendered subaltern, profoundly disrupted, abolished in law but not in life.

"Indigenous communities, rooted in their regional cultural traditions, had persisted for millennia before the Conquest. Indigenous empires rose and fell before European power. But communities were the economic and cultural basis of the empires of Mesoamerica and Spain," writes John Tutino, underlining the obvious fact that Spain's empire and kingdom would never have been what they were in later centuries—and even today—without their profits from the subjugation and exploitation of Mesoamerican and Andean communities.[32]

The category of "Indian" is necessary for this form of domination, and it is also present in a peculiar wage relation steeped in archaic ties of personal dependency. This category, says Bonfil, "is a total concept that claims to define in a single word the endless list of inferiorities attributed to a group or an individual in the eyes of whoever defines it or him as 'Indian.'"[33]

We are faced, then, with a racial construction of subalternity, an imaginary construction, that denies the dominated and negated civilization on the level of discourse but retains and needs it in the realities of domination and exploitation—while this civilization endures in the daily life of the subaltern, in their symbols, social relationships, and beliefs as in their multiple cultures of resistance and rebellion.[34]

6.

Subaltern civilization, like its various cultures of solidarity and work, gift and feast, deference and rebellion, can be negated or declared inferior in the discourse and behaviors of the dominant elites, whether these be colonial or nationalist, conservative or liberal. Nevertheless, the fact

---

32 John Tutino, "Comunidad, independencia y nación: las participaciones populares en las historias de México, Guatemala y Perú," in Reina, ed., *Los retos de la etnicidad*, pp. 125–51.

33 Bonfil Batalla, *Pensar nuestra cultura*, p. 92.

34 As Bonfil, who is not alone in pointing this out, writes: "The ways in which the inhabitants of *México profundo* manage their religious life offer many examples of how they have appropriated Catholic rites and images and given them a meaning different from their original one. They can imbue them with new meaning because they control them from their own religious perspective, which is not Christian but derived historically from an original Mesoamerican religion." *México Profundo*, p. 136.

is that in the production and reproduction of life, those subalterns are always present. They are the "doers," the ones who live by their hands, who make life possible. And yet they only figure in the historical record as a mass or at best a chorus, for record-keeping is a terrain occupied by the deciders and the scribes of the dominant elites, who alone keep a written tally.

The absence of the subaltern from the official record is not the result of any wickedness or conspiracy. It is simply that from where the elites are standing and taking note, they cannot make out the subalterns as anything more than shadows at the back of the stage. The only register of the subaltern, beyond a fragile oral history and a panoply of myths and legends, lies in their material cultural artifacts and in their actions, whenever these leave scars on the history preserved in the archives.

The most visible scars, if not the only ones, are those left by uprisings, mutinies, and revolutions. The history of the country now called Mexico, founded upon the geological fault line of that original antinomy, abounds with such mass events through both the colonial period and that of the Republic. Racially based dominance is brittle by nature because it prevents the definitive consolidation of an imaginary "we" in the consciousness of all, the dominated and the dominant, that is, a "we" made up of citizens equal in the eyes of a supposedly universal, impersonal, and abstract law.

At those moments when the subalterns enter the historical record with violence and in the first person, when the immense cast of bit-part actors occupies center stage, the ties that bind them together in action and the customs that organize them in the face of the dominant class become visible. These do not derive from the laws that are in force, from the statutes of republican policies, or from the party and institutional organs through which the prevailing structure of domination reproduces, renews, and perpetuates itself; they spring from their shared ancient past, that past which is, in Mesoamerica, likewise perpetuated and renewed through the subaltern civilization and its cultures.

The history of New Spain is not only a prodigious trove of riches, knowledge, and culture among the dominant classes. It is also a story of rural indigenous revolts and urban plebeian riots. Agrarian protest always evinced three traits, even when it erupted under Crown protection. It rested on the *existence* of an agrarian community predating the colonial order; on the *defense* of a traditional relationship to nature and territory (community lands, waters, forests, and pastures); and on the *preservation* of community autonomy against the encroachment of outsiders.

This is the world prior to the conversion of land, water, and woods into so many commodities; it is the world of reciprocity and redistribution that Rosa Luxemburg calls the world of natural economy, and others, the world of moral economy.

This world, a fabric of solidarities reproducing and renewing themselves, resists its own disappearance—as though it were a constant in human societies, a cloth woven in each case from the threads of history itself. In the commodity-crammed space of modernity, protest and rebellion are human acts and relations that resist being transmuted into goods or measured in monetary terms.

The modernity of digitized mercantile relations, including the buying and selling of labor power, also impinges on communications devices (and a social uprising is per se a communication among those who rise up): radio, television, the press, internet, transport. But an uprising is not coterminous with its artifacts. In it, we find continuously reproduced the fabric that made it possible: the collective intelligence and will that appropriate the artifacts for their own purposes. Such a will takes shape in areas that are not those of technology, in an education that is not that of the formal education system, and in other historic domains of the subaltern that have not yet been registered as history.

7.

Mexican revolutions and revolts have always broken out to defend the relations inherent in that earlier world. This is true of the Revolution of Independence itself, which was in substance a massive indigenous and agrarian insurrection launched as a counterblow to the modernization imposed through Bourbon reforms. These reforms, fed by enlightened notions of rationalization and centralized power, ripped apart the web of practices, compromises, and commitments governed by the customary relations of the Habsburg era.[35] However, in yet another paradox,

35   In his study of Andean social conflicts in the 1770s, which prefigured the great uprisings of Túpac Amaru and Túpaj Katari (1780–81), Sergio Serulnikov approaches the disruptive consequences of Bourbon modernization with some reflections helpful for thinking about the effects of the neoliberal modernization of dominion a couple of centuries later. His question is, why did those reforms, founded on enlightened ideas of rationalization and centralized power, trigger an indigenous rebellion in 1780–81 rather than a revolution led by the *criollos* who were affected by them? The native peoples, he says, viewed the reforms as "a major instrument of Andean resistance against entrenched structures of exploitation and political oppression in the rural villages," even as colonial

the thinking of the two Catholic priests who headed that revolution, Miguel Hidalgo and José María Morelos, was influenced by the French Revolution.[36]

The agrarian upheaval was so violent that the dominant classes retreated into their internal conflicts in a wholesale crisis of fragmented rule, rendering them incapable of aggregating the turbulent subaltern world into a nation until midway through the nineteenth century: it had escaped their control, and they feared it.[37] That subaltern world also turned in on itself to pursue its accustomed, immemorial life.

After Mexico lost half of its original territory in the war against the United States—the exorbitant tribute paid by the Mexican nation to the spatial formation of the US, the incipient Promised Land of capital—Benito Juárez's reforms founded liberal institutions, affirmed state power against the Church, and closed the doors of the Republic to the natives.

rulers sought to use such rationalizing projects for the contrary objective of fortifying their own control. "The key point, nonetheless, is that the most radical indigenous upheaval during the colonial times in the region was the outcome of the *intertwinement*, not the *clash*, between processes of social mobilization from below and political transformation from above. Seen from this particular regional context, the crisis of colonial legitimacy may have resulted less from the enforcement of a new colonial pact than from *the unintended ways in which this new hegemonic project helped to collapse the old one without consolidating in the process a viable alternative* [my emphasis—A. G.]. Bourbon policies increased the economic burden upon Andean communities at the same time that they empowered them to contest local authority." (Sergio Serulnikov, "Customs and Rules: Bourbon Rationalizing Projects and Social Conflicts in Northern Potosí during the 1770s," *Colonial Latin American Review*, vol. 8, no. 2, 1999, pp. 245–74).

36   Octavio Paz wrote in 1950: "The Revolution of Independence was a class war, and its nature cannot be understood correctly unless we recognize the fact that unlike what happened in South America, it was an agrarian revolt in gestation. This is why the army (with its *criollos* like Iturbide), the Church and the great landowners supported the Spanish Crown, and these were the forces that defeated Hidalgo, Morelos and Javier Mina." (Paz, *The Labyrinth of Solitude*, trans. Lysander Kemp [New York: Grove Press, 1961], p. 123.)

37   Regarding the period immediately after independence, John Coatsworth observes:

Although the native peoples and the liberals made Mexico ungovernable, neither group possessed the unity, political coherence, or economic resources to impose a new order on Mexican society. The indigenous population (as was the case with peasants everywhere in modern history) could only seize political power by allying with other forces in society. Mexican liberals were as frightened as the conservatives by images of the havoc wreaked by Hidalgo's movement, and so fearful of "caste war" that they failed to channel indigenous discontent to their advantage, except only at certain moments, in certain areas, and for short periods. Hence repression of indigenous revolts in the countryside was the agrarian policy of both liberal and conservative governments.

(John H. Coatsworth, *Los orígenes del atraso*, [Mexico City: Alianza, 1990], pp. 212–13.)

This Republic was constituted not only against the ancien régime but also, and above all, against the native world, that is, against the vast majority of the Mexican people. The Juárez era saw a new wave of campesino rebellions against the juridical dissolution of their communities and the conversion, by law or by force, of their lands, water, and woods into private property. In the northeast, the Yaqui continued to resist and defend their autonomy until after the Mexican Revolution, and in the southeast, the Maya remained on a war footing until the early twentieth century.[38]

8.

The advance of the railway during the last two decades of the nineteenth century, a classic symbol of progress, was marked by successive campesino revolts due to its repercussions upon their lives, lands, and economies. Protests and unrest also accompanied the creation of national boundaries in the same period, when the common lands of the pueblos became redefined as the property of landowners and boundary demarcation companies.

This progress—which is to say, the sustained expansion of capitalist relations via the privatization of lands, water, and forests—was considered a prerequisite for the establishment of modern republican political institutions and of a nation of citizens, with equal obligations and rights before the law, including the right to individual property. One result of this process was expected to be the overcoming of the "indigenous condition." In one of his last essays, Bonfil Batalla cites texts that seem like precursors, in negative, of the outbreak of the Revolution of 1910. Barely a year earlier, in 1909, one such text read as follows:

> There thus exists, on the one hand, great public wealth in stagnant or latent form, and on the other, a more convenient way within this wealth itself to pursue, as ever, the speedy regeneration of the Indian. Individualism must be created in him, relegating the community to its true function, for this imperfect and absurd socialism in which he lives and

---

38   In *México descalzo* (Mexico City: Plaza y Janés, 2002), Romana Falcón documents the territorial range and social depth of those rebellions, harshly put down under Benito Juárez and Porfirio Díaz. For an invaluable and up-to-date survey of the contentious relations between the Republic and native peoples, see Florescano, *Etnia, estado y nación*, especially Chapters 3 and 4.

where everything apparently belongs to everybody is what keeps the
Indian poor, with no real love of ownership, whatever his passion for his
plot . . . Communal property must be divided up.[39]

In other words, one ideological assumption of the reforms of nineteenth-
century liberalism and its heir, twentieth-century nationalism, was the
need to dissolve the social forms of the old regime and turn the natives
into citizens—into Mexicans who, in becoming Mexicans, would have
ceased being Indians, and, most importantly, would be stripped of their
commonly held lands and goods.

Nevertheless, at the start of the twentieth century, the sharp pen of
Captain Fournier, French military attaché to the United States, did not
mince words in recording his impressions of the army of the liberal-
oligarchic Republic of President Porfirio Díaz:

The Mexican nation is composed of three main elements: the Indians,
who make up the greater part of the population; the mestizos, a product
of the conquistadors crossed with the autochthonous race; and the upper
class, formed by individuals of the white race, largely of Spanish origin.
It was impossible to bring together in the proximity of the barracks such
socially disparate elements. As a result, the army recruits almost exclusively from among the Indians, in principle by voluntary enlistment
for three to five years, with the option to renew. Only the commanding
officers are drawn from other classes of the population.[40]

The soldiers of the Republican Army, that supposed foundry of citizen
equality without distinction of rank or wealth, at the age when youth
commits itself to serve the motherland, were none other than the natives,

39   Esteban Maqueo Castellanos, *Algunos problemas nacionales* (Mexico City:
1909), p. 93, as quoted in Bonfil Batalla, *Obras escogidas*, vol. 4, pp. 437–8. Bonfil cites
other examples of this mentality in the same essay. For example, on September 18, 1899,
in a front-page piece entitled "La raza indígena" (The Indigenous Race), the newspaper
El Siglo XIX scolded: "So many centuries of wretched ignorance seem to have withered
the brain of this race, which once boasted a civilization comparable to those of the
Ancient World and reached in Cuauhtémoc the summit of patriotic heroism. Today we
see them celebrate their hero with masquerades that would satisfy the inhabitants of
Timbuctoo or Kaffraria."

40   Archive Militaire de Vincennes, Inventaire Sommaire des Archives de la
Guerre, Série N 1872–1919. Attachés Militaires 7B 1727, Ambassade de la République
Française aux Etats-Unis, Washington, le 13 Dec. 1905. Le capitaine Fournier, Attaché
Militaire, 2ème Bureau, n. 4. Objet: L'armée mexicaine.

hustled into the draft by hoary ancien régime methods of deceit and coercion.

Indeed, in this liberal Republic, whose congress garlanded President Porfirio Díaz in 1905 with a Cordon of Military Merit and a gold medallion reading, "He pacified and united the country," indigenous peoples and communities were trapped in the very same racial and colonial subalternity as they had been a hundred years before in 1799, as testified by [Bishop] Manuel Abad y Queipo:

> We have already mentioned that the population of New Spain numbered roughly four-and-a-half million, which may be divided into three classes: Spaniards, Indians, and *castas* [mixed-race]. The Spaniards make up a tenth of the total and are the owners of almost all the property and riches of the realm. The other two classes, or the other nine tenths, can be divided into thirds, two made up of castas and one of pure-blood Indians. The natives and castas work in domestic service, agriculture, or the everyday offices of trades and crafts. That is to say, they are the servants or laborers of the first class. In consequence there arises, between them and the first class, that opposition of interest and feeling commonly found between those who have nothing and those who have everything, between dependents and masters. Envy, theft, poor service on the one side; disdain, usury, and harshness on the other. These outcomes are found to some degree in all the world. But in America they reach the highest pitch, for there are no gradual increments, no middle grounds; every man is either rich or destitute, noble or despicable.[41]

9.

Campesino and indigenous communities reacted with waves of resistance and rebellion against this continuity of colonial domination disguised as "republican equality," just as they had previously responded to Bourbon modernity in New Spain. This new republican modernity, whose overweening racism was denied in law and yet conspicuous in reality, was harmful at once to their lifeworld and to their own notions of equality and justice.

These successive uprisings culminated in 1911 with the irruption of campesinos and Indians into the armies of the Mexican Revolution, from the Northern Division [associated with Pancho Villa] to the Southern

---

41   As quoted in Florescano, *Etnia, estado y nación*, p. 276.

Army of Liberation [associated with Emiliano Zapata]. They joined in the name of a different Republic from that of the liberal, conservative, or nationalist elites. The practical outlines of such a republic were laid out by the Zapatistas and their peasant army in what came to be called the Morelos Commune, lasting from 1911 to 1919.[42]

Here was yet another rebellion of "custom" against "progress," in search not of restoring the past but of a different future, one predicated on the deeds, sayings, and writings of the rebels. This antinomy remains a recurrent feature of twentieth-century Mexican history, from the reforms of President Cárdenas in the 1930s to the insurrection in 1994 of the Zapatista indigenous communities in Chiapas State. The latter rebellion prompted a radical reframing of these issues in terms of events on the ground, as well as a remarkable outpouring of studies and debates on the topic, as tends to happen when all of a sudden, amid all the words, there is a blaze of action.

These histories tell us that the condition of subalternity cannot be altered through mere legislation that springs from the political corpus of a republic founded on the existence and persistence of that same condition. Subalternity can only be modified or overcome through the constitution of the subaltern as an autonomous subject, an individual "able to make use of his own understanding without guidance from others" in daily life and activities, rather than in remote texts. Indeed, this encapsulates the essence of the long and tortuous struggle for the autonomous organization of labor in opposition to the joint rule of capital and its state institutions over the past two centuries.

This autonomous subject is in turn constituted through experience, in the negation, through concrete facts, of his subaltern condition and the existent domination. Such a negation cannot be enacted within the institutions that sanction and reproduce this subalternity in its juridical forms, even if these do not textually enshrine it but declare instead that all citizens enjoy equal rights.

The specificity of Mexican subalternity resides not in the laws but in the facts. The facts come first. New laws cannot change the facts. New facts can change the laws. The autonomy of the subject is constituted through *experience*, the one thing that can lend substance to any law that sanctions that autonomy.

---

42 [Gilly described the social composition and motivating ideas of these two great peasant armies in his classic work on the Mexican Revolution, *La revolución interrumpida*; see Adolfo Gilly, *The Mexican Revolution*, trans. Patrick Camiller (New York: The New Press, [1971] 2005), Chapters 3, 4, and 8.]

This factual negation of the existing subalternity requires a break with these institutions, with a view to changing or modifying them at their root. A rupture of this kind is called rebellion, revolt, or revolution, depending on the case and the conditions. A new form of domination may then ensue but never the restoration of the previous form. What does take place in the action, and because of it, is the transformation of the subaltern himself, the conquest of his autonomy, his free will, his capacity to decide for himself. The Mexican Revolution of 1910–20 was a long construction of subjectivities through experience and because of experience.

The subjectivity of the subaltern and their very condition changed throughout the twentieth century, constantly redefining itself—as was observed by, among others, Carlos Monsiváis in his chronicles of urban life. The ruling classes perceive disorder, peril, and threat in such developments; subalterns experience them with joy but also with anger and violence.

The paradox is that in community-driven rebellions, as the Mexican instances have always more or less been, the decision-making capacity has been attained in ostensible defense of older relations that subject human beings and their reasoning to the control of the community or corporation. However, the only organizational forms available to these rebellions are those transmitted through their history. Within this contradiction, Mexican subalterns have laid claim to their past, creating a different history, constructing a modern individuality with ancient tools, reconfiguring the old sense of community into novel forms, rather than allow it to dissolve unresistingly into a multitude of individualities united in the market by the impersonal ties of exchange value.

Seen from the outside, the revolts in Mexico look like archaic utopias brandished against progress, modernization, globalization. Seen from the inside, they are the terrain of experience on which modern subjects are formed and educated, subjects distinguished by their ability to decide for themselves and to organize the means to carry out their decisions.

Of all the ways of asserting the autonomous subject, twentieth-century emigration to the United States is by no means the least important. Those who undertake the journey are for the most part young and intrepid, both men and women, a self-selecting group based on their readiness to take action, risks, and individual decisions. The decision to "go to the other side" is not solely an economic one. It is also a barely veiled form of subaltern protest against a social order that forces people to forsake land and loved ones as the only way—again paradoxically—to keep them.

10.

As we have repeatedly heard from the authors cited in this constellation, subalternity is not synonymous with submission. It is an active condition in peace and in war, in compliance and in defiance. It shapes the present from within the past and is condensed as action. It is through their deeds that the subalterns, the makers, step into the future, with the tools bequeathed by their past; with these tools they make and reveal the future.

Let us return one last time to Walter Benjamin:

> The class struggle, which is always present to a historian influenced by Marx, is a fight for the crude and material things without which no refined and spiritual things could exist. Nevertheless, it is not in the form of the spoils which fall to the victor that the latter make their presence felt in the class struggle. They manifest themselves in the struggle as courage, humor, cunning, and fortitude. They have retroactive force and will constantly call into question every victory, past and present, of the rulers. As flowers turn toward the sun, by dint of a secret heliotropism, the past strives to turn toward that sun which is rising in the sky of history. The historical materialist must be aware of this most inconspicuous of all transformations.[43]

It is a question of knowledge and of justice to reflect on history against the grain, to accept its antinomies and paradoxes, to develop its negatives, to reveal what is written in invisible ink by the deeds of the subalterns, to read the palms of those who live by their hands: to salvage our heritage and our histories in their entirety.

---

43 Walter Benjamin, "Theses on the Philosophy of History," in *Illuminations: Essays and Reflections*, ed. and with an introduction by Hannah Arendt, trans. Harry Zohn (New York: Schocken Books, 1969), p. 254–5.

8

A Certain Idea of Mexico

The Presence, Nostalgia, and Persistence of *Cardenismo* (2002)

In memory of Rafael Galván

1.

The "*cardenismo*" that took shape during the mandate of President Lázaro Cárdenas was at once a consolidation of the new state form arising from the Mexican Revolution; the closure of a cycle of revolutionary social transformations that began in 1910; and the constitutive moment of a national ideology, program, and collective imagination that would last throughout the twentieth century in this country as an essential part of the consciousness and political modalities of successive generations.

In other words, Cárdenas's reforms crowned a thirty-year cycle (1910–40) that saw the overthrow of the liberal-oligarchic ancien régime and, amid the conflictual materiality of social life, discussions and debates about the nature of national and state community, leading to their reconfiguration.[1]

---

1 This period roughly coincides with the three decades that Arno Mayer has called the Thirty Years' War of the twentieth century—the years of iron and fire between the beginning and end of the two world wars (1914–45), when the ancien régime of the European continent collapsed at last, in prelude to the subsequent destruction of its colonial empires (Arno Mayer, *La persistance de l'Ancien Régime: L'Europe de 1848 à la Grande Guerre* [Paris: Flammarion, 1983]).

In the nation's memory and imagination, those three decades and their culmination under Cárdenas still endure as a presence, a nostalgia and a timeless utopia. It is the afterglow of a bonfire that is now extinguished; and no one knows if it could catch light again, for though its promises were left half-fulfilled, they were never taken back.

2.

Ten years of armed revolution (1910–20) condensed in the deeds and experiences of the subaltern population both knowledge and assurance regarding their own abilities to rebel, to organize, to practice leadership, to master the arts of war, and to overcome adversity. Horses and weapons—forbidden to so many of the subalterns in ancien-régime societies—were in many cases their first material conquest of revolution. This was the exercise and affirmation in lived experience of equality and individuality, or, in other words, of that non-material conquest that consists of respect for one and all as the condition for a harmonious coexistence.

Such an affirmation always necessitates a cycle of violence from the bottom up, as old offenses are avenged and present existences and wills accorded their due value. This type of violence is described in all its elemental, immediate truth in the great novel of the revolution *Los de abajo* [*The Underdogs* by Mariano Azuela, 1915–20], and in *Cartucho* [Bandolier, 1931] by Nellie Campobello.

In Morelos—before the Zapatistas had formulated their program in the Plan de Ayala, indeed before the southern revolution was even called Zapatista—as soon as the southern pueblos began to rise up in February 1911, their actions followed, without any prior coordination between them, a pattern as old as the peasant wars: capture a village; open the jail and free the inmates; requisition arms; burn the municipal archives; shoot a few people to appease old, festering injuries and hatreds; blow up the company store; set fire to the haciendas, and kidnap their owners and other rich people to finance the revolution; and execute political bosses and prefects. A recent study by Felipe Ávila, *Los orígenes del zapatismo*, offers a good account of this pattern.[2] The rage from below was then matched or outdone by the repressive fury of the army and the landowners.

2   Felipe Arturo Ávila Espinosa, *Los orígenes del zapatismo* (Mexico City: El Colegio de México-Universidad Nacional Autónoma de México, 2001).

The terror wielded from below, unplanned and without foreseeable limit, is the form in which insurgent subalterns who still lack a language and a program constitute themselves as subjects and lay claim to their existence as a collective body before all and sundry. Their violence constitutes a new "we," the "we" that had always been denied to the subalterns. As we know from contemporary chronicles as well as histories, this terror was also selective: some properties and some hated people met with destruction or paid with their lives, while others were spared, because the "underdogs" always retain memories of a different kind of treatment.

3.

The ten-year cycle of armed revolution thus tells the story of the formation of a new subaltern subject, one with whom the rulers who subsequently emerged would henceforth have to deal, as part of the great reconfiguration by violence of the national-state community. Both kinds of subject, rulers and subalterns, inherit historic forms of command and obedience, and yet they mutually determine each other, mold each other, and infuse the inherited forms with new contents.

The occupation of Mexico City, the immemorial seat of power, by the campesino armies led by Villa and Zapata was one climax of this formation of new subjectivities. Others were the rout of the Federal Army by [Villa's] División del Norte in the battle of Zacatecas; the organization of the autonomous Zapatista government in the south, and the existence in 1915 of at least three governments at once: those of Morelos, Chihuahua, and Veracruz, each with their respective administrations and legislation.

4.

In the vicissitudes of this cycle and in their dealings with revolutionary subalterns, a young ruling elite was trained and educated, quite unlike that which prevailed under the Porfiriato. The most paradigmatic figure among these was perhaps Álvaro Obregón, but there were many others, with very different personalities. They included Luis Cabrera, Felipe Carrillo Puerto, Francisco J. Múgica, Lucio Blanco, Plutarco Elías Calles, Salvador Alvarado, Joaquín Amaro, Juan Andreu Almazán, Saturnino Cedillo, Antonio Díaz Soto y Gama, Lázaro Cárdenas, José Vasconcelos,

Francisco R. Serrano, Luis Morones, Adolfo de la Huerta. All were flung into the whirlwind of the 1920s following the assassination of Emiliano Zapata, the violent death of Venustiano Carranza, the triumph of the Agua Prieta rebellion, and the retirement of Pancho Villa to his hacienda in Canutillo in 1920, three years before being murdered in Parral.

5.

The laws passed in Veracruz in January 1915, together with the Constitution of 1917, make up the ensemble of formal juridical norms that were eventually agreed upon by the ruling elite who emerged from the revolution, in order to enshrine their own rule and impart legal substance to a new hegemony, a new relationship of command and compliance with the subalterns who had themselves been transformed by that revolution.

This legal framework—notably in key areas such as Art. 3 (pertaining to education), Art. 27 (land and subsoil), Art. 115 (municipalities), Art. 123 (labor), and Art. 130 (the Church)—both encapsulated the promises and marked the limits of the new form of state community that governments sought to consolidate from 1920 on.

These legal dispositions leave open, and widen to an unprecedented degree, the scope of what is under contention in the state context—that which is yet to be defined in juridical and social debates, in disputes and conflicts, prior to being enshrined as a legitimate relation, meaning, one that is stable and acknowledged by all.

These spaces of contention are vast. They include the rules governing the tenure and ownership of lands, waters, and woodlands, and the pre-existent rights of campesino and indigenous villages and communities; the ownership of oil deposits, mines, and the subsoil of the nation; the juridical status of the relationship between capital and labor; the social and organizational rights of wage-earners; federalism and local government; the defense of the nation and its territory; the status of the armed forces in relation to political power.

6.

During the turmoil of the Mexican 1920s, this space of contention emerged and became settled both in its objects and in its methods. Through its institutionalized or demarcated violence (if we may use such epithets), a new relation was incubated and gradually established within the ruling elite—chiefly, but not only, composed of the generals of the revolution—and also between that elite and the subaltern classes, among whom the weapons of the civil war persisted as did its customs, including their particular sense of obedience and honor.

The twenties were the years of plots, rebellions, and purges among the military; of fierce strikes (the tram drivers in 1921, the oil workers in 1925, the railroaders in 1926); of agrarian wars and their caudillos, from San Luis Potosí to Veracruz; of Felipe Carrillo Puerto's socialism in Yucatán. These were years of uncertainty in relations with the United States and about the legal situation of Mexico's subsoil. The years of the Cristero War [against the new state's secularism] and the no-less-violent emergence of four-way relations among the state, the Church, the Vatican, and the Catholicism of the countryside: conflicts that were far more decisive than is commonly acknowledged for what would follow in the 1930s. The years of the education plans, designed first by [José] Vasconcelos and then by Moisés Sáenz; the heyday of the muralists, of the [literary modernists] Los Contemporáneos, and the intellectual bohemia in the aftermath of war and revolution.

As is often pointed out, the twenties also saw the founding of the institutions governing administration, banking, education, the military, political parties, and trade unions. These were unquestionably the years of rebuilding a state apparatus that, in the fields of diplomacy, finance, communications, and dealings with the country's productive apparatus, took up the legacy, experience, and national vision of the deposed ancien régime of the Porfiriato. This factor is not always given its due. Such was the turbulent period of reconstruction, as the Sonoran leaders called it.

Initially in the revolution as military men, then in the "reconstruction" as politicians and statesmen, Lázaro Cárdenas and Francisco J. Múgica came together with the rest of the group that would lead the great reforms of Cárdenas's six-year mandate. Nothing that they did would have been thinkable without that previous apprenticeship and without each man's capacity to absorb, into his ideas and his character, its lessons and experiences. Those were the two decades of training, for those on top and the underdogs alike, for what was to become the *cardenismo* of the 1930s.

7.

In his essay "Hegemony and the Language of Contention," part of a collection of texts on modern Mexico, William Roseberry studies Antonio Gramsci's understanding of hegemony and notes the concomitant formation process of ruling and subaltern classes as characteristic of the constitution over time of a state form, one of whose features is "spatial differentiation . . . the uneven and unequal development of social powers in regional spaces."[3]

In this process of formation, Roseberry writes, "Gramsci does not assume that subaltern groups are captured or immobilized by some sort of ideological consensus." On the contrary,

> the relations between ruling and subaltern groups are characterized by contention, struggle, and argument. Far from assuming that the subaltern passively accept their fate, Gramsci clearly envisions a much more active and confrontational subaltern population than many of his interpreters have assumed. Nevertheless, he places action and confrontation within the formations, institutions, and organizations of the state and civil society in which subordinate populations live.

Leading Roseberry to the following conclusion:

> This is the way hegemony works. I propose that we use the concept *not* to understand consent but to understand struggle; the ways in which words, images, symbols, forms, organizations, institutions, and movements used by subordinate populations to talk about, understand, confront, accommodate themselves to, or resist their domination are shaped by the process of domination itself. What hegemony constructs, then, is not a shared ideology but a common material and meaningful framework for living through, talking about, and acting upon social orders characterized by domination.
>
> That common material and meaningful framework is, in part, discursive: a common language or way of talking about social relationships

---

3   William Roseberry, "Hegemony and the Language of Contention," in Gilbert Joseph and Daniel Nugent, eds., *Everyday Forms of State Formation: Revolution and the Negotiation of Rule in Modern Mexico* (Durham: Duke University Press, 1994), pp. 359–60.

that sets out the central terms around which and in terms of which contestation and struggle can occur.[4]

It was this type of framework that was configured between 1910 and 1934, to be crystallized into the specific form taken by hegemony in Mexico during the era of President Lázaro Cárdenas.

8.

Official postrevolutionary historiography in Mexico, seen as the history of the revolutionary nationalist elites, focuses on the figure of Lázaro Cárdenas in this latter period [1934–40], just as the Indian equivalent does on the figure of Gandhi and the South African on Nelson Mandela. Such a historiography is open to Ranajit Guha's criticism of the historiography of nationalism in India, which he says has "for a long time been dominated by elitism—colonialist elitism and bourgeois-nationalist elitism."[5] Both, according to Guha, "share the prejudice that the making of the Indian nation and the development of the consciousness—nationalism—which informed this process were exclusively or predominantly elite achievements": that of the colonial government in the one case, and in the other, that of the personalities, institutions, actions, and ideas of the Indian elite.

Historical writing of this kind cannot, however, "explain Indian nationalism for us. For it fails to acknowledge, far less interpret, the contribution made by the people on their own, that is, *independently of the elite*, to the making and development of this nationalism ... What clearly is left out of this un-historical historiography is the *politics of the people*."

Throughout colonial India, writes Guha, there was another domain of politics in which the "principal actors" were

the subaltern classes and groups constituting the mass of the labouring population and the intermediate strata in town and country—that is, the people. This was an *autonomous* domain, for it neither originated from elite politics nor did its existence depend on the latter . . . As modern

---

4   Ibid., p. 361.
5   Ranajit Guha, "On Some Aspects of the Historiography of Colonial India," in Guha, ed., *Selected Subaltern Studies* (New York: Oxford University Press, 1988), pp. 37–44.

as indigenous elite politics, it was distinguished by its relatively greater depth in time as well as in structure.

In the case of the Mexican Revolution, this dimension of the "autonomous politics of the subaltern," set free by the initial revolutionary explosion and realized in the action of the armies and militias of the campesinos of the North and South, neither vanished nor was completely absorbed by the postrevolutionary state. It was, instead, actively present in what Roseberry defines and describes as "hegemony," that *common material, meaningful, and discursive framework* that "sets out the central terms around which and in terms of which contestation and struggle can occur."

But, even inside this framework, that autonomous dimension persists as the "hidden transcripts" of the subaltern in apparently non-political forms of daily activity and sociality, like a dark star whose presence determines many of the movements, reactions, precautions, or representations of the ruling elites, most often without the latter being conscious of it.[6]

Should the ruling classes, by miscalculation or necessity, happen to breach those frameworks, that is, should they systematically infringe on the flexible but precise norms of their own hegemony, then this dark star will veer from its orbit, and its movements will be violent. This is what happened in Mexico between 1910 and 1911, and without Cárdenas's reforms in the second half of the 1930s, it might have happened again, in another guise.

9.

Let us recapitulate. A number of complex processes contending among themselves came together in the social and institutional reforms of those days: a) a new relationship between rulers and subalterns; b) the consolidation of the institutions and functions of the state apparatus, from banking to administration to education; c) the consolidation and expansion of an industrial and productive structure whose foundations were laid under Porfirio Díaz; d) the confrontation of the state with the oldest institution in the land, the Catholic Church, followed by a

---

6   James C. Scott, *Domination and the Arts of Resistance: Hidden Transcripts* (New Haven: Yale University Press, 1990).

stabilization of their dealings; e) the unprecedented expansion of the
education system and the deployment of an army of service providers
and mediators between the government and the working populations,
both rural and urban: teachers, topographers, surveyors, work inspec-
tors, *ejido* [common land] authorities, trade-union organizers, health
professionals; f) the purging and gradual professionalization of the army;
g) the organization of the state party—first as the PNR, then the PRM[7]
—as the form and framework of the politics recognized as legitimate, i.e.,
institutional and corporate politics; h) the establishment of the juridical
framework for resolving disputes: the Federal Labor Law, the Concilia-
tion and Arbitration Councils, the fourteen points [of Cárdenas's speech
rebuking big business] in Monterrey in 1936, the Agrarian Code and
related provisions, the government as "arbitrator and regulator of social
life"; i) the establishment of subaltern class organizations backed by the
state: industrial unions, CTM (Confederation of Mexican Workers),
CNC (National Peasant Confederation); j) nationalist and autonomous
diplomacy and foreign affairs, notably the redefinition and stabilization
of the relationship with the US—an indispensable move for the consolidation of Mexican state sovereignty—and the extension of solidarity
and other kinds of support to the Spanish Republic from 1936 onward,
a deliberate political bet by the Cárdenas government on a shift in the
European and global situation in favor of the Mexican Revolution. It is
against this background that we should view Mexico's policy of grant-
ing asylum to Spanish Republicans, anti-fascist refugees, and victims
of Soviet persecution such as Leon Trotsky and Natalia Sedova, Victor
Serge and his children, Vlady and Jeannine Kibalchich.

10.

On this edifice of national and social contestation, of state institutions
and relations between people and government, the two great, fundamental reforms of the period were justified, implemented, and nurtured:
land distribution (1936) and oil expropriation (1938). These measures
originated in a different vision from that of the Sonoran chiefs, and they
resulted in the construction of a hegemony that was far more sensitive to

---

7   [The Partido Nacional Revolucionario (PNR, National Revolutionary Party)
was founded in 1929; it was reorganized and renamed as the Partido de la Revolución
Mexicana (PRM, Party of the Mexican Revolution) in 1938. This in turn became the
Partido Revolucionario Institucional (PRI, Revolutionary Institutional Party) in 1946.]

the presence and gravitation of the dark star: the autonomous existence of the subalterns and of their own politics, no matter the name they went by—agrarianists, trade unionists, *cristeros*, Yaquis, or no name at all.

Land distribution, with its specific forms of landholding—above all the ejido—was the answer to justice and war: there would never be peace if the land were not redistributed. Here was the realization of Romain Rolland's phrase, "Par la révolution, la paix," which became the title of the 1931 classic by Frank Tannenbaum, *Peace by Revolution*. This answer sprang from Mexico's agrarian and indigenous center of gravity, not from the modernity of Sonoran agriculture. It moved from the pueblos of the heartland and the south, from indigenous communities and Indian wars, toward the old military colonies of the north, the fierce cattlemen of the northern haciendas, and the Yaqui warriors of Sonora.

Land distribution, not barracks discipline, put an end to the pretexts for military coups. It linked land tenancy with campesino organizations (ejidos, ejido committees) and with the marketing of their products, state credits, and a secular, rational, "socialist" education system, as well as, in some cases, with the organized possession of weapons to defend people against the *guardias blancas* [paramilitaries] of the big landowners. The real redistribution was, as ever, implemented from below and with violence.

The expropriation of oil led to the definitive demarcation of national territory, the arena in which the sovereign power of the national state is exercised. Together with agrarian reform, that measure gave real substance to some, at least, of what Article 27 of the Constitution had sanctioned in the legal realm: that the rightful proprietorship of the territory falls to the nation, and, therefore, agrarian and mining rents and revenues belong to the nation. The (partial) appropriation of this revenue and its use by the state apparatus to fund a range of commitments (administrative and social, as well as to encourage the formation of private capital) cemented the new ruling class, whose form of existence, or "existential status," with respect to the national community had developed during decades of extreme turbulence.

11.

Nevertheless, *cardenismo* turned out to be more than just the culmination of the Mexican Revolution in a renovated hegemony and state form. It was also, and chiefly, a set of ideas and an imaginary among the

majority of the people, not simply the poor. It was a certain internal-
ized vision of a country, a society, and a national community, a vision
that was closer to the experience that had been lived by successive generations than to any written, official political program. The *cardenista*
people, a body whose contours are nowhere specified, might adapt for
themselves the peerless words with which General de Gaulle begins
his *War Memoirs*: "Toute ma vie, je me suis fait une certaine idée de la
France." (All my life, I have had a certain idea of France.) Likewise, the
cardenista people could say: "All our lives, we have had a certain idea of
Mexico."[8]

During the six-year term of President Cárdenas, *cardenismo* was the
visible presence, alternately dazzling and opaque, of that same, habitually
dark star—the autonomous politics of the subaltern. A politics that flared
up periodically, before and after Cárdenas's mandate, into outbursts,
among them Zapatism, Magonism,[9] Tejedism,[10] the Cristero War, the
epic of Nueva Rosita,[11] the railway workers,[12] the student uprising of 1968,
the great earthquake of 1985,[13] the presidential election and civic protests
in 1988,[14] and the numberless revolts and upheavals in the countryside
throughout the second half of the twentieth century, climaxing in the
indigenous rebellion of 1994 in Chiapas.

The presence of this autonomous "underdog" activity exerted a clear
influence on government policy during the Cárdenas administration,
with active lines of communication and dialogue between the two levels.
In its specific way, the government drew support from such worker and
peasant mobilizations against internal and external adversaries, but the

8   Adolfo Gilly, *El cardenismo: Una utopía mexicana* (Mexico City: Cal y Arena,
1994).

9   [A reference to Ricardo Flores Magón (1873–1922), leader of the anarchist
Partido Liberal Mexicano in the 1910s; imprisoned in the US under anti-subversive
laws, he died in the Leavenworth prison in Kansas.]

10   [A reference to the Mexican revolutionary general Adalberto Tejeda (1883–
1960), governor of Veracruz State and then interior minister in the 1920s; he ran against
Cárdenas in 1934 as a socialist candidate.]

11   [The six-month strike by the coalminers of Nueva Rosita, Coahuila, in
1950–51.]

12   [Mexico's railway workers were often at the forefront of strike activity, most
famously including the strike of 1959, harshly repressed by the government.]

13   [An earthquake in Mexico City on September 19, 1985 caused several thousand
deaths and severe damage; the government's inadequate response also highlighted the
PRI system's waning legitimacy.]

14   [Carlos Salinas's victory in the 1988 presidential election was marked by
serious irregularities, prompting a widespread belief that he had stolen the election
from Cuauhtémoc Cárdenas, candidate of a left coalition and also the son of Lázaro
Cárdenas.]

organizational forms through which it did so were also methods of state control.

As the world situation and the Mexican heads of state swung to the right during World War II (Manuel Ávila Camacho) and after it (Miguel Alemán), this state control of popular organizations undermined the chances of resisting the rightward turn. It also facilitated sudden authoritarian takeovers (*charrazos*) in the organizations, as well as their tight corporate subordination to the state apparatus and to the capital accumulation that apparatus had encouraged. In his essay "The 'Comunidad Revolucionaria Institucional,'" Jan Rus conducts a detailed survey of this process in Chiapas State.[15] Of course, this subordination of workers' organizations to the state was a widespread phenomenon following the war, by no means unique to Mexico.[16]

Cardenismo, as a set of ideas and an imaginary of the Mexican people, is the product of the back-and-forth between actions and ideas in everyday reality. It remained in popular memory as a very different, indeed antipodal, period from the domination that followed from Miguel Alemán onward. And so, the *cardenista* current lasted well beyond the general's term in office, not least because his life and conduct in subsequent years did nothing to belie the actions, ideas, and promises of that earlier period.

Between 1940 and 1970, in his political activities and ceaseless travels and works around the country, the general was the custodian of this wide-ranging heritage: supporting the Guatemalan Revolution [when it was toppled] in 1954, protecting Fidel Castro's expedition in 1956, backing the Cuban Revolution in 1959, and the defense of the Bay of Pigs in 1961. He was involved in the Russell Tribunal against war crimes in Vietnam, and in the foundation of the [peasant union] Central Campesina Independiente and the Movimiento de Liberación Nacional; he spoke up for political prisoners in 1968, and, in 1969, backed the political and trade-union struggle of the electricians' Tendencia Democrática group, led by Rafael Galván and speaking through *Solidaridad* magazine. Cárdenas did all this while steadfastly refusing to break with the state institutions he had helped establish during the 1930s—an attitude that

---

15   Jan Rus, "The 'Comunidad Revolucionaria Institucional': The Subversion of Native Government in Highland Chiapas, 1936–1968," in Joseph and Nugent, *Everyday Forms of State Formation* pp. 256–300.

16   In his Mexican exile, Trotsky described this trend based on his analysis of the Mexican case. See Leon Trotsky, "Nationalized Industry and Workers' Management" (1938), in *Fourth International*, vol. 7, no. 8, 1946, available at marxists.org.

a considerable part of the communist, Trotskyist, and Maoist left found themselves helpless to explain or understand.

General Cárdenas fortunately had the time, the energy and the presence to encapsulate this heritage by writing down ideas and proposals in a final "Message to the Nation," composed in August–September 1970 on the eve of his death, and read out by his son Cuauhtémoc at the memorial ceremony one year later, in October 1971.[17]

As an ideology made flesh in the deeds of a time that came to acquire a mythic status, *cardenismo* competed with *lombardismo*, *priismo*, communism, *sinarquismo*, and other tendencies for hegemony over the mind and imagination of the Mexican people.[18] In the end, it stands as the principal expression, rooted in history, of what is meant in Mexico by "the left." It is no surprise that the actual form in which a national left exists in this country should have originated precisely in its own, great twentieth-century revolution.

In using the word *"cardenismo"* here, I do not mean to refer, or to confine it, to any one of the political currents identified as such, though the term may include them. I mean a collective imaginary that is much wider, more deeply rooted, and more lasting: precisely "a certain idea of Mexico."

Therefore, that autonomous politics of the subaltern, found in action far more than in writing, found in the ejidos, in strikes, in shanty towns, in rural schoolteachers, in the pueblos, in workplaces and schools, in the fiestas, in misfortunes and emergencies, is still a great trove of countless imperceptible traces that have yet to be brought to light, both from the days of President Cárdenas and from those that followed.

By so doing, we shall be able to explain the presence, nostalgia, and persistence of *cardenismo* in the ways and political imaginary of *los de abajo*, the underdogs, and to elucidate as far as possible its multiple meanings and its periodic reappearances—in the past, more recently, and still to come.

---

17   Adolfo Gilly, "El general escribe en su despacho. Once escenas en la vida de Lázaro Cárdenas," in *Lázaro Cárdenas: Iconografía*, (Mexico City: Turner, 2007).

18   [Lombardismo: A reference to Mexican labor leader Vicente Lombardo Toledano (1894–1968). Priismo: the shape-shifting ideology of the ruling PRI party. Sinarquismo: the ideas of Mexico's National Synarchist Union, a fascist movement founded in 1937 and banned in 1949.]

9

The Indigenous Army and the Mexican State

(1999, 2002)

1.

As with all true rebellions, that of the indigenous people of Chiapas has revealed some profound features of the state against which they are in revolt. The primordial question in this case is not to establish why the rebellion broke out: few have ever expounded their reasons in as much detail as this one. The questions are, rather, why society accepted and protected it once it was underway, and why the government halted military action within a fortnight and opened a negotiation process that, both actively and in suspension, has lasted more than five years, and indeed has never been canceled, while the rebels have neither laid down their arms nor relinquished their individual anonymity.

If the state form is that which contains and frames the relationship between rulers and ruled in a given national community, what is the peculiarity of the Mexican form? What is it that sustains this ongoing relation with a small indigenous army in revolt, surrounded by a Federal Army of overwhelmingly superior force (50,000 men armed to the teeth) yet expressing itself with relative freedom through the national press and dispatching its propagandists up and down the country—5,000 of them, for the latest public consultation organized by the Zapatista Army—with no hindrance from the police or the military?

In other words, what does this specific relation *reveal* about this state form as a generic relation?

2.

Rebellions speak more readily in practice than in words. And they usually speak though practice alone, so that it falls to the historian or the chronicler (and sometimes the judge) to disentangle their true meaning. The indigenous uprising in Chiapas, besides stepping into the world with a formal declaration of war, introduced itself at the highest symbolic level with the capture of four cities: most significantly among these, San Cristóbal de las Casas, the old Ciudad Real (Royal City) founded in 1563, the former capital of the señores, seigneurs, landowners, and oppressors of the Indians of Chiapas.

Thousands of indigenous men and women in disciplined military formation, led by hundreds of armed and masked fighters, took the city in the small hours of New Year's Day, 1994, as the political heads of the national government—the president, cabinet secretaries, and military brass—were celebrating the entry into force of the North American Free Trade Agreement and with it Mexico's accession to the First World. The poorest of the poor rose up on the very day, hour, and minute when the country's powerful were cheering their arrival among the richest of the rich. Few drunken binges can have been followed by a worse hangover.

If I revisit this inaugural gesture, it is because it marked the whole subsequent course of the relation between the rebellion and Mexican society on the one hand, and between the rebellion and the federal government on the other.

3.

The rebellion of the Ejército Zapatista de Liberación Nacional (Zapatista Army of National Liberation, EZLN) set out a program of eleven points, none of which, individually or jointly, advocated the subversion of the Mexican state. All fell within the remit of the Constitution and the law. On the most general level, the program does not overstep the bounds of a welfare state with a democratic electoral system and an honest, independent judiciary.

The Declaration from the Lacandon Jungle, made public on January 2, 1994, listed eleven "basic demands": "work, land, housing, food, health-care, education, independence, freedom, democracy, justice, and peace."[1]

The first six of these demands pertain to individual rights, specifically recognized as such in the Political Constitution of the United Mexican States. They are found in Art. 3 ("every person has the right to receive education"), Art. 4 ("every person has the right to health protection," "every family has the right to enjoy decent and proper housing"), Art. 123 ("every person has the right to dignified and socially useful work"), Art. 27, sub-clause VII (on ownership of ejido and communal land), Art. 4 and Art. 123 (on food). The other five are general demands bearing upon Mexico's political and juridical regime, all of them likewise guaranteed under the Constitution.

Is it really necessary to take up arms in order to ask for what is already laid down in the Constitution and the law? The very mismatch between the moderation of the demands and the enormity of the gesture—seizing the city of San Cristóbal and declaring war on the Federal Army—points to an area of crisis in the political regime proper to a state form that had become increasingly incapable of guaranteeing the rights or satisfying the demands recognized in its most fundamental legal statute, that is, in its foundational pacts.

The armed rebellion of 1994 embedded itself in this crisis area, which, following the fraudulently decided 1988 elections, had been opened up by the civic rebellion of *cardenismo*.[2] They entrenched themselves in the area where the fundamental component of a state relation—*legitimacy*, or what the Chinese used to call "the mandate of Heaven"—had been broken.[3]

Zapatismo did not trigger this crisis of legitimacy. It merely implanted itself there with its facts, showing to the nation an old, forgotten dimension of itself, as though it were brand new: the exclusion and oppression of native peoples, who make up at least 10 percent of the population, the lowliest of the low.

From that position, it laid claim to its own national program. It did not proclaim it in words alone. It proclaimed it through the armed

1   "Declaración de la Selva Lacandona. Hoy decimos ¡Basta!" in EZLN, *Documentos y comunicados*, (Mexico City: Ediciones Era, 1994), pp. 33–5. [English translation available at: struggle.ws/mexico/ezln/ezlnwa.html, accessed April 2, 2021.]

2   [A reference to Cuauhtémoc Cárdenas, son of former president Lázaro Cárdenas, who became the figurehead of a new opposition movement after being robbed of the presidency by fraud in 1988.]

3   Adolfo Gilly, *México: el poder, el dinero y la sangre* (Mexico City: Aguilar, 1995).

capture of a city, the political anonymity of its masked leaders, and the vast poverty of the indigenous peoples. Weapons, masks, and poverty were the source of legitimacy for Zapatismo's discourse; they defined its position outside the state form and beyond the latter's ways of relating in the world of politics.

4.

The lowliest of the low, I said. "Chiapas is the poorest state in the country," writes Julio Boltvinik, and "the rural areas of Chiapas are the poorest state zone (of a total of sixty-three) in the country, closely followed by the rural areas of Guerrero and Oaxaca" (two states with a similarly high proportion of indigenous residents).[4] Boltvinik's study "Map of Poverty in Chiapas" is based on figures from the 1990 census. The poverty line has been calculated, approximately, as an income of US$2.7 per person per day, and the extreme poverty line at US$1.83 per person per day.

According to the 1990 census, the total population of Chiapas is 3.21 million, of whom 2.90 million (90.2 percent) live below the poverty line; only 314,000 are categorized as "not poor." Sixty percent of the latter live in urban areas and 40 percent in the countryside. Those who can be labeled upper class are few: 4,597 individuals, all urban dwellers.

Boltvinik continues:

Of the total of the poor, the majority, almost 83 percent (75 percent of the total population) are destitute. If to these we add the very poor, we find that 92.5 percent of the state's poor (83.5 percent of the total population) are living in extreme poverty. Only 7.5 percent of Chiapas poor (6.7

4 Julio Boltvinik, "Mapa de la pobreza en Chiapas," in Cesáreo Morales, ed., *Chiapas: Una nueva visión para una nueva política* (Mexico City: Senado de la República, Grupo Galileo, 1998), p. 11. This report contains sixteen essays gathered into eleven typed volumes, written by prominent academic specialists in each field and commissioned by the Grupo Galileo, fifteen senators affiliated with the PRI. As a corresponding clue to the nature of the Mexican state form and the fabric of its relations, it is worth mentioning that in 1980, the report's coordinator, Cesáreo Morales, was a professor at the Faculty of Philosophy and Letters of the UNAM and thesis director for Rafael Sebastián Guillén, whom the Mexican government alleges to be Subcomandante Marcos. That thesis began with a quote from Foucault's "The Order of Discourse": "Discourse is not simply that which translates struggles or systems of domination but is the thing for which and by which there is struggle." [Michel Foucault, "The Order of Discourse," in Robert Young, ed., *Untying the Text: A Post-Structuralist Reader* (London: Routledge & Kegan Paul, 1981), pp. 52–3.]

percent of the total) are moderately poor. As we can see, the structure is completely tilted toward the most acute poverty.

Following this observation, Boltvinik proceeds:

> In this regard, there is a marked contrast between town and country. Whereas destitution affects 86.8 percent of country dwellers, it stands at 57.7 percent in towns. In rural areas, 93 percent of the poor are destitute, a figure that is much lower in urban settings—67.2 percent—although this, too, is surprisingly high.

In just a few approximate figures, less telling than a glance at the indigenous world or a tale by Rosario Castellanos, we see the social dimensions of the rural world in which the rebellion began.[5] However, as is well known from E. P. Thompson's moral economy, this extreme poverty cannot itself explain the outburst or the form it took. Poverty was always there, but the armed rebellion came now. The social dimension is necessary but not sufficient. We must seek the explanation elsewhere, in a different, added dimension.

5.

Yes: as of its initial proclamation, the First Declaration from the Lacandon Jungle, the EZLN arrogated to itself the discourse of poverty:

> We have been denied the most elemental preparation so they can use us as cannon fodder and pillage the wealth of our country. They don't care that we have nothing, absolutely nothing, not even a roof over our heads, no land, no work, no healthcare, no food nor education. Nor are we able to freely and democratically elect our political representatives; nor is there independence from foreigners; nor is there peace nor justice for ourselves and our children.
>
> But today, we say: ENOUGH IS ENOUGH![6]

---

5 [Rosario Castellanos (1925–74): Mexican poet and novelist raised in Chiapas; author of several works depicting the interaction of white, mestizo, and indigenous worlds, including *Balún Canán* (1957), *Ciudad Real* (1962), and *Oficio de tinieblas* (1967, translated into English as *The Book of Lamentations* [1998]).]

6 Subcomandante Marcos, *Our Word Is Our Weapon* (New York: Seven Stories Press, 2002), p. 13.

With that last word, "¡Basta!"—Enough!—the discourse of poverty flows into the recourse to rebellion. This recourse, legitimized by all the founding myths of the Mexican nation—the Revolution of Independence of 1810, essentially an agrarian rebellion, and in that sense an aggregate of indigenous revolts; the Mexican Revolution of 1910–20; the long history of peasant and indigenous uprisings since Cuauhtémoc's legendary resistance to the Spanish Conquest—rests on four discourses with which the Zapatista movement addresses society and confronts the government. They are:

a) The discourse of *resistance*: "We are a product of 500 years of struggle," the Declaration begins. In other words, the story of Mexico is not only one of oppression but also of resistance. Resistance is the spiritual and material dimension that, in the relation of dominance/subordination that sustains every state form, occupies an intermediate place between the two terms and prevents, almost always invisibly, the free will of every community and individual from being ground down by the friction between them.[7]

b) The discourse of *dignity*: Domination and oppression engender humiliation. And it is from nothing else than an intolerable, un-tolerated humiliation that rebellion springs. The revolt against humiliation appropriates the discourse of the fundamental dignity of humanity. From its first proclamations, this dignity has shaped the Zapatista discourse. One month after the uprising, the EZLN addressed the indigenous people of Guerrero State as follows:

> We saw our fathers with fury in their hands, we saw that not everything had been taken away from us, that we still had what was most valuable, what made us live, what made us step over plants and animals, what put the stones beneath our feet, and we saw, brothers and sisters, that all we had was DIGNITY, and we saw the shame was great to have forgotten it, and we saw that dignity was good for making men once more be men, and dignity returned to live in our hearts, and we were still new, and the dead, our dead, saw that we were still new and called us once more to dignity and the fight.

c) The discourse of *history*: Starting with its very name, Zapatismo undertook to wrest national history and the Mexican Revolution from

---

7   See the earlier work by Antonio García de León, *Resistencia y utopía: Memorial de agravios y crónica de revueltas y profecías acaecidas en la provincia de Chiapas durante los últimos quinientos años de su historia* (Mexico City: Ediciones Era, 1985).

the state regime that used them to legitimize its existence. The first great Zapatista public meeting, held in rebel territory before thousands of people from around the country, was named the Convention of Aguascalientes: a reference to the Sovereign Revolutionary Convention [in the city of Aguascalientes] that in October 1914 backed the campesino armies of Villa and Zapata and their entrance into Mexico City that December—as distinct from the Constituent Congress of February 1917 [in the city of Querétaro], which produced the founding constitution of the current form of the Mexican state. In the official history, the 1914 convention was the forerunner of the 1917 congress. But in the history of rebellion, the latter was the negation of the former, even if in order to prevail, it had to incorporate into its text the former's social provisions.

d) The discourse of *myth*, *custom*, and *language*: The EZLN, particularly Subcomandante Marcos, reprised indigenous mythology as a sign of identity and difference, a mark of cultures predating the Conquest and Christianization, whose cornerstone is rituals, customs, and ethical judgment. He does not set these in opposition to religion; he merely places them before and on an equal footing with it.

Some think that this constant allusion to myth is little more than a literary gesture. I say the opposite: while Marcos uses literary language in order to be more effective, the discourse of myth is addressed to a specific dimension of indigenous culture, understood as the context in which human beings give signifying sense to their actions and experiences and ascribe meaning to their lives. This dimension is present in Mexican cultural and spiritual life at large, if more dilute and diffuse, as well as in the unique popular Catholicism practiced in this country.

Here, on pain of being overlong, I shall quote Carlos Montemayor, author of *Guerra en el paraíso* (War in Paradise).[8]

> I have explained on several occasions that we are not taught to know what is, or is not, or is still, indigenous. Culture is a complex weave encompassing diet, kinship, moral values, worldviews. We who are not Indian have always held forth about the Indians, trying to pin down what they are, what they aren't, what they think or don't think. We still do not know to what extent Mexico is indigenous, to what extent native spirituality has been gaining ground over time rather than losing it.

8 [Carlos Montemayor's 1991 novel depicts the "dirty war" unleashed by the Mexican government against leftist guerrillas in the southern state of Guerrero in the 1970s.]

For the Indians, the land is not something inert; it is a living thing, and man, or, better said, indigenous peoples, are at the service of the world. Earth, springs, rivers, rains, sowing and harvesting represent processes of living entities of the visible and invisible worlds inhabited day in, day out by native communities . . . Their relationship to the world is a relationship between living beings. These peoples' way of understanding their commitments to the land is, therefore, substantially different from our own.[9]

The same can be said of history:

For the West, the calendarization of history is obvious: we believe that what happens once happened only that once and has nothing to do with the next instant. For indigenous culture, time evinces a different nature, a different speed (or perhaps slowness), and this is one of the secrets of the cultural resistance and combative capacity of those peoples. For them, the past takes place in a separate dimension that coexists with the present. Indigenous memory is a form of revitalizing the past. Festivals, dances, prayers, oral tradition, all these are the strength of a memory that communicates with that other dimension in which things are forever alive.[10]

In its turn, this cyclical dimension of time infiltrated from below and permeated the Catholicism—whose linear time stretched from Creation to the End of Days—imposed in the sixteenth century by the conquistadors on pre-Hispanic religiosity. This mixture yielded the Catholicism of the Chiapanecos, an Indian religion, visible in local ceremonies, beliefs, and temples, distinct from popular mestizo Catholicism. Jan de Vos writes:

The roots of pre-Hispanic religion were too deep to be ripped out and replaced by another faith. In this respect, the solution found by the indigenous people of Chiapas was the same as that of other colonized

---

9   Carlos Montemayor, "Antecedentes históricos de los conflictos armados en Chiapas," in Morales, ed., *Chiapas: Una nueva visión para una nueva política*. See also, among many others, Guillermo Bonfil Batalla, "Historias que no son todavía historia," in Carlos Pereyra et al., *Historia ¿para qué?* (Mexico City: Siglo XXI, 1980); Bonfil Batalla, *México profundo: Una civilización negada* (Mexico City: Consejo Nacional para la Cultura y las Artes, 1991); Jan de Vos, "Las rebeliones de los indios de Chiapas en la memoria de sus descendientes," in Jane-Dale Lloyd and Laura Pérez Rosales, eds., *Paisajes rebeldes: Una larga noche de resistencia indígena* (Mexico City: Universidad Iberoamericana, 1995); and Enrique Florescano, *Etnia, estado y nación: Ensayo sobre las identidades colectivas en México* (Mexico City: Aguilar, 1997).

10   Montemayor, "Antecedentes históricos."

peoples in Mexico and Central America. The natives applied to the field of religion the same strategy as they used in other areas of their impoverished, downtrodden peasant lives: they incorporated into their world every element the masters viewed as indispensable but on condition of reinterpreting and appropriating them in such a way as to make them their own . . .

This unusual construct would be named *la Costumbre* (the Custom) by the indigenous themselves. It is, to my mind, the most original and valuable cultural monument they managed to raise in the midst of the very circumscribed space left to them by the colonial regime in their condition as poor, exploited peasants. For that reason, and in view of its endurance to this day, it is worth making a thorough study of the ethnohistorical texts devoted to its development. The Custom was a veritable feat of religious pluralism . . .

The Custom, distanced by an ethnic barrier from the political activism of the clergy and from the popular Catholicism of the ladino [mestizo] population, continued to incorporate whatever Christian ingredients suited it, without ever abandoning the double root of pre-Hispanic religiosity: the orientation toward Mother Earth, and the cyclical recreation of the universe, both human and natural, in its feasts. It was preserved precisely as a root, that is, in underground form, running beneath rites and prayers that seemed acceptably Catholic on the surface . . .

It would be a mistake to reduce the Custom to an exclusively religious phenomenon . . . The Custom is social organization, political participation, economic activity, and cultural creativity all at the same time, all permeated by religion in the original sense of the word *religare*, to bind, to maintain the ties that unite individuals and community with nature, with the rest of humanity, and with the beyond that transcends the visible. Hence it gave rise to the complex system of community offices and posts that so fascinates the cultural anthropologists who have flocked to Chiapas since the 1950s.[11]

Indigenous history, mythology, and religion also pervaded indigenous languages—the tongues of feeling and of everyday life, quite separate from the mercantile exchanges with the outside world that are conducted in Indian-inflected Spanish.

---

11   Jan de Vos, "La Iglesia católica en Chiapas, 1528–1998," in Morales, ed., *Chiapas: Una nueva visión para una nueva política*, p. 11.

6.

But what are the languages, apart from that Spanish, that these discourses pervade, and how many of them are there? The state of Chiapas,
with a surface of 73,887 square kilometers, occupies almost 4 percent
of Mexican territory and is divided into 111 municipalities. Of its total
population (3.21 million in 1990, an estimated 3.58 million in 1995), 26
percent are speakers of indigenous languages while the estimated indigenous population is 35 percent. In the region of the Zapatista rebellion,
the proportion of indigenous-language speakers rises to 70 percent in the
Lacandon Forest and almost 80 percent in Los Altos. Across the entire
state, an estimated 716,000 people speak one of eighteen indigenous languages. In descending order, these are: Tzeltal (36 percent), Tzotzil (31
percent), Chol (16 percent), Tojolabal (5 percent), Zoque (4.9 percent),
Kanjobal (1.4 percent), and Mame (1.2 percent).[12]

In the municipality of Ocosingo, whose capital was taken on January
1, 1994, by the EZLN, eight indigenous languages are spoken. In Las
Margaritas, another municipal center captured that day, they speak six.
Furthermore, the native population that does not speak Spanish accounts
for 38 percent of all indigenous-language speakers. Of these non-Spanish
speakers, 84 percent live in settlements of less than 500 people. Looking
at only the most populous language groups, 38 percent of Tzeltals, 36
percent of Tzotzils, and 34 percent of Chols know no Spanish. In every
case, these figures are almost doubled for women: 64, 63, and 67 percent
of the same groups.

The levels of illiteracy are dismaying. Of the 462,445 people aged fifteen
and over who speak an indigenous language, 54 percent cannot read or
write. Among women, this proportion rises to 68 percent. Schooling
fares no better. Fifty-three percent of indigenous speakers never attended
at all; 28 percent never finished elementary school. The remaining 19
percent finished elementary and may have had some secondary education. As for access to senior secondary and higher education, the barrier
is almost impassable for indigenous people: a mere 2 percent has attained
those educational levels and a paltry 0.6 percent has managed, thanks to
unimaginable family sacrifices, to enter university.

---

12   Arnulfo Embriz, "Los universos indígenas," in Morales, ed., *Chiapas: Una
nueva visión para una nueva política*. I am indebted to the same essay for figures on
indigenous languages, illiteracy, and schooling.

7.

I mentioned three discourses: *resistance, dignity, history,* and a fourth, *myth, Indian religion,* and *language.*

The first three connect the indigenous world with the national state. Resistance occurs within the state relation of domination/subordination; dignity is the response to the humiliation through which this domination manifests itself, and history is the argument over the common past of the Mexican state community.

In all three, the interlocutor and antagonist, explicitly or otherwise, is the state regime and its internal relations as they are lived by indigenous people. When these people organize to resist domination, to negotiate its forms, or to rebel against it, it is this interlocutor they are addressing, and then these discourses flow: they counter and at the same time they connect; they open the space of dispute, litigation, and negotiation.

The fourth discourse, that of myth, Indian religion, and language, is proper to the indigenous world. It has no interlocutors in the state relation. It does not communicate with the masters. It is the recourse used to negate and to counter. Its idioms are those in which what James C. Scott calls "the hidden transcripts" of the dominated take refuge—the discourses that the dominator cannot and should not understand, those in which real or imaginary conspiracies and fantasies of payback or revenge take place.[13] They are the reverse side, where the pride of the oppressed shelters in secret, where the humiliations, offenses, and affronts meted out by the masters' world are stored, for an individual explosion or collective rebellion on some indefinite but certain tomorrow.

This fourth discourse is nourished by the thought and imaginary of the enchanted world, whose reasons are impossible to translate into the masters' discourse of reason. These reasons are, by the same token, outside the state relation—but they secretly feed all the resistances organized within that state relation through the other discourses.

8.

Resistance, dignity, and history are the three great themes around which the indigenous people of Chiapas have for many years been organizing within the Mexican state form. The peculiarity of this form, a product

13   James C. Scott, *Domination and the Arts of Resistance: Hidden Transcripts* (New Haven: Yale University Press, 1990).

of the 1910–20 revolution and its *cardenista* continuation in the 1930s, is to encourage the organization of campesinos and workers around their social demands, confronting private landowners or companies within the state's legal framework, until a solution can be negotiated with the intervention of the federal government or that of the states within the Republic.

By positioning themselves as the arbiters at the apex of the above triangle, federal and state governments acquire power over the forces in contention and can negotiate with each side their own role as the guarantors of balance. This is not a neutral arbitrator: it must after all secure the motor and ultimate objective of the modern state, which is the valorization and accumulation of capital as the structuring agent of social life in all its commercial, material, and spiritual transactions. The balancing of organized forces is one of the pillars of the state's legitimacy, such as it emerged from the juridical architecture of the 1917 Constitution and its social implementation in the reforms instigated by Cárdenas. These reforms redefined the ample and indeterminate space of contention, meaning those disputes that can only be settled by litigation, occasion by occasion and case by case.

Such a balance requires a permanent process of negotiation, a process in which the state form dwells and on which it feeds: a ceaseless "negotiation of rule."[14] The Constitution and the law determine the frameworks of this negotiation, in which the state community and the state form are construed as part of a long-term process and not as a stationary edifice, fixed once and for all. Within these frameworks, it is the state that defines the meanings shared by both dominated and dominators in the state community (an illusory or imagined community) and through which the regulation of community relations operates, termed *moral regulation* by Corrigan and Sayer: "a project of normalizing, rendering natural, taken for granted, in a word 'obvious,' what are in fact ontological and epistemological premises of a particular and historical form of social order."[15]

In this specific moral regulation, ever since the Reform of the Benito Juárez period [1855–1867], the Church has been excluded or, more exactly, sidelined from the state: its worldly goods were expropriated (it

---

14   See Gilbert M. Joseph and Daniel Nugent, eds., *Everyday Forms of State Formation in Mexico: Revolution and the Negotiation of Rule in Modern Mexico* (Durham: Duke University Press, 1994).

15   Philip Corrigan and Derek Sayer, *The Great Arch: English State Formation as Cultural Revolution* (Oxford: Basil Blackwell, 1985), p. 4.

had previously been Mexico's biggest landowner) and its role as money-lender given over to modern, secular institutions. Nevertheless, religion continues to be intensely present in Mexican life, and hence the Church likewise, so that the secular state has never stopped having to negotiate and contend with it over the scope and purpose of moral regulation. One of the bloodier episodes of this endless negotiation was the Cristero War of the late 1920s. The reforms to Article 130 of the Constitution under Carlos Salinas de Gortari opened up afresh the terrain of contention between church and state.[16]

The post-revolutionary Mexican state spurred the organization of campesinos demanding land, whose right of ownership was enshrined in the Constitution. In the perpetual struggle to turn such rights into realities—with all the attendant benefits such as water, seed, credit, education, highways—organized peasants forged links with the relevant governments, taken to be the embodiment of the protective function of the state in its specific role as moral regulator. This notion of the paternal or protective state has deep roots in Mexican history, being a direct and living legacy of the Spanish Crown, whose form of domination had subsumed within it the older modes of relating to power practiced by pre-Hispanic peoples.

As in other regions of the country, the indigenous people of Chiapas did not get organized qua indigenous people but in accordance with the category that constituted them as interlocutors vis-à-vis the state: that of campesinos. Under President Cárdenas, the federal government directly promoted this process, and since then the indigenous campesinos in Chiapas have been organizing ceaselessly. With all its ups and downs and frequent violent clashes with governors and armed landowners, this has secured the creation of ejidos, cooperatives, trade unions, credit unions, and other organizational entities proper to the Mexican state relation. Court cases, negotiations, deals, fresh litigation: these are the intrinsic elements of the form in which this relation exists and is recognized and experienced by everyone within it.

But beneath and beyond all that, the indigenous world lived on, with its culture and its beliefs; the ancient agrarian community, enfeebled, dissolved, fragmented by migration in search of new lands and new frontiers, but remade all over again in that which pertains to it alone and is not shared with the state: in myths, beliefs, the Custom, the language.

---

16   [In 1992, the Salinas government amended the Constitution to give expanded rights to religious associations and their members, including the right to teach and to vote.]

Everything for which they are excluded becomes everything that unites them beneath and outside the state relation. We have to think how this deep tissue, hidden only because others cannot see it, sustains and revitalizes the organizational forms that are recognized in the dialogue and negotiation within the state.

In a remarkable essay, "The 'Comunidad Revolucionaria Institucional': The Subversion of Native Government in Highland Chiapas, 1936–1968," Jan Rus examines how the Partido Revolucionario Institucional (Institutional Revolutionary Party, PRI) and its governments acted to absorb and dissolve these community relations inside the state form embodied by the party.[17] It thought it had succeeded, until the Zapatista uprising said otherwise, heralding an epochal crisis for that mode of rule.

However, over decades of struggle and legal conflicts, peaceful or violent, and often bloody (the blood was always indigenous blood), the indigenous campesinos of Chiapas developed an *organizational culture*. Generation after generation spawned countless organizers, experts in arguing with the government, convoking assemblies and reaching resolutions, leading marches, seizing land, going to court, and protecting themselves from armed attack by police, army, and paramilitaries.

Those thousands learned, read, told, and heard the history of a Mexican Revolution quite unlike the official version. They made it their own. From below, they saw it for what it was: a ten-year-long peasant war, not victorious but not defeated either; a war whose peaceful aftermath was the *cardenista* reforms, viewed, likewise from below, as a matter of struggle and organization rather than as a freely granted government concession. This culture and this vision of national history bound the Chiapanecans to their fellow campesinos in every state of the Republic.

The historic culture that legitimizes the Mexican state harbors within it a culture of rebellion. To put this differently: by legitimizing itself through the history of revolutions and the promised fulfillment of promises made, this state form absorbs into itself but also legitimizes a culture of rebellion, whose roots lie not in the state discourse, but precisely in the history lived by successive generations—a history the state distorts and adapts for its own purposes but cannot negate or condemn. The discourse of power, built as it is everywhere upon history, shares living myths with the discourse of rebellions.

---

17   Jan Rus, "The 'Comunidad Revolucionaria Institucional': The Subversion of Native Government in Highland Chiapas, 1936–1968," in Joseph and Nugent, eds., *Everyday Forms of State Formation*, pp. 265–300.

Here is the inevitable reversal, implicit in the specifically Mexican state form: the instruments that were developed to ensure campesino support, the instruments that legitimized the new state's rule and thus made rebellion superfluous, became instruments understood and appropriated by all, to be employed, when the time came, to legitimize and organize rebellion. A civic and electoral rebellion, internal to the state, in the *cardenismo* of 1988; an armed rebellion, external to the state, in the Zapatismo of 1994.

That time came when the ruling class, whose new hard core was international finance capital, began to dismantle the juridical and material pillars of the erstwhile state form and to roll out a series of counterreforms: privatizations; liberalization of foreign trade; financial deregulation; changes to Art. 27 of the Constitution, which had underpinned the ejido system and land rights; economic integration with the US; cancellation of subsidies on basic goods for the poor; and elimination of price guarantees for campesino produce. The resistance to this was patchy at first, but soon it began to organize against the effects of this stripping away of a protective state which, however, still retained its attributes and modes of control. This is why, as Neil Harvey notes, when the EZLN uprising broke out in January 1994,

> the popular movements, including the peasant movements of Chiapas, had already created a democratic discourse through their insistence on respect for rights, associational autonomy, and the unfulfilled promises of the Mexican Revolution. The Zapatistas were able to draw on both the diverse and often contradictory elements of this political discourse, but they were also able to give them a new political meaning.[18]

"The economic struggles for land, credits, and fair prices, while necessary to build regional organizations, were increasingly articulated in a cultural-political discourse of indigenous autonomy," Harvey writes. "If there is one thing that these diverse struggles have in common it is their opposition to rural bossism, or caciquismo," whose "roots are to be found in the concentration of political and economic power."[19]

---

18 Neil Harvey, *The Chiapas Rebellion: The Struggle for Land and Democracy* (Durham: Duke University Press, 1998), pp. 199–200. See also, Carlos San Juan Victoria, "Las organizaciones campesinas en Chiapas: consideraciones y propuestas," in Morales, ed., *Chiapas: Una nueva visión para una nueva política*.
19 Harvey, *The Chiapas Rebellion*, pp. 204, 36.

In other words, these mobilizations, even as they occurred for decades within the Mexican state form, already called into question and came into conflict with informal institutions vital to the existence and the tactical maneuvers of this state form: the cacique as the mediator between the two worlds, say, or the tangle of alliances and family interests that buttresses the power of the Chiapanecan agrarian oligarchy.

"The Zapatista rebellion," Harvey concludes, "can be seen as the latest in a long cycle of popular demands for dignity, voice and autonomy."[20]

The migration to and colonization of the Lacandon Forest in search of a new agricultural frontier, far from the oppression of landowners and governments—a social and demographic movement that had been underway for decades—turned into a novel form of resistance and relationship with the state authority. According to Harvey, "the migration of colonists to the Lacandon Forest and their organization in community-level cooperatives through the Catholic Church can be interpreted as the remaking of community and ethnic identity."[21]

Of course, the fundamental antagonist to this indigenous discourse is the Chiapanecan oligarchy, with its state governments, its caciques, and its racism, none of which are part of the official national discourse of the Mexican Revolution. But that topic would take us beyond the bounds of this essay.

9.

There is another element that plays a decisive role in the Chiapas conflict, with one foot inside the state form and the other in the excluded indigenous communities of that state: the Catholic Church in Chiapas, headed by Bishop Samuel Ruiz. It is a long story, and it has been told before. Catholicism takes root in indigenous culture and religion and, without taking them over completely, connects them with the organized body of the Church and its bishop.

On the occasion of Pope John Paul II's visit to Mexico, Samuel Ruiz, bishop of San Cristóbal since 1960, wrote a pastoral letter in May 1993 entitled "In This Hour of Grace." In it he summarized his thirty years as the head of a diocese where the great majority of the flock are indigenous. He listed four phases in the process of change on which he and

---

20   Ibid., p. 37.
21   Ibid., p. 66.

his collaborators had embarked with the aim of coming closer to this population. The phases were, he explained: the renovation of pastoral action (1960–67); the revaluation of indigenous cultures (1969–78); the recognition of the sociopolitical dimension of their extreme poverty (1979–91); and the defense of their rights against the threat of neoliberal modernity (1992 onward).[22]

During the first period, more than 600 catechists were trained. In 1968, to take stock of what had been achieved so far, the catechists' opinion was sought. Their response was unexpected: "The Church and the Word of God have told us things to save our souls, but we don't know how to save our bodies. While working for the salvation of our own and others' souls, we suffer hunger, sickness, poverty and death." Jan de Vos writes:

> After that challenge, both the pastoral team and the communities entered into a dynamic in which the true predicament of the indigenous, as exploited campesinos whose culture was despised, became the axis of thought and action. This was also the moment when the Catholic Church started to diverge more and more from the Protestant churches in terms of pastoral emphasis and strategy.[23]

This was in 1968, when the Second Vatican Council and the Medellín Conference were recent upheavals.[24] The bishop of San Cristóbal was reading "the signs of the times":

> For Samuel Ruiz and his team, inspiration would henceforth come from two "theological sites," meaning realities in which, Christians believe, God is especially present in "the signs of the times": the gospel of Christ, rediscovered as a liberating announcement to the poor; and the indigenous communities, which, from their negated past to their wretched present, were at once the bearers and the receivers of this liberating announcement . . . In the words of Samuel Ruiz himself, "the whole of community life, its whole social, economic, political, and cultural

22   De Vos, "La iglesia católica en Chiapas."
23   Ibid.
24   [The Second Vatican Council, 1962–65, made significant reforms to Catholic liturgy, as part of a bid to modernize Church practices. The Medellín Conference of Latin American Bishops, 1968, took this reformist agenda further, endorsing one of the key postulates of liberation theology by stating that the Church should take a "preferential option for the poor," and supporting the creation of Christian Base Communities.]

reality was revealed to us as a theological site that conveyed through its various elements—the listeners' needs and wishes, their ways of talking, thinking, judging, and interacting with their fellows—the content of the announcement."[25]

The bishop's pastoral letter mentioned three further points that converged, as he saw it, into a single focus:

1) The need to "incarnate" the evangelical message in indigenous culture. 2) The conviction that traditional Christian "redemption" means the wholesale "liberation" of humanity, as much on the community as on the individual level. 3) The duty to work, over and above the interests of the Church itself, to build the "Kingdom of God" that is already beginning on Earth through the struggle for justice and peace.[26]

Samuel Ruiz explained as follows the reasons for converting his diocese to "the preferential option for the poor": "It wasn't any kind of decree nor was it a mere theological elucubration, just a simple reading of a lacerating reality: high poverty rates, illness, illiteracy, lack of communications, profound marginalization and racial discrimination." Let me quote Jan de Vos at length:

To describe this emergency in more detail, Samuel Ruiz resorted to the "burning word" of the native campesinos themselves, compiled over more than twenty years of reflection in the form of countless courses, workshops, and exchanges of ideas between pastoral outreach and the communities. The diagnosis reached by the congregation themselves was a denunciation of the multiple abuses committed by the authorities and the dominant sectors of the region on political, economic, social, and ideological levels . . .

The pastoral letter made it quite clear that this "lacerating reality" was what pushed the diocese into its "preferential option for the poor," also prompting an in-depth revision of its various pastoral labors, especially that of catechism . . . As Samuel Ruiz put it: "As they reflected upon deeply painful experiences, men, women, and children would speak all at once in loud voices, as is the indigenous way, until an 'accord' emerged that contained their vision of faith, their theological vision of reality."[27]

---

25   De Vos, "La iglesia católica en Chiapas."
26   Ibid.
27   Ibid.

This process eventually transformed the structure of the Church's activity, as well as its relationship with the indigenous communities:

> It was the communities themselves, now accustomed to thinking and deciding as a group, who pressured the bishop to not only appoint indigenous catechists but also ordain indigenous priests. They made this request invoking the old pre-Hispanic religion in which such a consecrated office had featured . . . As a result, Bishop Samuel Ruiz named more than 400 lay deacons—*tuhuneltik*, in Tzeltal—in hopes of seeing them one day ordained as deacons and then as priests. Today, alongside some 8,000 catechists, these constitute the pastoral cadres of a native Church with a presence in more than 2,500 communities.[28]

In clear contrast to the traditional liberal discourse of the state—mouthpiece of the power of white masters and ladinos—the discourse of Ruiz's church of the poor is one that connects to the indigenous world in its own languages, its religion, myths and beliefs, and its communal view of the world and of the relations between the world and human beings.

Embracing indigenous thought, which in turn incorporates and assumes it on indigenous terms, this discourse enables native people to find, in the idiom of an ostensibly shared religion, an anguished communication with the modern world. Although this communication is really a misunderstanding, given that indigenous religion is incomprehensible to the Catholicism of the señores.

The action of this Church is not confined to preaching: it also engages in organization, using forms, terms, and languages that can be appropriated by the indigenous through the affirmation of their own thought, not its negation.[29]

---

28   Ibid.

29   "The work of the catechists was complemented by the decision to train a large number of community deacons whose main responsibility would be to help the priests administer the sacraments. It was the communities themselves that expressed the need for their own deacons so they would not have to rely on the already limited supply of pastoral workers in the diocese. Each community would choose their deacon, or *tu'hunel*, through consensus, and generally they elected those who had served well in other capacities. The diocese agreed to ordain deacons after a three-year trial period. The importance of the deaconhood was that it was made a permanent feature of community organization, whereas prior to the 1970s it represented more of a temporary solution to the lack of priests." (Harvey, *The Chiapas Rebellion*, p. 74.)

10.

In Chiapas, at least two modes of organization, combined and complementary, expanded and overlapped for years: that of peasants within the Mexican state relation, and that of indigenous people (who are the same as the first group) within the religious structures of the church of the poor. It is here that cadres were formed, experience gained, and demands formulated for the indigenous uprising of 1994.

In this fertile soil the small guerrilla band led by Subcomandante Marcos put down roots. The guerrillas had the capacity to understand it, learn from it, and adapt to it. At the same time Marcos managed to couch their demands in a voice that, at its best, conveys a connection between the enchanted world and the modern world, and reconciles them: "a world with room for all the worlds." In this message, the four discourses of rebellion are blended: resistance, dignity, history, and myth. One reason why it hit home among such diverse societies and audiences is because it also managed to be a discourse of diversity.

Without the group of militants who found a way to fuse with indigenous and campesino organizers, without their imaginative, logistical, and political abilities, no rebellion like that which took place would have been possible. However, to seek the explanation for the rebellion in only that small group, or in the Church of Samuel Ruiz, or in a conspiracy between the two, is to revert to the racism of old and dismiss those who were and are the protagonists of the rebellion: the indigenous peoples, with an army supported and sustained by their own villages and communities.

These communities, condemned to extinction by the modernity of capital, found in armed rebellion the way to break the enclosure and immobility of the crisis-ridden Mexican state form and project their voice into the wider world beyond. Their discourse, nurtured in the humus common to the vast majority of human beings, challenges the state's prerogative of moral regulation, its right to define time and its claim to name the world and imprint its own meaning on it.

Having always been excluded from the Mexican state, the indigenous peoples used their rebellion to expose to their country, Mexico, and to everyone else, the two-faced and deceitful nature of that state and its constitutional promises.

11.

The long negotiation between the Mexican government and the EZLN has been a site of encounter and missed encounter between two worlds and two times. These talks, after many twists and turns, culminated in the San Andrés Accords of March 1996, signed by the representatives of the federal government and the EZLN respectively. An all-party commission of lawmakers appointed by Congress, the Comisión de Concordia y Pacificación (Concord and Pacification Commission, COCOPA) would present the document before Congress for approval as a law of the Republic.

The content of the Accords is remarkable.[30] For all the latent ambiguity of many passages, they propose a reconstitution of the juridical bases of Mexican society by recognizing indigenous peoples as holders of their own political, social, and historical rights, on a par with individual citizen rights. To ensure full access to these, the Accords ultimately stipulate, native peoples require the legal acknowledgment of their existence as such.

As a general provision, the existence of these peoples is recognized in the Mexican Constitution in the chapter dealing with individual guarantees. Article 4 declares:

> The Mexican nation has a multicultural composition, which originally stems from its indigenous peoples. The law protects and promotes the development of their languages, cultures, practices, customs, resources, and specific forms of social organization, and guarantees to their members effective access to the jurisdiction of the state. In any lawsuits and agrarian proceedings that involve them, account will be taken of their juridical practices and customs in the terms laid down in law.[31]

The San Andrés Accords signal a far-reaching change to these statements, with regard to effective recognition of the existence, the jurisdictional customs, and the rights of indigenous peoples. I note here some of what the Accords contain.[32]

30   *Los Acuerdos de San Andrés* (Mexico City: Ediciones Era, 1998).

31   [Gilly is citing the text of Article 4 as amended in 1992; the Constitution was amended once more in 2001, when it was a revised version of Article 2 that recognized "the right of indigenous peoples to free determination ... within a constitutional framework of autonomy."]

32   Adolfo Gilly, "Los zapatistas en el Palacio de Minería," *La Jornada*, March 19, 1999.

- A wide recognition of rights that, taken in their true sense, affect all the inhabitants of the nation and not only the indigenous: the right to identity, diversity, community, and, above all, the explicit separation between rights and money.
- The revaluation of the word "autonomy": we claim self-governance and self-determination in everything that has to do with us. "Peoples as such are entitled to the right of self-determination," the Accords say. "Autonomy is the concrete expression of the exercise of the right to self-determination." And with the autonomy of native peoples, other issues return to the agenda, such as municipal autonomy, university autonomy, trade-union autonomy, and the twofold idea of autonomy as something already conquered, already being enjoyed, and autonomy as something yet to be constructed in the reality of Mexico.
- The recuperation of the term "peoples" for the judicial system: "The recognition of indigenous peoples as social and historical subjects implies altering the constitutive bases of Mexican society, by adding to the principle of citizenry the principle of indigenous peoples."[33]
- The restoration of Article 27 of the Constitution to its original sense, as the relationship of the Mexican people with itself, with its form of government, and with its territory as the original patrimony of the nation.
- The recuperation of the concept of sovereignty, no longer as property but as a complex identity linking nation, people, culture, history, and territory.

The government signed the draft of the Accords to be submitted to Congress on behalf of the four parties represented there, including the ruling PRI. Since this version did not address all the EZLN's demands, perhaps the government expected a rejection. On the contrary, the Zapatistas accepted the text as it stood. Signed by both parties, the Accords should then have passed automatically into law.

However, for reasons that were never explained but can be imagined, in December 1996, the executive power withdrew its signature from the Accords and proposed re-opening the discussion. The EZLN maintained its endorsement and demanded the implementation of what had been

---

33   Luis Hernández Navarro, "Serpientes y escaleras: los avatares de la reforma constitucional sobre derechos y cultura indígenas," in *Los acuerdos de San Andrés*, p. 216.

agreed. The negotiations and discussions have remained in suspension ever since. The indigenous peoples of Chiapas continue to live under siege, suffering shortages, harassment from paramilitaries, kidnappings, and murders. And they continue to resist.

Faced with the test of an indigenous rebellion, the state form came up against one of its limits. It was unable to admit into its frameworks the San Andrés Accords without going into crisis and disavowing the pledges it had made. Any future extension of rights, autonomies, and democracy will require a rupture, a reconfiguration, and a complete change of direction toward a new state form.

12.

In 1938, Graham Greene traveled around Mexico and came away with the dark impression of a country that threatened his Western rationality with some atavistic enigma he was helpless to decipher. He recorded this vision in his account of the journey, *The Lawless Roads*. Crossing the Chiapas highlands on muleback, he reflected on how the indigenous people had adopted the Catholic faith that was also his own. He wrote the following lines as part of his description of a country and of his own soul, troubled and confused by the contemporary presence of an ancient, enchanted world:

> And there was an even older world beyond the ridge: the ground sloped up again to where a grove of tall black crosses stood at all angles like wind-blown trees against the blackened sky. This was the Indian religion—a dark, tormented, magic cult . . . Here, in the mountainous strange world of Father Las Casas, Christianity went on its own frightening way. Magic, yes, but we are too apt to minimize the magic element in Christianity— the man raised from the dead, the devils cast out, the water turned into wine. The great crosses leaned there in their black and windy solitude, safe from the *pistoleros* and the politicians, and one thought of the spittle mixed with the clay to heal the blind man, the resurrection of the body, the religion of the earth.[34]

---

34 Graham Greene, *The Lawless Roads* (Harmondsworth: Penguin [1939] 1985), pp. 170–1.

Epilogue

In the general elections of July 2000, the PRI lost the presidency and with it, its status as the party of government. The new president was Vicente Fox, the candidate of the Partido Acción Nacional (National Action Party, PAN). One of his campaign pledges was a rapid resolution of the Chiapas conflict. He took office on December 1, 2000.

Barely three months later, on February 25, 2001, the March of the Color of the Earth, organized by the EZLN, set off from San Cristóbal toward Mexico City. It was led by twenty-three commanders, male and female, and Subcomandante Marcos, unarmed but with their faces always covered. They walked across the country from Chiapas to the Federal District, holding crowded rallies in cities along the way; they attended the National Indigenous Congress in Nurio, Morelos State, and on March 11 reached the capital of the Republic, where they convened a mass event that totally filled the huge Zócalo. The delegation stayed in the National School of Anthropology and History and met with a range of personalities and organizations.

After more than two weeks of tense waiting, on March 28 an EZLN delegation was received at a joint session of both chambers of Congress. From the podium Comandanta Esther spoke for the EZLN, her face covered by a balaclava. She voiced the reasons and arguments justifying congressional approval of the legal text that would enshrine the Accords of San Andrés as the law of the land. After that, the Zapatista delegation immediately returned to its home territory of Chiapas to await the decision of Congress.

This decision was unfavorable. The indigenous law approved by both congressional chambers (unanimously in the Senate, by a majority in the Chamber of Deputies) retained largely formal aspects and omitted substantial points of the Accords, notably those dealing with autonomy and the constitutional recognition of indigenous peoples as legal persons.

The Mexican state—the state whose administrations had negotiated or coexisted with the rebellion since 1994, without ceasing to harass the Zapatistas—had thus refused, once again, to modify its juridical essence consisting in the exclusion of the indigenous as such. Notwithstanding the changes in the sphere of representational politics (competitive elections with a plural slate of parties, alternation in the presidency), the legislative organs of this state had reaffirmed the continuity and permanence of its defining traits as a specific state form, rather than its much-vaunted transformation. Accepting the indigenous challenge would have meant opening the door to genuine change. Neither the legislative nor the executive powers were prepared to countenance it.

Since then, an armed truce has continued between the federal government and the indigenous army with its support base in the villages. Some see this situation as a dead end for the indigenous movement. Others see it instead as further evidence of the movement's resilience, its ability to wait things out and withstand adversity in a temporal dimension different to the time of the state and its institutions.

10

A Twenty-First-Century Revolution

(2004)

The Revolution is what is right for everyone. It is like the Old Condor of the high mountains with his white crest, who will protect us all beneath his powerful wings.

Francisco Chipana Ramos, 1945

1.

In its forms, protagonists and contents, the insurrectional movement of September–October 2003 in Bolivia appears as a product of the transformations imposed by the neoliberal restructuring at the end of the twentieth century on society and the economy, and above all on the lives, territories, and relationships of the subaltern classes. It is a new movement, with hitherto nonexistent actors, evincing an unprecedented capacity to link the most pressing demands to the most general national agenda—gas, water, hydrocarbons, coca, the republic—and whose methods of organization and confrontation have a venerable lineage but are also informed by all that new technologies have to offer.

The Bolivian uprising displayed a unique combination of ancient and modern features and a new utilization of popular violence. Rather than explain the insurrection on the altiplano by comparing it to revolutions of the past, it should be analyzed in relation with the transformations of society and of the modes of capitalist domination that have been underway since the last decade of the twentieth century.

This being the case, the violent and victorious Bolivian uprising that climaxed in October 2003 constitutes the first revolution of the twenty-first century. We must attempt to decipher its contents, its motives, and its portents.

2.

On October 17, 2003, Aymaras, peasant farmers, workers with and without jobs, street sellers and stallholders, indigenous students, mineworkers, and migrants from everywhere—in short, *la indiada*, the dreaded Indian rabble—with the violence of their bodies and their dead, took La Paz and overthrew the president of the Republic of the Lords and the Wealthy, Don Gonzalo Sánchez de Lozada.

Those people, yes, the ones who had been blocking roads since the beginning of September, and on general strike since October 8. With the violence of their bodies, yes, because apart from stones, sticks, slings, a couple of old rifles, and some dynamite, they had no weapons. With the violence of their dead, yes, because the army, which in order to clear the roads had started killing Indians again on September 20 in Warisata, in the altiplano of La Paz, slaughtered them once more in El Alto on October 12.

Those men and women, yes, the ones who on Monday 13, while the army was still busy killing down in La Paz, had carried their dead to the atriums of their churches and to the patios of their homes; they had held wakes; they had told each other, and told whoever wanted to listen, about the army's atrocities and their bare-handed resistance; and with rage in their eyes, they had shown reporters handfuls of bullet casings collected from the streets of El Alto, as if making an offering; and they had conferred in low voices and counseled one another all night long. And on the morning of Tuesday 14, they had filed through the dusty streets, carrying their dead to the churches, and had crowded to hear the Requiem masses; and they had talked to their leaders in neighborhood meetings. And then they had decided that now was the time to go down to La Paz, were it to cost another 500 dead—that was the number they said—and this time they would overthrow the hated, murderous president. With the violence of their dead, I said, with the violence of their bodies.

3.

They would go down to La Paz, I said. La Paz lies in a hollow, 400 meters below the altiplano where on the very edge of the gully clings El Alto, a town of 800,000 people, with self-built houses and the splendid snow-caps of the Cordillera behind. The slopes, plunging steeply toward the capital, are completely covered on this side by the old workers' neigh-borhoods—Munaypata, Pura Pura, Villa Victoria—which have known their share of struggles and massacres: Villa Victoria was bombed from the air in 1950.

Down avenues and streets and alleyways and paths the Aymara torrent flowed. It was Wednesday 15. The local people cheered them as they passed, gave out sodas, water, food, and many joined them. On the 16th, the tin miners of Huanuni would arrive, after negotiating and threatening their way past the army roadblock a hundred kilometers back in Patacamaya. In the end, the military detachment let through, without attacking, sixty truckloads of miners including *palliri* men and women [gleaners of mine tailings], from the mining capital of Oruro. Let through, I said, a sign of hesitancy that did not go unnoticed.

By then, tens of thousands of Aymara peasant farmers had arrived from Omasuyos province and other places on the altiplano, having blocked the highway for a month. Others flocked from the rebel strong-hold of Achacachi, site of several massacres over the years, where there stands a statue of Túpaj Katari, the Aymara chief who laid siege to La Paz in 1781 and was on the verge of capturing it when he was defeated by the Spaniards. Brigades of coca growers also came up from the Yungas valleys and other hot or temperate regions. Students from the Public University of El Alto (UPEA) were everywhere, milling between the bon-fires of old tires and barricades built from pedestrian bridges brought crashing down by the strength of many arms pulling ropes.

This time, October 2003, La Paz was under siege from Aymara Indians and the road closures and the general strike. No food supplies, commercial goods, or gasoline were allowed in. The demands were: the resignation of the president; an end to gas exports via Chilean ports; an end to the eradication of coca plantations (mainstay of the *cocaleros*, popular consumer product and sacred plant of ancient civilizations); a constituent assembly to re-found the Republic; and eighty further items of all kinds, submitted by each sector and community. The Aymara language, gestures, and even flag—the *wiphala*—had become receptacles and bearers of the great national demands.

Ever since 1781, Indians besieging the city has been a phantom terrorizing the imagination of the dominant classes: "The nightmare of an Indian siege continues to disturb the sleep of Bolivian criollos," wrote Silvia Rivera Cusicanqui twenty years ago. Now the nightmare had come true. Further south, meanwhile, where La Paz's river flows into more temperate climes and the wealthy have their homes, the ring closed in around them as the Indians from the lowland valleys, the *comuneros* of Ovejuyo, went through the nice neighborhoods without throwing a single stone, breaking a single window, or picking a single flower. They simply flowed, like a stream in reverse, on their way to overthrow the president.

4.

To break the siege, dispel the nightmare, punish the culprits, and allow gas and supplies to come back into the city, the army entered El Alto on the 12th. It came to kill, in that sprawling city built over twenty years by the hands of the displaced and the victims of neoliberalism: rural migrants from the altiplano, mine and factory workers who had been "resettled" from Oruro and Potosí, office workers from La Paz, poor and middling traders. In the most recent census (2001), 80 percent of all these had declared themselves to be "indigenous," Aymara or Quechua from various communities.

In 1950, as the inhabitants of Villa Victoria were being bombed by plane, El Alto had a population of 11,000, hanging there on the edge of the gully. By 2001, according to the census, it had risen to 650,000, in a country of 8 million people. And it kept growing. "Of the whole working population of El Alto, 69 percent are active in the informal sector, in precarious conditions, and in a semi-entrepreneurial or family setting. Despite this, just over 43 percent of Alteños are workers or employees, which makes this the city with the highest proportion of workers in the country," notes Álvaro García Linera.[1] It is a youthful population: 60

1 Álvaro García Linera, "El Alto insurrecto," *El Juguete Rabioso*, year 3, no. 90 (October 12, 2003). [García Linera went on to become vice president of Bolivia under Evo Morales, serving from 2006 to 2019.]

percent are under twenty-five years old and only 10 percent are over fifty. Sixty percent of homes lack plumbing and sanitation, healthcare is patchy, education likewise. Nationally, El Alto has the highest rates of child labor and highest average rate of employment per household. Even so, 60 percent of households live below the poverty threshold and half of those are destitute. Pablo Mamani, an Aymara sociologist who teaches at the Public University of El Alto, writes:

> El Alto is a city made by its inhabitants in terms of their manual and economic contributions to the construction of its streets, avenues, markets, soccer pitches, etc. In addition, we find a particular social construction of everyday life, based on wide kinship networks, relations of godparenthood throughout the urban space, young people's friendships across different barrios, and fairly common relationships stemming from shared backgrounds in the *ayllus* and communities of the altiplano or the valleys and subtropical Andean regions.[2]

El Alto, Mamani adds, asserts itself through its Aymara identity:

> In social protests, there are . . . forms of Aymara expression in the idiom of clothes and their meanings: the full skirts, the hats, and the language of symbols—*yatiri* [healer], coca, *pututus* [conch or bullhorn instruments], and wiphalas—which generate, from a position of social banishment, ceremonial and ritual alternatives to the elements symbolic of the state.[3]

This young, modern, defiant city, erected by the hands of its residents, resulted from the neoliberal phase of capitalism after the liberalization of trade and the economic restructuring launched in 1985 with Decree 21060—deeply hated today by the people—whose provisions withdrew support from rural and artisanal economies, crashed the prices of their products, closed mines and manufacturing, cut wages and jobs, privatized hydrocarbons and public services, triggered massive external and internal migration, and ripped apart the popular social fabric that had been woven since the Revolution of 1952.

In this way, neoliberal capitalism unwittingly created the popular mass, the territorial scope, and the social conditions of the insurrection.

2   Pablo Mamani Ramírez, *El rugir de las multitudes: La fuerza de los levantamientos indígenas en Bolivia/Qullasuyu* (La Paz: Aruwiyiri, 2004), p. 140. See also Luis Gómez, *El Alto de pie* (La Paz: Comuna, 2004).

3   Mamani, *El rugir de las multitudes*, p. 139.

Destroying the old forms of institutional bargaining, it brutally imposed a new domination. However, the coercion by which it did so did not meet with the consent of the dominated. The neoliberal mode of domination is one that seeks to disorganize and atomize its objects, refusing to negotiate anything with anyone, preferring to deal with isolated and defenseless individuals. But, as things turned out, it failed. The new mass began to organize all over again in its new territories, with the help of its ancient wisdom that did not reside in the dismantled institutions but in the minds and bodies of the mass. The new domination failed to establish a hegemony, failed to create consent to accompany and mediate coercion—as Peronism had succeeded in doing in Argentina fifty years before, or as the PRI had in Mexico, or even as the 1952 Revolution and the Movimiento Nacionalista Revolucionario (Revolutionary Nationalist Movement, MNR) had in Bolivia itself. On the other hand, the norms of the new domination ruled out, for the time being, military dictatorships as a "legitimate" solution to conflicts or as a means of administering the state—a shift that had been duly noted by the dominated.

5.

Against this "domination without hegemony" (the historian Ranajit Guha's term for the long colonial rule of the British in India), against this neoliberal domination of a formerly colonial state that the oligarchic caste was trying to force on Bolivia with tanks and guns at the beginning of the twenty-first century, the Bolivian people rebelled. As of the year 2000, they rebelled by means of successive "wars," the telling military name they gave to their movements: the war against privatized water supplies in Cochabamba in 2000; the war to defend the coca plantations in the Chapare against army and police in January 2003 (thirteen coca farmers dead, sixty wounded); the war against income taxes in La Paz in February 2003 (more than thirty dead); the gas war in September and October 2003 (eighty dead), leading up to the climactic capture of La Paz and the fall of the government that same year. Moreover, this mode of domination exacerbates the congenital fragility of a racist, ex-colonial state like Bolivia.

In this modernizing neoliberal rule that fails to assert its hegemony, we may perhaps hear a distant echo of what happened with the Bourbon reforms of the eighteenth century, shaped by Enlightenment ideas of rationalization and centralization of command. In the Andean region, the response was the huge indigenous rebellions led by Túpac Amaru and Túpaj Katari in 1780–81. A thought-provoking study by Sergio Serulnikov, "Customs and Rules," posits that, in the Andean region, the new rules were interpreted one way from the standpoint of Spanish and criollo interests, and another way by Indian interests. The latter saw them as "a major instrument of Andean resistance against entrenched structures of exploitation and political oppression in the rural villages," while the colonial rulers used these rationalizing projects for the contrary objective of consolidating their grip.[4] The key point for Serulnikov, however, is that

> the most radical indigenous upheaval during colonial times in this region was the outcome of the *intertwinement*, not the *clash*, between processes of social mobilization from below and political transformation from above. Seen from this particular regional context, the crisis of colonial legitimacy may have resulted less from the enforcement of a new colonial pact than from the *unintended ways in which this new hegemonic project helped to collapse the old one without consolidating in the process a viable alternative* [my italics]. Bourbon policies increased the economic burden of Andean communities at the same time that they empowered them to contest local authority.[5]

Could this latest altiplano insurrection, with no visible leaders, without party direction, without big trade-union backing, and without taking power, have been a violent flower that bloomed for a day? Or will it, like the revolutions of 1781 against the colonial power and of 1952 against the oligarchic state, prove to be the precursor to similar responses to the current neoliberal domination elsewhere in this part of the world?

If only to find the answer to that question, we must pay close attention to the movement, and above all, not abandon it.

6.

On October 12, to break the siege of La Paz, the army went into El Alto to kill, I said. There was no other solution for them because El Alto, that city of uprooted migrants, was astonishingly well organized in those days:

---

4 Sergio Serulnikov, "Customs and Rules: Bourbon Rationalizing Projects and Social Conflicts in Northern Potosí during the 1770s," *Colonial Latin American Review*, vol. 8, no. 2, 1999, pp. 247–8.

5 Ibid., p. 248.

closures of streets and highways, neighborhood councils on every block, volunteer vigils on every corner summoned by megaphones, barricades piled with stones, wire, and tires, independent radio stations broadcasting day and night, people's guards to prevent looting of stores, and assemblies held in the streets, trade-union offices, and parish churches. Among their meager belongings, the migrants had brought with them the immaterial heritage of organizational know-how.

"The community organization brought in from the altiplano and the mining centers stymied the government completely, so that it had to resort to the discretional use of force to break the stranglehold of the protest," wrote the conservative paper *La Razón*, with a certain lucidity, two weeks later on October 30.

It was a fair summary, but it left a good deal out. For this community wisdom is also materialized in the organizational forms that have been forged over decades, with as many highs as lows, by its bearers: the Central Obrera Boliviana (Bolivian Workers' Central, COB), weakened but alive, headed by Jaime Solares; the Central Obrera Regional de El Alto (COR), a decisive actor in this movement, headed by Roberto de la Cruz; the Confederación Sindical Única de Trabajadores Campesinos de Bolivia (United Trade Union Confederation of Bolivian Peasant Workers, CSUTCB), a strong force in the Aymara altiplano, led by Felipe Quispe, "el Mallku" [condor; a traditional authority]; in the coca zone and elsewhere, the Movimiento al Socialismo (Movement Toward Socialism, MAS), headed by Evo Morales; in the central valleys were the irrigation farmers under Omar Fernández; in Cochabamba and its periphery, the factory workers and the Coordinadora del Agua (Water Coordinating Group) led by Óscar Olivera, at the forefront of the water wars of 2000.

This might be seen as a fresh episode of what Silvia Rivera Cusicanqui calls the "difficult and contradictory process" of the "synthesis between *long memory* (anticolonial struggles, the pre-Hispanic ethical order) and *short memory* (the revolutionary power of the peasant unions and militias after the Revolution of 1952)."[6]

And yet the rebellion of El Alto was not carried out by these bodies or their leaders. It was local people and their neighborhood councils who articulated the entire movement. This was picked up by *La Razón* and other press and radiophonic media. And that is why the army cracked down indiscriminately on everyone, not bothering to seek out leaders who did not exist. The retrospective account in *La Razón* continues:

6   Rivera Cusicanqui, *Oprimidos pero no vencidos*, p. 11.

And so, at dawn on Sunday 12, a vast military operation in the northern zone began the killing that by that evening had claimed the lives of
twenty-eight people. The convoy of tanker trucks, led by well-equipped
tanks and armored Caimans [military transport vehicles], rolled down
Avenida 6 de Marzo toward the Ingavi barracks, firing machine-gun
rounds that were met with homemade dynamite sticks, firecrackers, and
stones, leaving a trail of dead and injured.

With the violence of their bodies and their dead, I said. "The political
movements and the trade unions were largely absent from the conflict,"
the newspaper continues. "It was local residents who organized this rad-
icalization. On the night of Wednesday 15, the enraged people moved
nine train carriages, each weighing ten tons, and pushed them off the
bridge onto Avenida 6 de Marzo, closing off that route."

Enough is enough. No more convoys through here, goddammit.

And then more people went down to the city: the locals, the relatives
and friends and acquaintances of the dead, the injured and the persecuted, the incandescent mass created by years of neoliberalism, the heirs
of community organizing and trade-union struggles, the Aymara and the
Quechua, the *indios* and the [mixed-race, plebeian] *cholos*, those who
live by their hands, those who are so many things except rich. Meanwhile, at the other end of the city, the native *comuneros* trekking up from
the south closed off the bottom of the funnel that is La Paz.

7.

By that stage, following the massacre of October 12 in El Alto, something was happening in La Paz that would prove decisive. First tens,
then hundreds and hundreds of professionals, academics, artists, writers,
journalists, and other sectors of the middle class had begun to set up
"pickets"—their word—inside churches, announcing their hunger strike
"in solidarity with the city of El Alto and the families of those who were
murdered," as their first communiqué stated. It went on to denounce the
"guilt of the political class" and to demand the resignation of "Sánchez
de Lozada and his government."

The instigators of the hunger strike feared an imminent clash between
the crowd, which now filled the streets and squares, and the army. At day-
break on the 17th, that mass had blocked the entrances to Plaza Murillo
and were threatening the Palacio Quemado [government palace], while

a frontline of police and a second and third line of soldiers protected the presidential residence. According to Ana María Campero, the former People's Defender, a prominent political figure, and leader of the hunger-striking "pickets," between the 16th and the 17th the latter were worried enough to mobilize, so as to "convince both sides not to fall into a confrontation that would have meant great bloodshed." One week later, on October 24, Campero published an article in *Pulso* magazine that explained the "mediating" role of the hunger strikers, as she experienced it from her position in the conflict:

> While some of us tried to contact the social leaders on our cell phones, Sacha Llorenti, Ricardo Calla, and Roger Cortés went forward to meet the marchers, who assured them that they would not do anything to provoke a clash. I managed to call General Juan Veliz, the army commander-in-chief, and had a long conversation with him, starting with: "Please, General, don't have your men fire on the people." Juan Ramón Quintana did the same with other top military chiefs. According to reports, the military told Sánchez de Lozada that very night that they were going to withdraw to barracks. During the afternoon in Patacamaya, they had let a contingent of mineworkers go through unimpeded.[7]

Someone said to me weeks later, speaking from the left, that the sudden involvement of professionals, intellectuals, and artists masked a mixture of fear and hypocrisy. Certainly, I said, there's fear everywhere, from Los Altos to the arty Sopocachi neighborhood. But classes don't act out of hypocrisy.

"Here in Villa Ingenio, we were afraid," a priest in El Alto, Father Wilson Soria, told me. He and his parishioners of Christ the Redeemer risked their lives dodging bullets to rescue the wounded, and later, along with other neighbors, he signed an exceptional manifesto that asked for nothing less than "the gradual dissolution of the army" out of "respect for human dignity and brotherhood in cultural plurality." We may be sure that Father Soria would not have been granted an interview by General Veliz, and that this would not in any case have been an aspiration or a duty in his eyes.

"Everyone was scared in La Paz," I was told by Jenny Cárdenas, a peerless singer of Bolivian music and another promoter of the pickets. "But

---

7   Ana María Campero, "Los piqueteros de la esperanza," *Pulso*, October 24–30, 2003.

I didn't join the hunger strike out of fear but because I don't want to live in a country where they can only govern by killing the people." It was not fear. It was the sudden move of one class toward another, characteristic of all great social upheavals. It was like January 12, 1994, in Mexico City, when the multitude packing the Zócalo called for a ceasefire and a halt to the military slaughter of the Zapatistas and the indigenous communities that had risen up in Chiapas.

This turnaround in La Paz, replicated on October 15 and 16 in Cochabamba, Oruro, Potosí, Tarija, Sucre, Santa Cruz, and other cities in the Republic, finally isolated the president, the army, the US embassy, and the irreducible hubs of oligarchic racism that gather around that trio. When the military command stepped aside, the president and the embassy were on their own. Despite the explicit support of the State Department in Washington, the collapse was inevitable.

8.

On Thursday October 16, the whole of downtown La Paz, boulevards, plazas, and side streets, teemed with the crowds of those who had converged there from El Alto, the altiplano, Oruro, the Yungas, the southern valleys, the working-class shanties, the universities and schools, the markets—from over the hills and under the earth.

La Paz, a captured city. With the violence of their bodies and their dead, I said, the insurgents had conquered the city. They were now preparing to capture, literally at any cost, the abode of the president and his closest subordinates, in particular Defense Minister Carlos Sánchez Berzaín, mastermind of the killings. Preparing to hang them, they said. The pair were protected only by a fractured military command, which had already had to execute indigenous soldiers for refusing to shoot at their fellows and well knew that the invaders meant it about the 500 more dead; and that after that slaughter, there could be nothing but disarray and dishonor.

Early in the morning of October 17, the reports say, "the military were highly reluctant to continue firing on the population." The president was informed that the generals had "flexibilized" their position and wished him to step down. The streets buzzed with rumors of a resignation. At 13:00 hours, Sánchez de Lozada penned it. Three hours later, accompanied by his closest minsters, he escaped from the building in a helicopter. That same night they flew to Miami from the airport of Santa Cruz de la

Sierra. Once the plane had taken off, someone faxed the president's resignation letter from the airport to the Chamber of Deputies. In the final scene of this postmodern operetta, the fleeing president's farewell railed against the social organizations for fomenting "national disintegration," "corporatist and trade-union authoritarianism," and "fratricidal violence."

That was the end of it. The insurgents had won. Vice President Carlos Mesa, having distanced himself from his boss on the 13th, assumed the presidency. Over the following days he promised a referendum on gas exports, the constituent assembly, and other demands of the popular movement. The campesinos went back to their communities. The miners went back to Huanuni, saying as they left, according to people in El Alto: "Any time another president needs overthrowing, just let us know and we'll be back."

The new president was not one of their own. But nor was he the mass killer. They had not "taken power." They had suffered eight dead and 400 wounded. And yet they had achieved what they had been out to do ever since the rebellion of February 2003 in La Paz, which had itself cost thirty-three lives, many of these cut short by army sniper fire. This time they had toppled the murderer. They had won.

The question poses itself again: Was this insurrection a violent season of a single week, snuffed out after the return to everyday domination by the state and its routine oppressions, or was it a harbinger of something that will come or is already on its way?

I cannot answer this question now. But what I will say is that the feeling of having won is perceptible, strong, and lasting. With this strange, unaccustomed sensation, which does not appease the anger of having obtained so little while the political class reverts to its old tricks— with this sensation, the October insurgents are going about their work and gathering in discussion: how do we proceed now, what's the next step, and don't lower your guard because this bunch won't do a thing, they just make promises to get our votes. So, what about all those who died, who were left wounded or broken, just for them to win some elections and some seats while everything goes on as it was? Was it for that, that we put our bodies and our lives on the line?

Violence continues to incubate in Bolivia, the violence of those who won but did not vanquish, those who do not want to be fooled again by the upper crust, the "whiteys," q'aras, eternal masters of the racist and oligarchic domination of capital; and the other violence, too, that of the masters, who are using this unstable interregnum to regroup and plot their revenge.

9.

But was this a revolution? How could it be, when the state apparatus and its repressive forces were not destroyed, when a revolutionary workers' party did not take power, when there were no leaders and no proclamations? How was this a revolution, when all it did was remove a president and his coterie of killers? How, if the insurgents left La Paz, went back to their communities and farms, their mines and workshops, their barrios and homes, in short, to their ordinary lives? What just took place in Bolivia is as old as rebellion and at the same time new, radically new. All the questions are valid. Let us attempt some answers.

A revolution is not something that happens within the state, inside its institutions and among its politicians. It comes *from underneath* and *from outside*. It happens when those who are, precisely, always underneath and outside burst onto center stage, with the violence of their bodies and the fury of their souls: the forever-deferred, the led, whom the leaders treat as nothing but a quantity of votes, an electoral clientele, malleable matter to be bused around, poll fodder. It happens when they irrupt with their own political goals, when they organize in accordance with their own decisions and knowledge, and, with lucidity, thought, and violence, force their world into the world of the rulers and achieve, as in this case, what they had set out to do. What happens next will happen next.

If revolution only took place when a new ruling elite conquered state power, where would that leave the revolutions of 1848 in Europe, the 1857 Revolution in India (which the British labeled a "mutiny"), the 1905 Revolution in Russia, the 1919 German Revolution, the 1936 Spanish Revolution, the 1944 Greek Revolution, the Hungarian Revolution of 1956, the Guatemalan Revolution, the Salvadoran Revolution, and so many others canonized in the histories of the left?

In July 1917, faced with the imponderables of an unprecedented mass movement unfolding in Russia, Vladimir Ilyich Lenin asked himself: "What defines a revolution?" This was his answer:

> If we take the revolutions of the twentieth century as examples, we shall naturally have to recognize the Portuguese and Turkish revolutions as being bourgeois ones. Neither of them, however, is a "people's" revolution since the mass of the people, its enormous majority, has in neither of them come out actively and independently to any notable extent with its own economic and political demands. By contrast, although the Russian bourgeois revolution of 1905–07 registered no such "brilliant" successes

as at times fell to the lot of the Portuguese and Turkish revolutions, it was undoubtedly a "real people's" revolution since the mass of the people, its majority, the very lowest social strata, who were crushed by oppression and exploitation, rose independently and placed on the entire course of the revolution the imprint of *their own* demands, of *their own* attempts to construct a new society in their own way in place of the old society which was being destroyed.[8]

Vladimir Ilyich knew that he was looking at something new, prompted by the expansion of capital in recent decades and the violence of capital's wars: the first revolutions of the twentieth century. He did not define them by their orientations, programs, or outcomes, but by their protagonists, dynamics, and events. He was trying to define and name what was new. At the start of the twenty-first century, after another expansive wave of capitalist domination in recent decades, we stand once more before the unknown.

10.

It is hard to grant the name of "revolution" to this Bolivian insurrection. Hard to go back to that old story again, just when it seemed that everyone had "reached a consensus" that revolutions were a thing of the past and from now on there would only be elections, democratic transitions, good governance, pacts, and consensuses. It is hard having to deal once more with the intractable: revolution is back, just as violent, chaotic, dirty, badly dressed, underfed, ill-spoken, and stinking of poverty as it ever was, hurling its bodies, its dead, into our faces all over again.

Better to say that this was not a revolution at all, it was a massive riot, a rebellion, an insurrection that made mistakes and lacked a party to guide it; it was only about the gas and the coca plantations, a popular movement, a troublesome mob and not much more.

Let us turn, then, to the balance sheet drawn up by that clear-sighted conservative organ *La Razón* on October 30:

> In a confused, disjointed, bloody conflict lasting forty-one days, the Bolivian president resigned, defeated by a battle he never led, suffocated by his inner circle, cut off from the people but convinced that he had not

---

8   V. I. Lenin, *The State and Revolution* (London: Penguin, 1992), pp. 35–6.

put a foot wrong during his second term that began on August 2, 2002, and lasted 437 days.

Betraying a certain disenchantment at this collapse devoid of honor or glory, the writer adds: "Presidential conservatism was imposed, animated by the technocratic administration of the state and a passion for household surveys."

"Confused, disjointed, bloody": every observer describes, in the words and with the feelings proper to each, what they see from where they stand and what they perceive from within the consciousness of their social location. The consciousness of *La Razón*'s commentator is one unmistakably dispirited by the events his perception has registered.

I, however, still believe that this was a revolution, whose moment of victory was the taking of La Paz and the fall and flight of the Sánchez de Lozada government on October 17, 2003. I don't know what will happen next. I know that revolution is back on Latin American soil again, even if to conservative eyes it looks like "a confused, disjointed, bloody conflict."

11.

The *indios*, the *cholos*, the men and women of the subaltern classes, with their ways of organizing and taking decisions, with their multilevel formations or without them, with the leaders that they had to hand, with the violence of their bodies and their dead and the fury of their souls, took La Paz, paralyzed the army, and overthrew the president and the government of murderers. No matter what happens next, and we don't yet know what it may be, the word for that is *revolution*. To dispute the word is tantamount to disputing the hard-won victory of the protagonists: the *indios*, the *cholos*, the men and women of the subaltern classes in Bolivia. We would do better to trust them.

11

Intermittent Insurrections

(2009)

1.

The continuing revolution in Bolivia is a process deeper than politics, reaching well beyond the elites and the economy. It questions the very basis of the historical domination by those elites, old and new. It comes from far below. It is propelled by an ancient fury. It can be halted neither by massacres nor by fragile agreements with the racists of the "Media Luna."[1]

The killings of September 2008 in Pando; the scenes of public humiliation, pain, and punishment meted out to indigenous people in the main square of Sucre and the streets of Santa Cruz de la Sierra; the walls daubed with large signs shouting "*¡Collas, raza maldita!*" (Collas, damned race!), put the whole country on notice, loud and clear, that the oligarchic minority knows exactly what it is defending: its power is nonnegotiable, its lands are untouchable, and its despotic right to rule springs from skin color, not the citizens' vote.[2]

---

1 [Literally "Crescent Moon," the term refers to Bolivia's four eastern departments of Santa Cruz, Beni, Tarija, and Pando, which have a lower proportion of indigenous inhabitants. After 2005, these departments became the center of opposition to the Morales government. Their demands for greater autonomy prompted a crisis in mid-2008 that brought revanchist maneuvers from the right and countermobilizations by government supporters.]

2 [The term *colla* is used, often pejoratively, to refer to indigenous or mestizo people from Bolivia's five highland departments, in contrast to the *cambas* of the lowlands.]

This minority is not prepared to alter anything about its despotic right. It relies, furthermore, on poor white sectors whose one and only "asset" is the skin color that separates them from the Indians. It is still less prepared to redistribute property or wealth. Here is the nub of the protracted dispute around the new Bolivian constitution.

The old dominant class knows very well that it is not a matter of making some "democratic extensions" to the law. It faces instead a revolution that challenges its power and privileges and the "grid of inheritance" of its despotic rule.[3] Because a revolution is one of those climactic moments when the uprising of a people touches the very foundation of domination, it endeavors to destroy it and manages to fracture the dividing line where this dominating power is hinged in the society concerned.

I do not mean the line that separates the rulers from the ruled, which is a political question, but that which separates the dominant from the subaltern. The classic term of social revolution refers to the subversion of that social—not just political or economic—domination. This dividing line is clearly and deeply etched in Bolivia. It is more than a class domination, although it is that, too. It is above all a racial domination, implanted in colonial times and ratified by the oligarchic republic from 1825 onward.

Under conditions of racial domination, to be a full citizen means to be white or if mestizo, assimilated. In order to become a citizen, the Indian must cease to be an Indian and recognize himself, and be recognized, as white; he must break with his concrete historical community, encompassing the Aymara, the Quechua, the Guaraní, and the many other indigenous nations of Bolivia; he must enter the abstract community of citizens of the Republic as a freshly arrived subordinate. Indians are expected to renounce their own being and history and join the republic of the whites, the rich, the schooled, the Spanish-speakers—where, in any case, the ineffaceable color of their skin will always condemn such men and women to the rank of second-class citizens. That is the nature of the domination that the new constitution claims to have abolished.

---

3   I use this term in the sense given to it by E. P. Thompson in "The Grid of Inheritance: A Comment," in E. P. Thompson, Jack Goody, and Joan Thirska, eds., *Family and Inheritance* (Cambridge: Cambridge University Press, 1976), pp. 328–60.

2.

The strength and coherence of the revolution in Bolivia are nourished by an ancient civilization that endures in languages, customs, beliefs, solidarities, and communities, in urban as well as rural settings. Bolivia's new Political Constitution acknowledges the existence and rights of that civilization and its cultures.

In the mountains and valleys of Upper Peru, the dark-skinned and dominated were not imported from elsewhere. They were there before. They were, and are, the original Andean civilization. The filmmaker Jorge Sanjinés made an unforgettable work in which he calls them "the clandestine nation." In Mexico, Guillermo Bonfil Batalla spoke of "Deep Mexico, a negated civilization." Taking my cue from him, I called it a "subaltern civilization" in my book *Historia a contrapelo* (History Against the Grain).[4]

Whether clandestine, denied, or subaltern, its social and cultural grid of inheritance, present in everyday life in the form of custom, emerges violently when it comes to organizing the revolts and rebellions of its heirs and carriers, for these revolts are as deep-seated as racially based domination is profound and persistent.

The dominated and the subaltern, when their time comes, rise up again and again to seize the rights that this racial republic refuses to grant or curtails: dignity and respect, spaces of freedom and organization, the natural resources of their land, education, and health care—everything that would constitute the social fabric of a republic of equals.

The old republican motto "liberty, equality, fraternity" finds in such uprisings its indispensable twin: "land, justice, solidarity." For there can be no freedom in those latitudes without land redistribution, no equality without justice for all, no fraternity without solidarity, the internal solidarity of the many communities and of the entire community of that nation of nations known as Bolivia. This does not only imply a new political and economic order. It is a call for what in the Bolivian context would amount to a new social order. Hence the bestial violence of the reactions of privileged groups and their henchmen.

Indigenous and popular movements are on the march in Bolivia; some are literally on the warpath. The confrontations occupy the terrain of a revolution whose makers and protagonists refuse to allow it to be snatched or bartered away. The landowners and white minority are now

---

4   [See the essay reproduced as Chapter 7 of this volume.]

trying to undo the results of the constitutional referendum.[5] If they do not give up this effort, the outcome will be settled in the streets and the fields, as it was in October 2003, and as the warlike determination of the people's siege of the city of Santa Cruz showed again in September 2008.[6]

3.

Working-class indigenous rebellions, seeking both to change the conditions of life under colonial and racial dominion and to subvert the latter, are not new in Bolivia. Sergio Serulnikov, among others, has researched the native insurrections (led by Túpac Amaru, Tomás Katari, and Túpaj Katari) that fought to impose governments of their own in the colonial world of the eighteenth century. He posits that such an indigenous government entailed "the activation of political practices that undermined the founding principle of colonialism: the belief in a clearly defined link between power and culture, cementing dominion on the inherent superiority of European civilization."[7] Then as now, that is where the radicality of subversion lay.

The campaigns of Tomás Katari in Chayanta toward the end of the eighteenth century installed a short-lived but real and region-wide Indian government that remained symbolically within the frame of the Spanish Crown. Nevertheless, Serulnikov writes, it called into question

> the entire edifice of colonial hegemony: the use of cultural difference as a signifier of racial inferiority and of the notion of racial inferiority to justify the right to political domination. Only when that threat vanished, and solely in order to domesticate its original subversive content, did republican rulers venture to incorporate the great campesino movements into their own historical narrative.[8]

---

5   [Held on 25 January 2009, the referendum approved the new constitution by 61 percent to 39.]

6   [Gilly is referring to a blockade of Santa Cruz by tens of thousands of MAS supporters, seeking to counter the autonomist agenda of the opposition.]

7   Sergio Serulnikov, *Conflictos sociales e insurrecciones en el mundo colonial andino: El norte de Potosí en el siglo XVIII* (Buenos Aires: Fondo de Cultura Económica, 2006), pp. 442–44. See also Sinclair Thomson, *We Alone Will Rule: Native Andean Politics in the Age of Insurgency* (Madison: University of Wisconsin Press, 2002).

8   Serulnikov, *Conflictos sociales*, p. 444.

Next came the heyday of the "Indian statue," erected as part of the story of the modern nation, in which native history is depicted as a rehearsal of national independence and the antecedent of the white and mestizo republic. The native is subsumed into the national, negated and cut short as a history on its own terms. As Guillermo Bonfil Batalla noted in 1980, "Nineteenth-century evolutionist theories supplied a splendid rationale for this new exclusion: Indian peoples were laggards of the historical process and required the redemption, no longer of the Christian faith, but of progress."[9]

Redemptive progress was thus presented as an infinite process of civilization that would never be completed, given the natural inferiority of the natives posited since the Valladolid Debate of 1550 between Ginés de Sepúlveda and Bartolomé de las Casas. Indian insurrections, with their characteristic intermittence, challenged that essential postulate of colonial domination on the ground rather than in learned polemics.

In Andean uprisings, according to Serulnikov,

> what the *criollos* would rapidly learn, and their nineteenth-century descendants not forget, was that the autonomous mobilization of Andean peasants and the installation of one of their leaders as the supreme authority were incompatible with the perpetuation of the mechanism of colonial subordination, whatever the overarching formal political regime might be.[10]

These insurgents declared fealty to the Crown in order to legitimate their movement; they went before the colonial courts to demand their rights; they attempted to forge alliances with elements among the criollo elites. All in vain. Serulnikov concludes that

> by de facto challenging their subordinate place in the natural scheme of things, the natives' mobilization destroyed any common ground between the colonizers and the colonized. Once again, the analytical problem consists in shifting the axis of programs and ideas to the field of relations of power, where ideas acquire their true significance.[11]

---

9 Guillermo Bonfil Batalla, "Historias que no son todavía historia," in Carlos Pereyra et al., *Historia, ¿para qué?* (Mexico City: Siglo XXI, 1980), pp. 227–45.

10 Serulnikov, *Conflictos sociales*, p. 442.

11 Ibid., p. 443.

4.

Every rebellion is nourished by organizational forms and cultures whose roots lie in accumulated, transmitted experience. Every rebellion, in its own specific way, embodies these all over again, transfigured and altered by time.

These cultures and forms long precede the policies and parties of the present day. Whenever political parties have genuinely come to be tools at the service of the subaltern, it is because they were equal to seeing and receiving that inherited experience, and able to assimilate it to the present so as to lend substance and reality to their programs and to their own organizational forms. This is the only way for them to pass the test not just of theory but of reality. A program can only be real if by means of these forms and cultures it succeeds in embodying and expressing itself in its own epoch.

These organizational cultures spring from the grid of inheritance of working people. They differ in the histories, places, and countries concerned; they are alike—even in the worlds of modern industry—in their communitarian and solidaristic content. They constitute an *organizational knowledge* and an *affective education* shaped and polished over successive generations in the urban and rural places where labor lives, thinks, feels, and makes.

5.

Domination is never a stone laid on top of inert matter. It is always a cloth woven in time and extending through space. The dominant elite, presuming itself to be the weaver of life and history, regards the subaltern as little more than the unthinking yarn of which the cloth is made. Colonial domination, moreover, has its own rule: the right to command, based on a presupposed racial superiority by reason of birth or background.

And so, when the subalterns of the underside of the cloth burst to the forefront, the teleological colonial or national histories judge it to be an anomaly of the weave, a knot or defect deriving from the coarseness of the materials used—the subaltern—or else a momentary hitch in the machinery of domination.

The colonial power thought it had found rough but docile hands in the indigenous population of the Andean region. What it actually found were hands that think, intelligent modes of obedience to imposed rule without which no human work is possible, subjections coerced but alive, with a history and thinking of their own, hands and intelligences underpinned by an ancient civilization whose history and cultures long predated colonial domination and its fabric.[12]

The threads of indigenous history are part of that weave, contribute to sustaining the whole fabric, and protrude at times with their own particular patterns and colors. They are not severed from the threads of colonial and national history. But they are different, older, perhaps less visible today, originary and original threads of a history that is marked and traversed by the other histories and inseparable from them, and yet as persistent as language, as custom, as the fruits of earth and heaven.

6.

The history of humanity is not a single entity, nor does it course down a single expanding channel.[13] It is made up of multiple histories, which, looked at in the *longue durée* of millennia, converge, intertwine, and knit into one another in accordance with the wandering of the human species through places and eras.[14]

For Miguel León-Portilla, there are multiple but not many originary civilizations:

The concept of civilization in the anthropological sense is not counterposed to culture but is a more developed form of culture. A civilization harbors urban life, that is, cities, and more complex forms of social, political, economic, and religious organization; it features labor specialization and such creations as exact time measurement, writing, educational institutions, and the production of what today we call art. Now then, among the civilizing processes developed by the human race, a certain number must be recognized as originary, meaning that they came autonomously into being. All other civilizations, no matter how highly developed, must

12   Miguel León-Portilla, "Mesoamérica: una civilización originaria," *Arqueología Mexicana*, vol. 14, no. 79, May–June 2006, pp. 18–27.

13   Ranajit Guha addresses this topic in *History at the Limit of World-History* (New York: Columbia University Press, 2002).

14   "The multiplicity of histories resembles the multiplicity of languages. Universal history in the present-day sense can never be more than a kind of Esperanto. The idea of universal history is a messianic idea." (Walter Benjamin, "Paralipomena to 'On the Concept of History,'" in *Selected Writings, vol. 4: 1938–1940*, trans. Edmund Jephcott et al. [Cambridge, MA: Belknap Press, 1996], p. 405).

be regarded as derived or set in motion by various civilizational nuclei. There are only a few instances of originary civilizations in world history.[15]

León-Portilla identifies six: Egypt (the Nile); Mesopotamia (the Tigris and Euphrates); India (the Indus); China (the Yellow River); the Andes; and Mesoamerica.

As in all the worlds and territories where an originary civilization emerged, indigenous life and history in Bolivia are supported and sustained by this preexistent, persistent civilization—muffled no doubt but not suppressed. The specific forms of different modernities are steeped in it. It shows up in the gestures of everyday life and the peculiarities of celebration, love, mourning, protest, rebellion.

After that, it seems to hide or to slink away to the back of the stage. But no. There it remains, affirmed in its hard desire to endure. Until the next time that this permanence becomes impermanence,[16] and in the spirit, the revelation, and the action of the revolt we once more see the quotidian and the extraordinary as parts of the same unit of historical time.[17]

This unique alternating rhythm of permanence and impermanence informs the histories of the subaltern—clandestine, obscure or negated, but ineradicable, because they took place. Just as the rise and fall of the seas are governed by the Moon, so too in history, it is the hidden side that regulates the tides.

---

15   León-Portilla, "Mesoamérica."

16   Raquel Gutiérrez Aguilar, *Los ritmos del Pachakuti* (La Paz: Yachaywasi, 2008), discusses this singular form of the historical process in Bolivia from a vantage point of experience and reflection. As Walter Benjamin wrote in 1940: "The history of the oppressed is a discontinuum. The task of history is to seize hold of the tradition of the oppressed. [. . .] The continuum of history is that of the oppressors. Whereas the representation of the continuum leads to a leveling, that of the discontinuum lies at the basis of authentic tradition. Consciousness of historical discontinuity is the characteristic of revolutionary classes at the moment of their action." Walter Benjamin, *Écrits français* (Paris: Gallimard, 1991), p. 352.

17   "The domain of the quotidian, which is also the domain of the seeming perpetuity of subordination, is circumscribed by a limit beyond which lies the extraordinary, apocalyptic, timeless moment of a world turned upside down. It is the historical record of those brief moments of open rebellion which gives us a glimpse of that undominated region in peasant consciousness and enables us to see the everyday and the extraordinary as parts of a single unity in historical time." Partha Chatterjee, "The Nation and Its Peasants," *The Nation and Its Fragments: Colonial and Post-Colonial Histories* (Princeton: Princeton University Press, 1994), p. 171.

Part III

Between Past and Future

12

Bolivia Fifty Years On

(2003)

Interview by Sinclair Thomson and Seemin Qayum

When did you first go to Bolivia?
I arrived on April 7, 1956. I was twenty-seven years old. I remember the date because it was two days before the anniversary of April 9.[1] I can still see it, the myth parading past. The myth of permanent revolution—the workers' militias! "Can this be real?" I said to myself. The miners marching past with helmets and rifles. Tears came to my eyes as I watched; I found it deeply affecting.

But, well, that was the myth. All the same, the miners retaining their rifles meant that the monopoly on legitimate violence had been broken. Keeping their weapons ensured a remarkable balance of power for quite some time. There was a mineworkers' territory. You couldn't go in without requesting permission from the mineworkers' government, the mineworkers' union.

What was it like, arriving somewhere so different in 1956?
I went to the mines later on. At first, I was in La Paz, which was already completely different from my hometown, the city of Buenos Aires. I had spent a lot of time among Argentine workers. And so the world of mining was not alien to me, any more than that of the workers of La Paz. Had I landed in the campesino world, it would have seemed far stranger. But the workers in La Paz, the urban leftist groups, the world of mining . . . nothing was all that unfamiliar.

---

1   [Gilly is referring to the anniversary of Bolivia's National Revolution of 1952.]

What I did find alien was the whole Bolivian universe. It took me a while to understand that there was nothing wrong with it . . . I was slow in rooting out the underlying thing in me, the idea of "progress." As in, "Well, they're like this now but only because they haven't gotten yet to being like that, but everything in due course, etc." A progress that also features to some extent in Trotskyism. Not as deep-seated as in traditional Bolshevism, but you do get the notion of advanced countries and backward countries, as they call them. The backward ones being set to reproduce the development of the advanced ones, albeit via different paths.

I never thought it was a matter of "superstition." I just felt stunned. I tried to understand: "What *is* this?" I tried to understand why everyone turned up to meetings an hour or two late, and that was normal. Back then I saw it as unpunctuality, disorderliness, peasant ways, what have you . . . No! It's a different way of being in time.

I remember in 1960, after a few weeks in Amsterdam, a Dutch friend suddenly asked, "What do you find is the biggest difference between Amsterdam and La Paz?" And without thinking, rather to my own surprise, I replied: "The way all the public clocks here tell the same time, while over there each one tells whatever time it wants."

Were you aware of how you were changing? Or is that something you understood afterward?
What I learned in Bolivia, I only understood later. I realized later that I'd behaved like a barbarian. The thing is, the Bolivians are very polite. They have an amazing refinement, like all ancient peoples. They don't tell you off. They don't get mad. They keep quiet. A respectful silence, always. After a while, when there was that silence I'd think, "What appalling thing did I just do?" And I remember above all my impatience. You are not taught in Argentina to be very patient. That impatience may have come over as arrogance, and possibly it was arrogance.

Was your learning process personal, or at the same time ideological? For example, with respect to the idea of progress, of the role of the vanguard.
No. I belonged to a Trotskyist group in Argentina that had no time for that idea. It was a very ordinary organization, the Partido Obrero (Trotskista) (Workers' Party [Trotskyist]). Most of the members were workers. The leaders were almost all industrial workers. There was no arrogance— if anything they were anti-intellectual, but not to excess. I didn't go to Bolivia with any intellectual arrogance. That was an advantage. I had a

certain humility because I had already lived with working people. In that world you learn to look properly, to know who you're speaking to and where you're speaking from.

What do you remember about the compañeros you met?
In La Paz I was welcomed and offered accommodation by Hugo González Moscoso and his partner, Delia Quiroga. And by Fernando Bravo, a teacher from Oruro, and his partner, Elsa Cladera. They had two daughters, one named Bolsha, the other Nadezhda. And there was Amadeo Vargas, who was imprisoned for a time in the La Paz Panopticon, and after that was always traveling around the altiplano from mine to mine. Their organization was called the Partido Obrero Revolucionario (Revolutionary Workers' Party, POR), and its paper was called *Lucha Obrera* (Workers' Struggle). There was a different Partido Obrero Revolucionario, led by Guillermo Lora, which published a paper called *Masas* (Masses) and whose main base was in the Catavi-Siglo XX [tin mine]. These were all outgrowths of a single original trunk, which also gave rise to a group of Trotskyists who joined the Revolutionary Nationalist Movement, including Edwin Moller and Lidia Gueiler; the latter eventually became president of Bolivia.

In Oruro, the members of the Partido Obrero Revolucionario–Lucha Obrera were mineworkers and railwaymen. One, Paulino Joaniquina, was organizing secretary of the union of the San José mine, right next to the city. This guy was involved in the POR, and he was also involved in the Diablada ["Dance of the Devils" folklore troupe]. It was 1958, and he regularly came to the Trotskyist meetings. One day, Paulino doesn't show up.

"Why isn't he here?" I ask.

"He's busy with the Diablada . . ."

"What do you mean, busy with the Diablada?"

"Yes, he's rehearsing, because it's Carnival in a few weeks."

I was flabbergasted. Go figure: a Marxist, a Trotskyist, and now he's busy with the Diablada. One day I went over for a look, and there was Paulino with his devil mask on, skipping and dancing. Paulino wasn't dancing with the Diablada out of "entryism." He was in the Diablada just because he was in it!

Paulino went on being a union leader for a long time. He was a very good man, much loved by the miners. He lived with his partner and children and whenever the kids saw me coming up to the house, they'd run out, shouting: "Dad, the gringo man's here!"

Not until much, much later did I realize that in this relationship, the guiding hand belonged to this group of miners, and the instrument guided by that hand was me, because some of my skills could be useful to their struggles. Sure, when we were drinking chicha or chatting neither of us was thinking that way, but that's not the point: today I can see that it was so.

There was another guy called Nina—Nina being his alias. His real name or his last name was Velarde, I think. He was a textile worker, but he'd been a miner and had all the training. He belonged to the Trotskyist organization of La Paz. At the time he was living with his compañera, who had a *wawita*, a baby. He lived up there in Villa Victoria, which was the toughest shantytown. There were armed groups in there as well. For a long time, the government couldn't even enter that shanty by force. La Paz felt perpetually threatened by the idea of Villa Victoria sweeping down on it, armed.

One day I dropped in on him. The house was one room, with a dirt floor and the odd mouse running around. His partner had lost her job at the Said [textile] plant and had used her severance money to buy a typewriter, a portable Olivetti.

"Why did you buy that machine?" I asked her.

"For the kid."

"The kid, why, he's not yet . . ."

"When he grows up, I want him to know things—and how to write properly."

She was an indigenous textile worker, in a bowler hat and with her baby on her back. She bought the machine like a good mother. Imagine, buying him a typewriter—it's precisely a mythic notion, because she wants him to know, to write. That's what things were like in '56 and '57.

Constantino Morales was a mineworker at San José, near Oruro. He lived in the miners' district, four or five hundred meters away from the pit, in a little adobe house with a dirt floor. It had just one room. I spent two or three days there.

There was only the one bed. When it was time to sleep, Constantino's wife spread some ponchos on the ground for herself. Straight off I said, "No way, I'll sleep on the floor. It wouldn't be the first time." They refused, saying a guest could not stay on the floor. I had been sufficiently civilized by then to know that I had no business arguing with what they had settled between themselves. So Constantino and I shared the bed, one with his feet this end and head that end, the other in reverse [*laughs*]. And the lady—in her hat and full skirts—on a blanket on the floor . . .

It was an insoluble problem. If the guest must have the bed, well, the woman must sleep on the floor! You could interpret that as evidence that women are subaltern. But, if you think about it sensibly, there was no other way.

Constantino was working fourteen hours a day at the time, doing a ton of overtime inside the mine. Because he was a *preste*, a sponsor in the next fiesta that was for Easter, I believe, for Holy Week. So he had to make it a grand fiesta.

Constantino was committed to his preste duties, and he was a miner, sure, a Marxist, a Trotskyist, and yet . . . It's like the other fellow with his Diablada. He was a preste and those were the social relations in the mineworkers' district. Community relations: how could he not be a preste?

He had to get up early and go to work. Every morning he would tell me his dreams. I can recall two that he described. Well, one was a dream, the other was a project he had.

The dream went like this: "Last night I dreamed that some gringos came along to visit the mine. They were shown in, so they could see what it was like. I was down the other end, we were busy working, and there was a lever there. So, I said, 'I'll push this lever down and see what happens.' I push it down. Boom! Big explosion where the gringos are, all blown to kingdom come!" As for the other dream, the project, it was to obtain electricity for the mine from a hill, the San José hill just behind the pit.

"See, you pump the water up, fix a torrent so the water falls down, put a dike in, which produces electricity, and we got power for the mine!"

What was I supposed to say? I knew enough not to start arguing, "And how would you pump the water uphill? With what energy?" Of course, I didn't say a word. He had come up with that old dream of workers from the dawn of the industrial era: the idea of perpetual motion.

One day, an Interamerican Health Service ambulance stopped on the corner near his home. It was running a children's vaccination program. "Constantino," I said, "do you plan to vaccinate them? Why not send them over? The jab is free."

"Are you crazy?" he said. "Who knows what garbage the gringos are putting into us just to make Bolivians dumber and easier to exploit." He was adamant. It's to do with the way progress comes about. The Iraqis would later say the same about the aid workers: who knows what they're peddling? But Constantino harbored dreams of progress, like the electricity idea. He was by no means a stickler for traditional myths.

What conclusions do you draw from these stories?
The three anecdotes I just relayed are about modernity. One about electrifying the mine. One about the ambulance vaccination program. And the dream about blowing up all the gringos. The most modern dream was about how to obtain electric power. And at the same time, the guy was a preste, as well as belonging to a left-wing organization. These are pure dreams of modernity. The miners are a part of modernity but a peculiar kind of modernity.

Now that you've made me think back—what was this modernity?—it's remarkable how egalitarian people were. I'm not saying the campesinos are not egalitarian, but that was a different world. More impervious to where I was coming from. Whereas the mineworkers' manner was the working-class one I was used to, same as the metalworkers or textile workers, and I felt wholly at ease. It was how industrial workers treated each other.

However, I don't mean industrial workers in the American or Argentine sense. Those guys would never double as prestes. It's closer to the Gramscian model, in which the south overlaps with the north. In 1950s and '60s Italy, workers from the Mezzogiorno flocked to the expansion of Fiat. They were the *terroni*, assumed to be "backward," whom the priest had fixed up with car factory jobs. The northern workers looked down on them a bit . . . they'd brought these country ways with them. And it was they who kicked up all the trouble in the early 1960s, they were the hotheads who always led the fray. Lacking all subordination to trade-union discipline, they dragged everyone else along. Union discipline is twofold: on the one hand, it's what empowers you to struggle; on the other, it restrains. And the "backward" people went in for brawls, dragging the union along. They displayed the most radical tendencies. Ultimately, both groups merged in the factory councils, and the union turned into the "union of councils."

How did the other twentieth-century revolutions influence the Bolivian one?
The Russian Revolution had a dazzling effect, initially, on Latin America. It is hard to imagine today. Here was a utopia that could never become a reality, and yet they'd made it real. Even in the '50s, the Russian Revolution was the concrete embodiment of that World Social Forum slogan: "Another World Is Possible."

I'm not suggesting that the Bolivians were thinking about the Russian Revolution. It was simply there, a myth in people's heads until the '60s. I was coming from the youth wing of the Argentine Socialists, and never had any faith in the Soviet leadership. For many people after the war, though, the crushing of the Hungarian uprising by Soviet tanks in 1956 was the first great crack in the mythic image.

Some leaders certainly did have the Russian Revolution in mind. For example, in their way of reading political developments in Bolivia.
There was much discussion among specialists and the whole Trotskyist community about the character of this revolution. Just like the Bolsheviks used to bandy around references to the French Revolution: "Here comes Thermidor." "No, this is not Thermidor." Not the least connection! [*Laughs*] But these were shared references, part of the common imaginary. In Bolivia, during the Revolution of 1952, for people with that cast of mind April 9 was the February Revolution, to be followed by October . . . It's a narrow framework of thought in the end, and a bit religious. I am not saying the Russian Revolution influenced Bolivia—there was no influence whatsoever. Still, there was the immanent presence of the fact that more than one power existed in the world. It's hard to believe we've lost that.

The dream of the Bolivian nationalists of the Movimiento Nacional Revolucionario (National Revolutionary Movement, MNR) was to achieve a revolution like that of Mexico, or more exactly a state like the Mexican revolutionary state. They said so explicitly. They wanted a party like Mexico's, they admired it tremendously. The Mexican Revolution exerted far greater mythic influence over the Bolivian nationalist elites than the Russian did. Among the nationalists, both elite and leftwing, the argument was about whether or not to nationalize the mines, whether or not to implement agrarian reform.

Tell us more about how you saw the mineworkers after the revolution.
Between 1956 and 1960, I recall constant efforts by the nationalist government to gain control over the miners and the peasants . . . As of '55 or '56, the mineworkers began buying radio transmitters, and at least until the early 1960s every pit had its own radio station with music and news— no broadcasting propaganda all day long. It was the kind of thing every local radio puts out: "Francisco sends many happy returns to Juanita on her birthday . . ."

The radios were a useful means of communication whenever strikes broke out. A chain of mine radios was set up that proved quite effective— this was the 1950s, not the 2000s! Because to organize several factories in struggle is one thing: factories are interlinked, a city's factories are in that city. But to organize a mineworkers' struggle, when the mines are dotted all over the altiplano, is considerably more complex. There were debates over the radios, too—should we do this, or that—as well as propaganda and trade-union publicity. But it was not so much undiluted political radio as normal stations with syndical and political functions. The radio was a great tool for taking possession of space and life, everyday life. It would play some *huayno* [popular Andean dance] music or whatever, but that music was coming from *my* station, no one else's. And it was a union station.

I think the transmitters were largely bought with members' dues and sourced in Eastern Bloc countries. That's why I say the myth [of the revolution] is enduring. It formed, albeit improbably, a counterweight to capitalist power. But there was little Soviet and Communist influence. It was no greater than the Trotskyist influence; in fact, it was smaller.

What I see as an analyst is the struggle to control the workers. Now, approaching it from the miners' point of view, the resistance was focused on the defense of spaces. First came wages, labor conditions, grocery stores, while always driving a hard bargain. To put it in more general terms—they wouldn't use those words, but it's how they acted—those were the spaces controlled by the mineworkers, spaces of political autonomy, in the sense of the Indian historian Ranajit Guha. Those spaces are what they defended. I find this aspect is very well conveyed in the book by Domitila [Chungara, Bolivian labor leader and feminist].[2] She tells it in such a fresh way.

Spaces of autonomy—nobody called them that in those days. In Trotskyist terminology the phrase was rather "dual power"—a mineworkers' power and a national power. There is, in this view, a situation of dual power, in which one must end up eliminating the other. I know, now, that this is not the right expression for the case that concerns us. Spaces of autonomy were intended to bear upon the decisions of the state in all areas relevant to them or to make decisions in this space without state interference; they were not to create a parallel national power, which would amount to something quite different.

The only way to get rid of the space of autonomy, to truly get rid of it, was to get rid of the mines—an objective that eventually coincided with changes to the economy toward the end of the 1970s. But until they finished off the mines, the space of autonomy persisted. In 1980, under

    2   [Domitila Chungara, *Si me permiten hablar: Testimonio de Domitila, una mujer de las minas de Bolivia* (Mexico City: Siglo XXI, 1978). Published in English as *Let Me Speak!*, trans. Victoria Ortiz (New York: Monthly Review Press, 1978).]

the dictator García Meza, the last pocket of mining resistance was in Viloco. It was bombed. The last mineworkers' stronghold finally had to be bombed before it would fall . . .

That's also how they took the Central Obrera Boliviana (Bolivian Workers' Central, COB).[3] They flattened the place with their cannon. Why on earth did they destroy the HQ on the Prado [promenade] in La Paz? It was totally symbolic politics. One of the facts that demonstrates the existence of a space of autonomy is the necessity to smash the COB offices, stupidly, with a cannon, when it could easily have been occupied by a dozen soldiers, job done.

What was the relationship between mineworkers and peasants at that time?
As I recall, in any dispute the miners could always count on campesino solidarity, of course. The campesinos would show up with sacks of potatoes and maize, food to sustain the strike. Then you've got the solidarity resolutions repeated by the unions, but that was at an institutional level; it was the institutional reflection of what was happening in the spaces of autonomy. And there were also internal conflicts. I remember a classic confrontation between two campesino trade unions in Cochabamba, the leftist one and the one with links to the MNR, each with its own militias.

The mineworkers were very connected to the countryside. A miner is a kind of industrial peasant, the same as a fisherman. In Cuba I went out one day on a small boat with the fishing fleet and when I saw how the men behaved, I thought: "But these guys are campesinos!" This was hardly a new discovery, but for me it was. Like the miners, they were deep inside the natural world with its random risks and perils. They depended on the sea the way the miner depends on the mine.

The campesino world remained close at hand: all the miners had family in the country. And they knew they would retire there. When you stop going down the pit, you return to the countryside, the campo. Some of them would become campesino leaders. When a miner got too old, that is, at the age of forty-five, he returned to the campo, where he'd be a well-respected figure. They are a very curious breed, miners, in Bolivia and everywhere else.

How would you characterize the subalternity of the Bolivian miners during those years?
As bloody-minded! Sure, they might be subaltern, but no one was going to push them around! All subalternities, by definition, possess spaces

---

3   [Formed in 1952, the COB is still the main trade union federation in Bolivia.]

of autonomy, reflecting the way each subalternity is constituted. The constitutive form of subalternity after the conquest of Mesoamerica and the Andes, defined according to a racial divide, is a very screwed-up, violent constitutive demarcation, which in turn spawns a certain form of rebellion. When rebellion comes to these lands, it comes with racial vengeance.

In Argentina, on the other hand, subalternity was constituted in the last decades of the nineteenth century and involved immigrant workers. It thus resembles the subalternity of workers in the United States in the past and no doubt today. It emerged differently, in the subalternity of the wage earner without ties of personal dependence, who is part of the factory organization and defends his spaces within that factory organization. There is a whole world inside the factory. And there is a whole world in the workers' neighborhoods, a world of places, bars, encounters, canteens, conversations. As soon as conflict breaks out, everyone knows where they have to go, where they're supposed to meet. Worker subalternity is very precise. And that, at least, looks the same everywhere.

What might be the specific traits of Bolivian mineworkers?
Well, that they are so mingled in with campesino and indigenous forms, as indeed the whole of Bolivia is. Worker subalternity is likewise mingled in with the territory of the workers' barrio, a zone of the city that gives its own special flavor to urban life. Whereas the miners' barrio is the mine, the mining encampment, and that's it. That's their world. They are the masters of a territory that includes the town of Oruro, right next to the mine. In Catavi-Siglo XX, Pulacayo, Santa Fe, in any Bolivian mine, you find a working population that has its own territory. Maybe that's what enabled the militias . . . added to the fact that they handled dynamite. And that they were used to risking their lives: they risk their lives every day, generation after generation.

In 1960-something, after my time in Bolivia, I was in England. I went to visit a mining family who even put me up for the night. I went inside and found the house so similar in the layout of utensils, the organization of space, half working-class and half countrified, that I thought to myself: "I'll be damned, these places are so alike." In England I saw an ancient mining culture with similarities . . . with a whiff of the Bolivian about it. But English factory-worker culture was more like the Argentine version. In 1987 I remember Perry Anderson coming to Buenos Aires and attending a rally in a workers' neighborhood. He came back excited: he had seen, he said, the English working class of twenty-five years previous.

In the fall of 1981, I toured various factories in Detroit at the invitation of Harley Shaiken. We went for some beers with two or three shop stewards. I felt thoroughly at home. We were speaking a different language, and yet the ways of cracking a joke, of chugging a beer, of relating to one another, were just the same . . . The car factory workers of Detroit were just like the workers in the big Argentine factories. The same thing happened to me in Italy. Right at home, right away.

Speaking of Detroit, Buenos Aires, England, or Italy, these are urban working-class cultures forged during the heyday of heavy industry, back in the nineteenth century. The miners' case is somewhat different, harking back to colonial times and even earlier. This is also an effect of the presence of campesino culture.

During those years, did you feel you were living in a revolutionary culture?
During those years, I don't know. But the young man I was at the time certainly felt that. Mind you, that youth was a thoughtless fool . . .

In what sense?
He thought that the revolution was just around the corner. Within six months . . . Within a year, two years . . . That was how the miners lived. The utopia of revolution was lodged inside their heads. I say "the miners" but it's rather *those* miners in particular, the ones who were fighting. And there were plenty of them, for whom the revolution had not ended.

They had already had the National Revolution of 1952 . . .
But the socialist revolution was still to come.

But in 1956, '58, '60, did the miners believe that the National Revolution had fallen short?
"The miners," that covers a lot of people. I can only speak about the ones I met. And then about what I picked up from their behavior, their common way of being. The miners wanted to achieve more gains. I do believe they thought they could go further. And rule. The idea of wielding power, as in the title of your book, Sinclair, is very old: *We Alone Will Rule.*[4] Because that was the answer to humiliation. Over on the other side, they read it as a desire to call the shots, but it's not that simple.

It is more a matter of no more humiliation of anyone. The Bolshevik vanguard sought to take power and reorganize the world, and with this

---

4   [Sinclair Thomson, *We Alone Will Rule: Native Andean Politics in the Age of Insurgency* (Madison: University of Wisconsin Press, 2002).]

ambition they headed the greatest revolution of the twentieth century. I suspect that the rest, the people who rise up in every revolution, are thinking: "Nobody's ever going to humiliate us again." Túpac Amaru's old vow—"The lord will never again grow fat off our sweat"—crops up again verbatim in peasant revolts in Mexico a century later. The point is not to rule but to know that "they will not do this to us again." And if in passing we get to rule, so much the better! [*Laughs*]

Did they feel humiliated in those years?
No, but they felt there was injustice, that people were better off in La Paz, that their wages were inadequate. They were caught between trade-union struggles and the myth of revolution, which endures as a myth even when it is realized.

It seems to us that Bolivia is unique in many ways, despite having elements in common with other Latin American countries.
You find shared aspects, such as the Spanish form of domination. There is a *racial* form of subalternity that is imposed everywhere. Five hundred years are not enough to expunge that memory from consciousness, especially as through all those centuries that racial divide has reproduced itself constantly in successive forms of domination, right up to the present day. These peoples hold this fact somewhere in their memory. Worker subalternity lacks this racial aspect. Here is an entire people, who regard themselves as a people; the workers are not a separate people. Who have their own language; the workers do not speak a separate language. Who are subjected to forced labor; the workers are paid a wage. Who are humiliated in their day-to-day existence; workers cannot be humiliated in the same manner, and when they are, all hell breaks loose. More than half of workers' struggles are against humiliation. But with Indian subalternity, you see centuries of pitiless humiliation and resistance taking a range of forms that are not those of working-class struggle. You see that everywhere. I still remember my initial, outsider's amazement on encountering it in Bolivia.

In Peru there's this grand coastal oligarchy, ever since the Viceroyalty of Peru. It had no equivalent in Bolivia, whose ruling class was far less wealthy and where there was none of the pomp of Lima's court. And none of that long coast. Chile is another matter. In Mexico you have the rich court and culture of New Spain, one of the great wonders of Latin America. While Bolivia sits somewhere up there, landlocked and impoverished. A whole different world. Bolivia was the altiplano, Cochabamba, and Sucre—no oceans, ports, or wider world. The altiplano, mining, and the valleys that fed it. Bolivia took a long time to constitute itself around what looks like a mining enclave; it had to win permission to get its products out to the sea, the markets, the world.

It is an astonishing country. I know how unique and concentrated it is. Every country is different. But Bolivia is different in a specific way. I wouldn't be able to define it. But I know exactly what you're talking about, and the funny thing is that it's a massive spiritual intensity. And that spiritual intensity can kill you . . . You go there and . . . you suffer like anything. You become steeped in the huge spiritual force of that place. Where the hell does it come from? Who knows. But it is a truly terrific intensity, and it stays with you for life, like an education of your soul and feelings.

What are your thoughts on the role of memory in oral history?
Much of what people tell you fifty years after the event is a mythic construct. And they're not aware of doing it, because the memories have already hardened into that. Almost everything the old Zapatistas related were mythic constructs . . . Rather like the way I talk myself, mythologizing a little. You tell exemplary stories. The things you remember are exemplary stories that you've been telling for years, and maybe they changed somewhat in your recollection. We all tell exemplary stories.

In all that you've been saying, what do you mean by myth?
When I say myth, I don't mean a lie or a falsehood. I really mean the distillation over time of countless lives, an imaginary, meaningful condensation of the presence of that past inside us, a coded imprint of the untold history, quite possibly indecipherable by now but undoubtedly real. Jorge Luis Borges, in his "Parable of Cervantes and Don Quijote," writes: "In the beginning of literature is myth, and in the end as well."[5] At the beginning and at the end of history, too.

5   [Jorge Luis Borges, *Labyrinths: Selected Stories and Other Writings* (New York: New Directions Publishing, 1962; rev. ed. 2007), p. 242.]

13

Destinies of a Revolution

(2017)

Preamble

At the end of August 1990, I published a fragment of Victor Serge's poem "Confessions."[1] It was written in 1938, in the midst of the delirium of the years he called "midnight in the century," as old Russian revolutionaries were confessing to strings of improbable and outlandish crimes at the Moscow Trials. I was struck, then, by how many people felt touched by those words from another era:

> If we roused the peoples and made the earth of continents shake,
> shot the powerful, destroyed the old armies, the old cities, the old ideas,
> began to redo everything with these defiled old stones,
> these tired hands, and what little soul we had left,
> it is not in order to haggle with you now,
> sad revolution, our mother, our child, our flesh,
> our decapitated dawn, our night with its stars askew,
> with its inexplicable Milky Way torn asunder.[2]

---

1   [An earlier version of this chapter was published in Gilly's essay collection *El siglo del relámpago* (2002); Gilly revised it for publication in an October 2017 special supplement to the Mexican newspaper *La Jornada* commemorating the centenary of the Bolshevik Revolution. The title is an allusion to Victor Serge's *Destin d'une révolution* (1937), translated into English as *Russia Twenty Years After*.]

2   Victor Serge, *A Blaze in a Desert*, trans. James Brook (Oakland: PM Press, 2017), p. 55.

And yet Serge wrote this in 1938, in an attempt to make sense of the unbelievable confessions of the old heroes, saying that the Moscow Trials and the crimes of Stalinism in the Spanish Civil War spelled the final agony of the revolution. Those who had made and led the revolution were physically exterminated during those years, to the point that Soviet artists recall 1937 as the darkest year of the cycle inaugurated in 1917. The year of prison bars, barbed wire, firing squads, and crosses.

Socialists will only be able to understand the Soviet collapse and its paradoxically liberating content once they have recognized that the October Revolution was put to death during the 1930s, along with the great majority of its leaders. What crumbled in 1989 was something else, namely, the privileged and oppressive political regime set up by the gravediggers of that revolution, the embalmers of Lenin's corpse, the men who sat down at Yalta with the United States and Great Britain to divide world domination and the subordination of countries between them, and who pursued, from then on, the policies of a great power.

The notes below outline a reflection upon the origins and antecedents of the disaster that was the Soviet Union and its gravediggers, together with thoughts on the destiny of socialism, that human ideal of freedom, equality, and fraternity, both before and after the cycle of the Soviet state.

1.

The Russian Revolution of 1917 was a huge explosion of liberation: it finished off an empire, swept away landowners and capitalists, destroyed armies and built them, unleashed the powers of creation of workers and the downtrodden, invented new forms of democratic governance, fed the hopes and struggles of the world's oppressed, proclaimed ideals of equality, justice and freedom, and called—not merely in words but above all in great historic deeds—for the construction of a world devoid of exploitation, oppression, or humiliation.

The political regime that succeeded the revolution ended up in wholesale retreat, leaving what remained of that revolution to the power and authority of finance capital. It was not defeated in war, but by the global market, the universal circulation of goods (including the commodity of "labor power") and capital.

The state that emerged from the October Revolution—whose avatars this is not the place to analyze—proved unable to vanquish capitalism on the single and ultimate terrain on which the confrontation between two modes of production is decided: that of productivity as measured on the world market.

2.

That defeat, resisted and postponed for decades by the extraordinarily heroic defensive stands of Marxists, socialists, and the Soviet peoples, appears in retrospect as a series of disasters for the original conception of socialism: justice and liberty.

From the mid-1920s at least, the Soviet regime began clamping down on urban and rural workers alike. There was oppression, repression, and mass deportations of the nations within the USSR, making it as much a "prison of peoples" as the Tsarist Empire; ideas were crushed, trials falsified, and socialist opponents and dissidents exterminated inside and outside the Union; a network of prison camps and colonies for internal exile and forced labor was created. Nations and national liberation movements were invaded, suppressed, or persecuted—the Baltic countries (1939); Germany (1953); Hungary (1956); Poland (1956); Czechoslovakia (1968); Afghanistan (1979). Revolutionary movements were infiltrated, sold out, or strangled, the most notorious cases being Spain (1936–39) and Greece (1944–47).

It would be superfluous to review here the parallel series of disasters inflicted on the whole planet, in the course of those same decades, by capitalism. The post–World War II socialist revolutions followed their own paths, rather than that dictated by Moscow: Korea (1945), China (1949), Cuba (1959), Vietnam (1975).

From the 1930s onward, Stalin's regime showed mounting brutality toward Russian and Soviet Marxists and socialists of every stripe: revolutionary socialists, Mensheviks, anarchists, communists, and Bolsheviks were jailed, deported, shot, silenced, and slandered. This repression extended to the entire world, including Mexico and the United States. Such policies expressed the interests and outlook of a new social class: the state bureaucracy. Covered in privileges and shielding behind the repression of its own people, this bureaucracy left a trail of ineptitude, crime, and catastrophe. As of 1989, it became overtly capitalist and transformed erstwhile privilege into property and capital, in Russia and in the global world of finance.

In November 1989, an uprising on both sides of the city tore down the Berlin Wall, an absurd defensive barrier erected in August 1961 by the repressive East German regime. Two years later, in December 1991, Boris Yeltsin dissolved the Soviet Union and launched a wave of privatization of state assets. At the end of eight more years of successive political crises, he resigned the presidency on December 31, 1999, and handed the power to his prime minister, Vladimir Putin.

That collapse gave birth to the capitalist Russia of today, financially, militarily, and scientifically mighty, the old territorial and military great power lying between Asia and Europe that had never been altogether suffocated beneath the Soviet mantle, as General de Gaulle maintained.

3.

After World War II, the existence of the USSR and its confrontation with the US, UK, and other imperialist powers protected a string of national revolutions in Africa, Asia, and Latin America. However, it forced those revolutions to accept conditions of subordination to its great-power interests and to its bureaucratic models.

These revolutions made the most of the contradictions between the Soviet Union and the United States. We should not forget, though, that the Russian Revolution of 1917, in the midst of the generalized wartime crisis of 1914–18, managed to prevail with none but its own forces to rely on, plus the solidarity of the workers of Europe and the world; and that the Chinese Revolution triumphed alone in 1949, against the advice and warnings of the Soviet leaders, in the midst of the anticolonial revolutions that swept Asia, Africa, and Latin America in the period following World War II.

The bureaucratic regime in the Soviet Union could only impose itself by quashing the resistance of Soviet Marxists of all tendencies. Unable to silence them, it was forced to imprison, exterminate, and defame them. The story of this heroic resistance has not yet been fully written. Marxists and socialists need to work on a thorough history, analysis, and comprehension of this fight to the death against socialist ideas. History cannot be dissolved by conjunctural explanations, or narratives that have had constantly to be replaced by other narratives.

4.

As of the 1920s, theoretical polemics in the USSR addressed every aspect of the construction of socialism, as well as the very idea of socialism.

No serious theoretical and historical task can be accomplished without recovering this.

The most superficial attitude has been to contend, with no evidence beyond one's own ignorance of the writings of Karl Marx, Rosa Luxemburg, Leon Trotsky, and Victor Serge, that Stalinism is already contained in Marxism, or that Stalinism and Trotskyism are mere "enemy brothers." I have never once found such affirmations, unless made in bad faith, to be based on anything other than substantial ignorance.

These debates are rooted in concepts of history, human labor, and socialism. Let me bring a couple of quotations to bear, not as a clinching argument but as a simple illustration of the topics being discussed, of the depth of those discussions and of their continued relevance:

> Reduced to its primary basis, history is nothing but a struggle for an economy of working time. Socialism could not be justified by the abolition of exploitation alone; it must guarantee to society a higher economy of time than is guaranteed by capitalism. Without the realization of this condition, the mere removal of exploitation would be but a dramatic episode without a future. [3]

So wrote Leon Trotsky in *The Revolution Betrayed* (1936). This economy of working time, this productivity of labor, can only be measured on a global scale. Already in March 1930, in the prologue to *The Permanent Revolution*, Trotsky had written:

> Marxism takes its point of departure from world economy, not as a sum of national parts but as a mighty and independent reality which has been created by the international division of labour and the world market, and which in our epoch imperiously dominates the national markets. The productive forces of capitalist society have long ago outgrown the national boundaries. The imperialist war (of 1914–18) was one of the expressions of this fact. In respect of the technique of production, socialist society must represent a stage higher than capitalism. To aim at building a *nationally isolated* socialist society means, in spite of all passing successes, to pull the productive forces backward even as compared with capitalism. To attempt, regardless of the geographical,

    3   Leon Trotsky, "The Stakhanov Movement," in *The Revolution Betrayed: What Is the Soviet Union and Where Is It Going?*, trans. Max Eastman (New York: Merit Publishers, [1936] 1965), marxists.org.

cultural, and historical conditions of the country's development, which constitutes a part of the world unity, to realize a shut-off proportionality of all the branches of economy within a national framework, means to pursue a reactionary utopia.[4]

5.

Already during those years, the arguments of Left Opposition Marxists in the Soviet Union demanded full recourse to the market and to democracy as correctives and testing grounds of economic planning. As Trotsky wrote in October 1932, in *The Soviet Economy in Danger*:

> The innumerable living participants in the economy, state and private, collective and individual, must serve notice of their needs and of their relative strength not only through the statistical determinations of plan commissions but by the direct pressure of supply and demand. The plan is checked and, to a considerable degree, realized through the market. The regulation of the market itself must depend upon the tendencies that are brought out through its mechanism. The blueprints produced by the departments must demonstrate their economic efficacy through commercial calculation. The system of the transitional economy is unthinkable without the control of the rouble. This presupposes, in its turn, that the rouble is at par. Without a firm monetary unit, commercial accounting can only increase the chaos.[5]

As early as 1932, then, Trotsky maintained that only the coordination of these three elements—state planning, the market, and Soviet democracy—could have ensured a correct steering of the economy during the transition to socialism. In 1936, in *The Revolution Betrayed*, he added:

> These functions of money [accumulation], however, bound up as they are with exploitation, are not liquidated at the beginning of a proletarian revolution but in a modified form are transferred to the state, the universal merchant, creditor and industrialist . . .

4   Leon Trotsky, Introduction to the German edition of *The Permanent Revolution*, trans. John G. Wright (London: New Park Publishers, [1930] 1962), marxists.org.

5   Leon Trotsky, "Conditions and Methods of Planned Economy," in *The Soviet Economy in Danger*, trans. Max Shachtman (New York: Pamphlet Pioneer Publishers, [1932] 1933), marxists.org.

The role of money in the Soviet economy is not only unfinished but, as we have said, still has a long growth ahead. The transitional epoch between capitalism and socialism taken as a whole does not mean a cutting down of trade but, on the contrary, its extraordinary extension . . . All products and services begin for the first time in history to be exchanged for one another . . .

The raising of the productivity of labor and bettering of the quality of its products is quite unattainable without an accurate measure freely penetrating into all the cells of industry—that is, without a stable unit of currency.[6]

Khrushchev's reforms and those that followed were belated and inefficient statist versions of those long-ago proposals by Soviet Marxists back in the 1930s. They came too late for socialism but not for yesterday's Soviet bureaucrats transformed into the Russian capitalists of today. In that same work of 1936, *The Revolution Betrayed*, Trotsky clearly summarized the elements of this crisis:

Two opposite tendencies are growing up out of the depth of the Soviet regime. To the extent that, in contrast to a decaying capitalism, it develops the productive forces, it is preparing the economic basis of socialism. To the extent that, for the benefit of an upper stratum, it carries to more and more extreme expression bourgeois norms of distribution, it is preparing a capitalist restoration. This contrast between forms of property and norms of distribution cannot grow indefinitely. Either the bourgeois norm must in one form or another spread to the means of production or the norms of distribution must be brought into correspondence with the socialist property system.[7]

6.

The return to capitalism of the USSR and its satellites sprang originally from the theory and practice of the construction of socialism in each country, formulated in 1924 by Stalin and his associates. In 1930, in *The Permanent Revolution*, Trotsky wrote:

6   Trotsky, "Money and Plan," in *The Revolution Betrayed*.
7   Trotsky, "Not Yet Decided by History," in *The Revolution Betrayed*.

From the standpoint of principle, the departure from Marxism by the Stalinist "school" on the issues of socialist construction is no less significant and drastic than, for example, the break of the German Social Democrats from Marxism on the issues of war and patriotism in the fall of 1914, exactly ten years before the Stalinist turn. This comparison is by no means accidental in character. Stalin's "mistake," just like the "mistake" of the German Social Democracy, is *national socialism*.[8]

This vision prompts the identification of socialism, not with a social relation that is superior to capitalism in terms of culture, liberty, and productivity, but with each state that proclaims itself to be socialist. Socialism thus ceases to be the democratic self-organization of society and becomes the actions and directives of the "socialist state," whose officials cannot countenance any initiative that escapes their control.

The national state thus becomes the subject of socialism and its apparatus is counterposed, on the one hand to capital as self-valorizing value, and on the other to socialism as labor self-organized in democracy and autonomy. The notion of the existence of a "camp of socialist states" and, its corollary, the idea of "two world markets" was merely the absurd generalization of this statist concept of socialism. In this way the Marxist vision of an integral, complex period of global transition to world socialism, comparable to the many centuries of transition toward capitalism, is wholly lost.

This vision is present in Marx, from *The German Ideology* to the *Grundrisse*, in his correspondence with Engels, and in his last letters to Vera Zasulich and the Russian Populists. Such a universal vision came to be replaced by the idea of a succession of "socialist" national states. Trotsky used to say that the latter notion amounted to believing that a pile of dinghies could be built up to form an ocean liner.

7.

The Communist Parties of all countries, along with their political or intellectual "fellow travelers," organized around this theory and this program. At one time or another they justified, defended, and proposed as a model the statist socialism of the Soviet Union. All of them ignored, covered up, or in too many cases participated in the crimes of the Soviet

---

8 Trotsky, introduction to the German edition of *Permanent Revolution*.

bureaucracy. The damage inflicted for decades by its apparatuses on the very idea of socialism has been incalculable.

This is not to deny the heroism, the struggles, and the sincerity of countless communist activists and leaders. They devoted their lives, they died fighting for the socialist ideal and against the horrors and oppressions of capitalism in their tens and hundreds of thousands. But it is important, in the face of a universal catastrophe for socialism, to distinguish theoretical and political error from the rectitude of intentions and the heroism of personal conduct.

The Stalinist parties and their theorists and propagandists justified the dictatorship of the bureaucracy, denied its crimes, and argued for the idea and practice of the one-party state; they were silent about monstrous events like the division of Germany, the Berlin Wall, and the crackdown on the various national groups within the Soviet Union; they minimized and at times went so far as to justify the crimes committed against the idea of socialism on behalf of the power, privileges, and policies of a bureaucratic caste composed of upstarts, oppressors, and exploiters; and they denied a monstrous reality inside the USSR: the prison camps where hundreds of thousands of political prisoners, deliberately mixed with common criminals, lived, suffered, and died. In 1956, Khrushchev's "Secret Speech" publicly acknowledged a reality that had long been denounced by researchers, writers, and former inmates of those hellish places. Prominent among such survivors is Varlam Shalamov, whose *Kolyma Tales* offer vivid, terrible, truthful testimony to his years in the forced-labor and concentration camps of the penal universe known as the Gulag.[9]

When the house is falling down around you, you don't just look at which recent repair was botched. You must investigate its construction and structures and get to the bottom of any flaws resulting from deceit, self-interest, or ignorance. All socialists, that is, all those of us who believe in a possible world of justice, equality, and freedom among human beings, have an obligation to do so.

8.

During the great days of 1989, that magical year of the twentieth century, from the student and popular movement culminating in China's Tiananmen Square to the fall of the Berlin Wall, that caste of exploiters

9   Varlam Shalamov, *Kolyma Tales*, trans. John Glad (New York: Penguin, 1994).

and its regime of oppression were besieged, shaken, and in some places defeated. These social processes have to do with the great shifts that occurred around the world from the mid-1970s: the global restructuring of capitalism, radical technological innovations, the transformation of labor conditions, devastating crises in the dependent or less developed countries (then called the "Third World"), the wholesale domination of finance capital, ecological emergency, rearmament.

However, the decisive fact for any future perspective is this: those bureaucratic regimes were not wiped out by capitalist weapons or over-thrown by an all-embracing war whose destructiveness had sent the idea of socialism packing into the distant future. They collapsed from the inside. Their peoples forced them to retreat, in the economic sphere due to their ineptitude and their privileges, and in the political sphere through democratic mobilization and insurgency.

The distinction is a radical one. Capitalism's plan for combating socialism and destroying the regimes that challenged it under the social-ist banner was war—not democratic revolution. The war was averted, and the peoples found or invented their own paths as they rose up against statist, authoritarian, and oppressive regimes in search of the same ancient ideas: justice and liberty.

If those ideas currently fit into an idealized view of the market as the alleged instrument of fairer, less arbitrary distribution, this *inverted view of reality* should be blamed on the former regimes that had symbolized for their peoples the negation of justice and liberty. But it also takes time, and painful experience, to become versed in the privileges, injustices, and exclusion of the capitalism that emerged from those ruins.

9.

Luciano Galicia, a revolutionary and trade-union organizer in Mexico since the 1930s, drew my attention some while ago to a document of the Left Opposition in the Soviet Communist Party. Written as early as 1927 and circulating illegally at first, it speaks with bold, stylish lucidity:

> A whole series of future five-year plans will leave us far from the level of the advanced countries of the West. What will be happening in the capitalist world during this time? [. . .]
>
> If you admit the possibility of its flourishing anew for a period of decades, then the talk of socialism in our backward country is pitiable

tripe. Then it will be necessary to say that we were mistaken in our appraisal of the whole epoch as an epoch of capitalist decay. Then the Soviet Republic will prove to have been the second experiment in proletarian dictatorship since the Paris Commune, broader and more fruitful, but only an experiment . . .

The European proletariat needs a far shorter period for its take-off to the seizure of power than we need to catch up technically with Europe and America . . . We must, meanwhile, systematically narrow the distance separating our productivity of labour from that of the rest of the world. The more we advance, the less danger there is of possible intervention by low prices, and consequently by armies.[10]

History, as ever, turned out to be more knotted and complex. The European proletariat did not seize power; World War II happened, and then came the reality of the market, of labor productivity and global market prices, and then other things happened. And yet, the clarity, scope, and far-sightedness of that long-term assessment are startling.

A second, gigantic Paris Commune! This bold prophecy, almost a century old, has ultimately been borne out in strange, apocalyptic, planetary forms, as is always the case with good prophecies. Today its evident clairvoyance contrasts with the obtuse idea of a socialism in each country.

10.

The present worldwide offensive of capital does not only aspire to wreck what remains of the social revolutions in Russia, China, Vietnam, Cuba, and elsewhere. It seeks to wipe the very idea of socialism from the minds and the dreams of human beings.

But it cannot. The socialist ideal, which animated the Paris Commune and the October Revolution, is resurgent day after day in the urban and agrarian revolts against the exploitation, dispossession, oppression, and local and global injustice of the capitalist-dominated world.

However, it is also the case that socialism will only succeed in reclaiming its place in human hopes, and Marxism its place as a *theory of revolution, liberation, enjoyment, and freedom,* by means of a profound

10   As quoted in the appendix to Trotsky, *The Revolution Betrayed.* (Emphasis added.)

critical reorganization of socialist ideas and the recuperation and actualization of Marxist tenets, the first of which is the concept of that liberation as an entire epoch.

One hundred years on from the October Revolution, our twentieth century of revolutions and counterrevolutions must become the object of renewed Marxist study around the world. As an organized political force, socialism will be unable to advance without political alliances and agreements of the most various kinds, in a range of concrete situations, with the other forces and ideas thrown up by the social and political crises proper to the universal dominance of finance capital. Ecological disaster already featured in the long-term forecasts of Marx, and subsequently those of Rosa Luxemburg. And now it is here, wreaking havoc with nature and life.

Marxism is not simply a political idea. It is a theory of capitalist society, its forms of exploitation and alienation and its irreconcilable contradictions; a theory of human relations of dominance and subordination and the conditions for their abolition; and a theory of the emergence under capitalism of a modern class of white-collar workers (in addition to blue-collar workers) that is today demographically universal, in whose relations of cooperation and solidarity lies the seed, latently present in this global reality, of the relations that would prevail in a future society of freely associated producers, free and equal women and men. Such relations exist already in uprisings and in solidarity organizations, in the selfless indignation that motivates social movements, and in the varied and ubiquitous rebellions of women for liberty, equality, and the enjoyment of the goods of the Earth by all.

Today we are living through an unprecedented expansion, in depth as in breadth, of the knowledge, the culture, and the number of white-collar workers in a context of changes to the organization of work and production. A confirmation and a mutation of the contradiction between living labor in all its forms and capital as the ambit and ascendancy of finance. This confrontation, which remains opaque for many of those affected, colors all the other complex contradictions and relations between human beings and between humans and nature, each of which ought to be treated on its own merits rather than lumped with any other. We are in the throes of an all-encompassing technological revolution, spreading with unprecedented velocity around the planet. While this does not alter social relations, it does exacerbate their confrontations and contradictions, which are adopting new forms and engendering new global dangers.

11.

We who are socialists and Marxists have come a long way in the course of the century of the October Revolution. Over those hundred years, the socialist idea changed the world. It enabled the conquest of ineradicable gains that have become a habitual part of social life. It illuminated the greatest liberation movements humanity has ever known. And against the humiliations, oppressions, and exploitations meted out by the owners of power, it gave a living, century-long actuality to the immemorial yearning for justice, freedom, equity, solidarity, knowledge, and enjoyment of the multiple worlds of life.

Socialism has acted as both impetus and guide of the most generous sentiments, dreams, and deeds of our era. In the epochal change now underway, the crisis entails the devaluation of old ideas, of past forms of knowledge, and of the intellectual workforce that carried them, in tandem with the start of a new accumulation. We are witnessing the beginnings of a new cycle of theoretical accumulation that is not marked by any foundational work but rather and above all by the reality of planetary events.

But Marxism is not only a theory. It is also a practice. It therefore demands an ethics, which other bodies of knowledge and other theories do not. There has never been and never will be a reorganization of the socialist ideal and of Marxist theory without a moral fundament. Nothing can be rebuilt upon ignorance, concealment, mendacity, covetousness, and calumny.

Any critique of the ideas is also a critique of the practice, and this last is possible only when governed by an ethics of socialist political conduct—an exigency that is unknown, unnecessary, or antagonistic to other schools of politics. Such is, too, the great lesson of the disaster of the bureaucratic dictatorships and the lies and falsifications of "socialism in one country."

There is no future for any discussion that covers up the past, wholly or in part; that refuses to see and criticize errors of theory and their inexorable and fatal practical consequences; or that attempts to curtail the universal instrument of criticism on behalf of particular interests.

The peoples of revolutionary countries and lands harbor, in their lived experience and in their social and individual thought, possibilities yet to be revealed. These will only appear to us, illuminate us, provided we place no artificial or arbitrary limits on our criticism, our knowledge, and our learning of the past.

12.

As someone who has lived through the twentieth century, my "homeland in time," I can see no valid reason for the despondency, desolation, and bewilderment that have overtaken so many socialists. Have we forgotten what already lies behind us?

The twentieth century was the century of Fascism and Nazism, of extermination camps and crematoria and the Jewish genocide; of the millions of dead under Stalinist repression, as testified by Nikita Khrushchev; of colonial wars and metropolitan torture; of famines in Africa and the devastation of nature across the world; of two World Wars and countless wars between nations; of the deportation and genocide of entire peoples; of Franco's barbarism; of the Japanese invasion of China and Korea, and the atomic bombs dropped on Hiroshima and Nagasaki; of the martyrdom of Vietnam at the hands of the French and the Americans, and the Sino-Vietnamese conflict; of the atrocities perpetrated by the Chilean and Argentine military against their own people; of the entrance of Soviet tanks into Budapest and Prague, and the massacre of communists in Indonesia; of the unending tyranny in Guatemala and the long dirty war waged by the Salvadoran army against that country's democracy and population.

13.

As with Walter Benjamin's "Angel of History," this accumulation of ruins appears when we look behind us in our time. From every one of those ruins there also rises an architecture of devotion, heroism, and solidarity erected by human beings in their ceaseless quest for justice and freedom. Starting with the Mexican Revolution of 1910, the Russian Revolution of 1917 and the German Revolution of 1919, moving on to China in 1949, Vietnam in 1975, Nicaragua in 1979, and Eastern Europe in 1989, the twentieth century was also the century of revolutions. Let us not deny that heritage.

It was likewise the century of a worldwide insurgency of women, one which continues to spill over like a high tide throughout this epochal change. This is an everyday, ongoing, sometimes invisible insurgency that challenges the most archaic forms of oppression and injustice, and transforms dreams and demands of equality, justice, and liberty into aspects not of politics but of life.

During that century, too, the idea of and clamor for democracy put down universal roots. Democracy was by no means given to us as a subproduct of the market. Respect for the vote was not a favor granted to us. It was seized, fought for—yesterday and today—in arduous struggles waged by workers, peasants, women, youth, and the poor against agrarian oligarchies and a militaristic, barbaric capitalism.

14.

Latin American socialism and Marxism are presently engaged in the wholesale recovery of their historical memory. We thus recuperate the revolutionary syndicalists, those women and men who from the beginning of the century in the United States, Mexico, Cuba, Brazil, Argentina, Chile, Peru, Bolivia, and Uruguay organized trade unions, workplace strikes, and general strikes throughout the continent; the agrarian socialism of Emiliano Zapata and his campesino commune in Morelos; the communitarian and civilizing ideals of Pancho Villa and his military settlements; the organizers of peasant movements in each country, and the great figures of our long and complex socialist lineage, themselves marked by points of light and shadow like all humans who ever lived.

Shattering the Night is the title under which Osip Piatnitsky's 1925 *Memoirs of a Bolshevik* was published in Spanish.[11] In it, Piatnitsky recounted the heroic, silent, clandestine Bolshevik combat against Tsarist autocracy and censorship during the early years of the last century. In 1937, Victor Serge was writing *Midnight in the Century*, his chronicle of the horror of Stalin's dictatorship. And *Out of the Night* is the title of Jan Valtin's 1941 account of his escape from the twin hells of Stalinism and Nazism.[12]

The ambiguous metaphor of the night alludes to the origins of socialist rebellions, at once enlightened and romantic. Our times are those of lost illusions for some and dissolved nightmares for others. This is not

---

11   *Rompiendo la noche: Memorias y revelaciones de un bolchevique, ayer y hoy, el mundo mañana* (Mexico City: Ediciones Pavlov, 1950). Published in English as *Memoirs of a Bolshevik* (London: M. Lawrence, 1933). [Osip Piatnitsky (1882–1938) joined the Russian Social Democratic and Labour Party in 1899 and took part in the 1905 and 1917 Revolutions, serving as a top Comintern official from 1921 until his arrest in 1937; he was executed the following year.]

12   Victor Serge, *Midnight in the Century*, trans. Richard Greeman (New York: New York Review Books, [1939] 2014); Jan Valtin, *Out of the Night* (New York: Alliance Book Corporation), 1941.

enough. In order to liberate socialism from the night, it is necessary, now as before, to re-establish truth, reason, and memory, and—once again—to recover history, install the republic in conditions of democracy, protection, and equality for all, and endow words with their fullest freedom.

14

Ernest Mandel: Memories of Oblivion

(1995)

On the morning of July 21, 1995, in Horefto—a small Greek town on the shores of the Aegean—Michel Pablo (real name Michael Raptis) was telling me about how he met Ernest Mandel in Paris during World War II. Michel Pablo, a Greek national born in Alexandria and raised in Crete, a Trotskyist since 1936 and a delegate to the founding congress of the Fourth International in 1938, was living in the German-occupied city under the tenuous cover of a study grant while convalescing from tuberculosis. In 1944, he was thirty-three, with a degree in urban planning. Ernest Mandel, born in Germany in 1923 and brought up in Belgium by Jewish émigré parents, was twenty-one; he had dropped out of university, carried away by revolutionary passion toward a different future. In Paris, he joined the International of which Pablo was already a leader.

A long friendship of life and struggle began at that moment between these two men of such disparate backgrounds, united by the same ideas and by different forms, as it turned out, of revolutionary passion: one was, at that point, the master; the other, his young and brilliant disciple. The story Pablo told me was, at the end of the day, an ancient Greek tale.

At 2:30 in the afternoon of that July 21, the telephone rang in my hotel room in Horefto. I heard Pablo's voice saying, "Je dois te transmettre une bien triste nouvelle: Ernest vient de mourir" (I have some sad news for you: Ernest just passed away). The conversation we'd had that morning about him was preserved on my tape recorder as part of a long interview.

CR

Last September 30, I was one of six or seven hundred people of diverse backgrounds, ways of thinking, and nationalities who accompanied the remains of Ernest Mandel to the old Parisian cemetery of Père Lachaise. His ashes were interred near the Communards' Wall, where many of the last-ditch combatants of the Paris Commune were shot in 1871. Among the crowd of young and old was Michel Pablo, come to bid farewell to the compañero with whom he had parted ways thirty years before, down the paths of Earth and life. Someone gave him a copy in Greek of Mandel's last book, *Power and Money*, which the author had sent him three days before his death. It was a splendid fall morning and, in keeping with the times, the cortege was singing in low, quiet voices the old funeral march of the German revolutionaries, like a song of long ago. Nevertheless, none of the men and women who were present felt crushed by the fall of the Berlin Wall, because they had spent their lives fighting from the left to bring it down. There were no happy faces (except perhaps for mine, because the sky was so blue), and no sad ones either. Afterward, some friends and I went off together for couscous in an Algerian restaurant.

When we were talking by the Aegean, Pablo had recalled the arrival of Mandel in occupied Paris in 1944. "Ernest was very young, very brilliant, as was Abraham Leon [the author of a memorable work on the Jewish question]. The pair were inseparable. Coming from a leftist organization of Jewish youth, they joined our movement together. From then on, Mandel and I were closely linked. He lived in Brussels and would travel in secret to Paris to attend meetings. He'd stay at our place, and then return to Brussels. He felt toward me as he would toward a father, and I felt toward him as toward a spiritual son. I felt very proud of Ernest's membership in the Fourth International. I met his parents, too. His father was a left-wing Jew, an admirer of Trotsky, a very brave man. He knew that his son and I were friends as well as comrades, and he used to say to me: 'Michel, you must allow my Ernest to go to university as well, I beg you.' He wanted his son to have a degree, which back then was something we couldn't care less about . . . Near the end of the war, Mandel was captured by the Nazis along with Abraham Leon. Leon was sent to a labor camp, where he died within months. But they didn't realize that Ernest was a Jew, and since he spoke perfect German, they made him an interpreter in a factory, from where he managed to escape."

CR

From then on, the life story of Ernest Mandel is first and foremost a story of ideas, linked to the Fourth International. In that postwar period, the second half of the 1940s, he and Michel Pablo together defined the three great lines of the organization's program: a democratic political revolution in the Soviet Union and the Eastern countries; a socialist revolution in the West; and a revolution of national liberation in the colonies and dependent countries, or what would be dubbed the "Third World." All three were understood as constituting inseparable parts of a combined process of socialist revolution around the world.

Under these banners, Trotskyists took part in the whole gamut of national and social struggles in their countries, always in the face of a double hostility: that of the Communist supporters of Moscow and Peking, and that of the repressive bodies of the capitalist states. It is hard to imagine today the vehemence with which that implacable Communist hostility translated, from the 1930s to the 1960s, into persecutions, assassinations, denunciations, imprisonments, and endless calumnies, all from within the left itself. Trotsky's followers were branded as agents of the Gestapo, of Franco, of British imperialism, of the CIA, of whoever you care to name, rather than being treated as a distinct political current of the left. Endorsed by Moscow and its client states and parties, this campaign sent many to jail or to their deaths. When the full story comes to be written, it will become evident that the cruelest crimes of Communism were those committed against its own kin, the people who stood up to oppose Stalin's murderous regime. It is not for nothing that, toward the end of his life, Trotsky ran out of words for expressing human ire and, turning to the Bible, called him Cain.

That hellish climate, endured by Mandel through the 1940s and '50s, became milder in the wake of Khrushchev's "revelations" about Stalin's crimes—"revelations" in quotation marks, since anyone who wanted to know already knew about them—but it continued to weigh on dogmatic Communists like a thick fog, with a curious mirror image in right-wing minds that persists to this day. It is a strange fact that one of the greatest political thinkers of this century, Leon Trotsky, continues to be almost unknown in universities where lesser figures have enjoyed greater acclaim, albeit transitory, overstated, and ultimately undeserved. But such are the ways of academia and the paths to salvation of well-meaning consciences. The works of Ernest Mandel, like those of Victor Serge, Isaac Deutscher, and a handful of others, have contributed significantly to breaching that steel ring of ignorance and prejudice, while making no concessions to habit or fashion.

CR

The father was right to insist that the son should obtain a degree. Thanks to his theoretical writings as an economist, Ernest Mandel far transcended the bounds of his political organization, and, especially after the mid-1960s, exerted a notable influence on both the thinking of the left and the academic media. I remember René Zavaleta Mercado, the Bolivian thinker and poet exiled in Mexico, telling me admiringly sometime in the mid-1970s about the vast scope of the author's knowledge reflected in the *Introduction to Marxist Economic Theory*. That work in particular was a protracted bombshell that served to demolish every Soviet and like-minded manual, with their degradation of teaching, contamination of minds, and aptitude for obscuring any theoretical Marxist vision whatsoever.

However, the work Mandel himself regarded as his masterpiece was *Late Capitalism*, whose preeminence among Marxist ideas was comparable to that given to the works of Rudolf Hilferding and Lenin on imperialism at the beginning of the century. In his later years he continued to work on his theory of long-wave cycles in capitalism, building on the relevant research by Kondratieff and Trotsky.

In the spring of 1960, when I met Mandel in Brussels, he was completing his *Introduction*, and pinned high hopes on it, rightly, as it turned out. I had come from Amsterdam to see him about something to do with the travel documents required by Algerian revolutionaries. As a young Latin American savage who had only just landed in the Dutch canals, I remember being struck by the old, European-style house where he lived with his mother, a kind lady who asked me to stay for dinner. Ernest had a surprising collection of Johann Sebastian Bach records in his study. That afternoon I roamed the city while he made time for us to meet. At a marvelous exhibition I discovered Alexander Calder's mobiles, the easy grace of their colors, balance, and movements. When I think back on it, I feel the same rush of unexpected beauty that filled me then.

The rupture between Mandel and his Greek mentor was a painful event for the latter and doubtless also, though I don't know for sure, for the former. It took place between 1960 and 1961, precisely when Michel Pablo was imprisoned in Holland for his activities in support of the Algerian Revolution. Moscow and the Communists viewed Algeria's War of Independence as a bourgeois-nationalist movement that merited no support; socialists formed part of the French government that was fighting it with blood, fire, and torture. The Algerians had to organize their own networks on metropolitan territory and even set up a secret weapons factory in Morocco, attracting Trotskyist metal workers from Argentina and Greece.

As ever in these cases, the breach between the two men was essentially a matter of ideas. Both believed, as did so many others, that the meaning of life could only lie in helping to change that life and the cruel, inhuman world we inhabit. Both, as I have mentioned, agreed on the big things. If I had to define them with an all-encompassing term, I would say they were classical humanists—one descended from the ancient Greek school, the other from the Enlightenment and its reason.

This is not the place to go into the details of their falling-out, some of which I may know better than anyone and other details not at all. I do know that over and above the two men and their feelings, the powerful forces of ideas pulled them in different directions.

To put it in the most abstract terms, and in a sense the most schematic, we might say that one, the Belgian, was convinced that the vector of the revolution that would change the world was the industrial proletariat. His thinking came from the Marx of the *Communist Manifesto* and *Capital*; his formative years had been spent in the tremendous manufacturing and mining environments of the Belgian metropole. The other one, the man from Alexandria and Crete, having grown up in a European border country with a long history of secular struggle for independence from the Turks, and a country closer to the so-called Third World than to an industrial nation and to the Middle East than to the West, understood the vast insurrection that shook the world during the 1950s and '60s as the very one Trotsky had glimpsed from inside Cárdenas's Mexico toward the end of his life: the rise of the teeming humanity of the colonized and dependent peoples against the imperial metropoles, in India, China, Indochina, Korea, the Middle East, Algeria, the Arab countries, the whole of Africa, and Latin America. His thinking came from the Marx of the *Grundrisse* and the last letters to Vera Zasulich.

I do not wish to suggest that these two strains of thought were antagonistic or mutually exclusive. Simply that when the inevitable test of practice came up, as unexpectedly as it always does, in 1959–60 in the form of the Algerian War, it would drive the two onto divergent paths. For one, the sign of the century lay in its proletarian and socialist revolutions; for the other, in its nationalist and anticolonial movements. As a result, although neither of them had planned it in advance, each derived a different set of priorities, visions, futures, ways of organizing and of fighting: one concerned above all with workers' councils and general strikes, the other with national conspiracies and insurrections. When the latter wanted to stake his fortunes on organizing the Algerian Revolution, the former demurred in various ways. The break, which was complex and messy, saw Ernest Mandel replace Michel Pablo as the primary leader of that strange organization, the Fourth International, while Pablo and his followers struck out for other shores in terms of ideas and actions in the wake of Algeria.

Both men had known Che Guevara in the 1960s. Mandel was invited by him to Cuba, which he visited in 1964, during the controversy over forms of moral and material stimulus to the Cuban economy. In Stockholm in 1975, he told me that their meeting had been the most remarkable interview of his life. Michel Pablo spoke with Che during a long night in Algeria, where Che was marshaling support and resources in preparation for his African campaign. In one of our talks by the Aegean, he said that Che had reminded him of the lines by Swinburne: "In his heart, wild desires. / In his eyes, the foreknowledge of death." A few days later I had the opportunity to ask Régis Debray whether his own recollection of Guevara was in any way like Pablo's. "Yes," he said without hesitation.

The year 1968 seemed to vindicate the school of Ernest Mandel. At least it did in France, where millions of workers on general strike occupied their factories under the emblem of the red flag; or in Czechoslovakia, where factory workers and councils acted as the hub of the national rebellion against Soviet domination. But 1968 was also the year of the Tet Offensive in Vietnam, the red students in Berlin and throughout Germany, the anti-war mobilizations in San Francisco and New York, and the student movement in Mexico—a great wave of young people from the peripheries of the planet and of industrial production who wanted to change the world in which they lived, not just labor relations, of which they had no experience yet.

Around that time, the Fourth International headed by Mandel expanded rapidly, at least in Europe and Latin America. In the 1970s Mandel was touring the universities of many countries; in Mexico City he filled the Che Guevara auditorium, among others. He had the honor of being banned from both the United States and the Soviet Union, as well as from the Eastern Bloc, France, Germany, Spain, and more, like an unintended homage paid to the rebel intellectual by an absurd, insecure, fearful world. The material, technological, ideological, and military counteroffensive of capitalism in the 1980s, sometimes called the global restructuring of capital, altered the direction of the tide and displaced the fears of the powerful to other areas, fears that have never quite evaporated since then.

The school of the Greek continued to give priority to the course of liberation movements. "Europe's '68," Michel Pablo said to me last summer, "was more than anything the result of the influence and pressure exerted on the youth of those countries by the colonial revolutions and national liberation wars of the 1950s and '60s: Africa, Algeria, Vietnam, Cuba, China. Not for nothing did they adopt Che Guevara as their symbol." He went on: "The most profound significance of the twentieth century has been that great movement of liberation for colonies, oppressed peoples, and women, rather than the proletarian revolution that had been our myth and our God."

Ever since Marx and the Russian Populists, this polemic has pervaded the revolutionary movements of the twentieth century. I am aware that for many it has lost its meaning, or never had one; time will tell, not the fashions of successive decades. I personally believe that in the present epoch, uncertain, restless, and impenetrably opaque as it is, that debate continues to be meaningful for those who, having learned in books or from experience that history lasts a long time, refuse to accept society in its present state, the law of money, and the universe of mercantile exchange as the only conceivable and possible frameworks for human interaction.

It was to this intricate, symbolic history that my memories led me, on that fall morning in Père Lachaise. Also present, standing silent and straight, belying his eighty-four years, was Ernest Mandel's erstwhile Greek compañero. And many others. We were saying farewell to a utopian, irreducible child of our time, who since his earliest youth had confronted by means of ideas, writings, and actions the powerful of this world, the lords and masters of East and West, and the inhuman windstorms of cynicism.

The city evening was mild. In a secondhand book kiosk, I found a novel by Oscar Vladislas de Lubicz Milosz that I had heard about but had never believed existed: *L'amoureuse initiation*.

15

Globalization, Violence, Revolutions: Nine Theses

(2001)

The tradition of the oppressed teaches us that the "state of emergency" in which we live is not the exception but the rule. We must attain to a conception of history that is in keeping with this insight. Then we shall clearly realize that it is our task to bring about a real state of emergency, and that this will improve our position in the struggle against Fascism. One reason why Fascism has a chance is that in the name of progress its opponents treat it as a historical norm. The current amazement that the things we are experiencing are "still" possible in the twentieth century is not philosophical. This amazement is not the beginning of knowledge—unless it is the knowledge that the view of history which gives rise to it is untenable.

Walter Benjamin, "Theses on the
Philosophy of History," Thesis VIII.

1.

According to Max Weber's classic definition, the state is "the form of human community that (successfully) lays claim to the monopoly of legitimate physical violence within a particular territory—and this idea of 'territory' is an essential defining feature."[1] Any state community (in modern terms, nation-state) contains within it a relation of dominance/ subordination, historically configured, in which an elite controls the exercise of this monopoly and oversees a fixed mode of extraction and distribution of the social surplus product. I define revolution as the violent rupture of this relation on the part of the dominated.

Every victorious revolution establishes a new relation of dominance and a new elite, rather than the abolition of all dominance. Such has been the norm of all known revolutions. It also establishes, if it is a social revolution, a new form and new bases for the distribution and allocation of the social surplus or excess product, beginning with rent and its derivatives. The form of extraction of the surplus does not necessarily change, being a function of social productive culture and technological development. Nor do those social and human relations, as distinct from the state-political relation, that are formed and transformed through the long, slow unfolding of history.[2] Through and beneath revolutions, wars and counterrevolutions, a lasting memory persists, along with the fabric and the material and immaterial heritage of civilizations and life.[3]

2.

The revolutions of the twentieth century (whether national or social) were chiefly propelled by the oppressed and subaltern of the rural world, often led by a small fraction of the educated urban elites—a germ of the new elite of the victorious revolution. The violent irruption of peasants and rural populations in those revolutions was not prompted by a detailed vision of a certain future but by the intolerable conditions of the present. "The masses go into a revolution not with a prepared plan of social reconstruction but with a sharp feeling that they cannot endure the old regime," notes Leon Trotsky in *History of the Russian Revolution*.[4]

1   Max Weber, "Politics as a Vocation," in Weber, *The Vocation Lectures*, trans. Rodney Livingstone (Indianapolis: Hackett Publishing Co., 2004), p. 33.
2   Rhina Roux, "Historia y comunidad estatal en México," *Viento del Sur: Revista de ideas, historia y política*, no. 15, July 1999, pp. 47–56.
3   If this is so, each state community can be figured as a great arch built over centuries, not in harmony but in permanent friction, conflict, and negotiation. See Philip Corrigan and Derek Sayer, *The Great Arch: English State Formation as Cultural Revolution* (Oxford: Blackwell, 1985) and Adolfo Gilly, *Chiapas, la razón ardiente: Ensayo sobre la rebelión del mundo encantado* (Mexico City: Ediciones Era, 1997).
4   Leon Trotsky, *History of the Russian Revolution*, trans. Max Eastman (Chicago: Haymarket Books, [1930] 2008), p. xvi.

As Walter Benjamin writes in his "Theses on the Philosophy of History," that violent force feeds on "the image of enslaved ancestors rather than that of liberated grandchildren."[5]

It is not in economics nor politics but in history (in each history) and in its weave of relations of dominance and dependency that the genetic code of each revolution may be deciphered. This is a view taken up in different ways by Barrington Moore, E. P. Thompson, and James C. Scott; by what might generically be called the school of "moral economics," as well as the school of subaltern studies; and by a range of US historians specializing in Mexico, of whom I will name only two who are no longer with us: Daniel Nugent and William Roseberry. All of them follow Benjamin's recommendation: "to brush history against the grain."

These national, agrarian, and social revolutions of the twentieth century have arisen, every time, against the universal dispossession embodied in the expansion of capitalist relations and the destruction of the previous human world of personal relations; against the transformation of every use value into an exchange value; against the commodification of every human relationship.

From this angle, if we harken to the imaginary of their protagonists rather than of their leaders, these revolutions resemble the vision of Walter Benjamin: "Marx says that revolutions are the locomotive of world history. But perhaps it is quite otherwise. Perhaps revolutions are an attempt by the passengers on this train—namely, the human race—to activate the emergency brake."[6]

This by no means entails a return to the past. Those who rebel seek to avenge the oppression of generations gone by but also to burst violently into a future of their own, something they can only imagine or glimpse as one of the forms of hope built from the memories of those generations. "What is at stake is not conservation of the past but the fulfillment of past hopes," write Max Horkheimer and Theodor W. Adorno in their 1944 preface to *Dialectic of Enlightenment*.[7]

Every social relation of domination and subordination encloses, as

---

5   Benjamin, "Theses on the Philosophy of History," in *Illuminations: Essays and Reflections*, ed. and with an introduction by Hannah Arendt, trans. Harry Zohn (New York: Schocken Books, 1969), p. 260.

6   Walter Benjamin, "Paralipomena to 'On the Concept of History,'" in *Selected Writings, Vol. 4: 1938–1940*, trans. Edmund Jephcott et al. (Cambridge, MA: Belknap Press, [1940] 2003), p. 402.

7   Max Horkheimer and Theodor Adorno, *Dialectic of Enlightenment: Philosophical Fragments*, trans. Edmund Jephcott (Stanford: Stanford University Press, 2002), p. xvii.

the two words indicate, two active components, each of which recognizes the other as its counterpart. Hence it is an active relationship. The element that denotes this activity is the resistance of the dominated, the vital name of the constant, multiform, and shifting friction between the two components of the relationship.

This resistance takes certain forms in the agrarian societies in which domination appears in the form of ties of personal dependency, visible and acknowledged by all. In modern society—the society of capital, the society of self-valorizing value—dominance presents itself disguised as a relation between individuals who are free and equal before the law and property, in a community whose interactions are mediated by money and where exchange value subordinates and subsumes use value, not as the stuff of a flourishing life but as mere material support for its instantaneous and ceaseless digital transfigurations. In his *City of Quartz*, Mike Davis portrays Los Angeles as a prime locus in which these transfigurations of value, outside human control, seem to dictate the norms of life.[8]

Each of these forms of dominance and subordination corresponds to various forms of hegemony (the recognition—always open to challenge —of the legitimacy of dominance under the ideology shared by the illusory community) and to various forms of the spontaneity and organization of resistance.

Now, only in exceptional circumstances will this resistance culminate in a rebellion or revolution aimed at breaking, provisionally or definitively, the prevailing social ties. In most cases, resistance devolves—with more or less lucidity on both sides—into a negotiation of rule and of its rules, of the accepted forms of legitimacy, and, less perceptible at times but always present, of the extraction and allocation of surplus product (tribute, rents, taxes, prices, profits, surplus value).

So, we have a relation, *dominance* and *subordination* (under the forms of legitimacy and hegemony), and a friction that is consubstantial to its existence, *resistance*, from which two variables emerge: 1) *negotiation* in normal times; 2) *revolution* in exceptional times.

3.

Revolution does not mean explosion or conspiracy, even if these may count among its attributes in some cases. Revolution means, above all,

---

8   Mike Davis, *City of Quartz: Excavating the Future in Los Angeles* (London: Verso, 1990).

organization and mobilization. The elemental forms of this organization are not defined by the parties or the elites who direct the movement. They exist already in the everyday activities of the people, in its social life. These forms are nourished by already-existing realities and organized activities. They are rooted in the ancient bonds of solidarity among the oppressed (almost merged with everyday life, though far from being its sole component) and in the ancestral yearning for justice, which is usually the same as their religious beliefs. In light of the accounts of its protagonists, the indigenous uprising in Chiapas that began in 1994 is a typical case of the above.[9]

The historiography of revolutionary elites has almost invariably left to one side—has literally not registered—this "autonomous domain" of the politics of the subaltern, whether in national or social revolutions; or else it has taken for granted that the politics of the elite leadership is the conscious reflection of the unconscious movement of the masses.

A rebellion supposes a common imaginary among those who rebel. This imaginary does not derive from the theories or programs of educated elites; rather, the elites can only occupy that rank in a rebellion or a revolution if they are capable of perceiving and understanding this historically sedimented imaginary and of making their own ideas and visions regarding the reorganization of society—whether religious or political or utopian—resonate with it. An implicit dialogue is underway here, too, a process of negotiation and creation in the incandescent intellectual and spiritual activity proper to a revolution; it is not the adaptation of some ideas to others. Thus is shaped the particular and innovative discourse of each revolution or dissenting movement, simultaneously old and new and shared by all: no to the conservation of the past, yes to the fulfillment of past hopes in the novelty of a revolution, its discourses and deeds.

The notion of the fulfillment or redemption of hopes, in this thinking, does not entail the advent of a redeemer so much as the arrival of a time of redemption (the still-not-arrived) as the achievement of the subaltern and the oppressed themselves. This suggests that in the relation of resistance—an active one by definition—a certain vision is generated and entertained (a perception, an unperceived imagination) of a possible overcoming/erasure of the domination that extreme resistance denies,

9   See, for example, "Historia de Marcos y de los hombres de la noche," interview with Subcomandante Marcos by Carmen Castillo and Tessa Brisac, October 24, 1994, in Adolfo Gilly, Subcomandante Marcos, and Carlo Ginzburg, *Discusión sobre la historia* (Mexico City: Taurus, 1995).

without managing to suppress it; the practical and unexpressed utopia of a "topsy-turvy world" that fuels explicit protests, angry interjections, and smothered discourses alike.

In the Marxist theoretical universe, one of the most acute observers was Rosa Luxemburg as she surveyed this difference between revolutionary elites and the people who sustain those elites while at the same time quite naturally conserving their own ambit and everyday forms of communicating, reflecting, coming to agreement, deciding, and doing. In the second half of the twentieth century, Frantz Fanon undertook his own foray into those two domains, which are superimposed but not merged in times of revolutionary mobilization, while distinct and separate in times of retreat.[10]

In India, Ranajit Guha has rebutted the representation of Indian nationalism as an enterprise in which the indigenous elite guides the people "from subjugation to freedom." This representation is essentially the same mechanism as that which underpins the various official narratives, including some on the left, of the Mexican Revolution and its aftermath under Cárdenas. "What, however, historical writing of this kind cannot do," says Guha, "is to explain Indian nationalism for us. For it fails to acknowledge, far less interpret, the contribution made by the people *on their own*, that is, *independently of the elite* to the making and development of this nationalism." Indeed, "What clearly is left out of this un-historical historiography is the *politics of the people*."[11]

Apart from the politics of the nationalist elite, Guha continues, there was during the colonial period another domain of Indian politics in which the "principal actors" were neither the dominant groups of indigenous society nor the colonial authorities,

> but the subaltern classes and groups constituting the mass of the labouring population and the intermediate strata in town and country—that is, the people. This was an autonomous domain, for it neither originated from elite politics nor did its existence depend on the latter. It was traditional only insofar as its roots could be traced back to pre-colonial times, but it was by no means archaic in the sense of being outmoded. . . . As

10   Frantz Fanon, *A Dying Colonialism*, trans. Haakon Chevalier (New York: Grove, [1959] 1965); *The Wretched of the Earth*, trans. Constance Farrington (New York: Grove, [1961] 1963).
11   Ranajit Guha, "On Some Aspects of the Historiography of Colonial India," in Ranajit Guha, ed., *Subaltern Studies No. 1: Writings on South Asian History and Society* (Delhi: Oxford University Press, [1982] 1996), pp. 3–4.

modern as indigenous elite politics, it was distinguished by its relatively greater depth in time as well as in structure.[12]

In elite politics, mobilization was achieved vertically, whereas the horizontal dimension pertained to the domain of subaltern politics. The first relied in the main on colonial or pre-colonial political institutions; the second "relied rather more on the traditional organization of kinship and territoriality or on class associations depending on the level of the consciousness of the people involved."

> Elite mobilization tended to be relatively more legalistic and constitutionalist in orientation, subaltern mobilization relatively more violent. The former was, on the whole, more cautious and controlled, the latter more spontaneous. Popular mobilization in the colonial period was realized in its most comprehensive form in peasant uprisings. However, in many historic instances involving large masses of the working people and petty bourgeoisie, in the urban areas, too, the figure of mobilization derived directly from the paradigm of peasant insurgency.[13]

This traditional model of organization tends, in turn, to set up its own command structures in line with the same rules of kinship and family or clan networks, whence there finally emerges the simultaneously protective and menacing figure of the cacique, ataman, or godfather—a virtually indispensable mediator when it comes to negotiations of an agrarian society with urban state institutionalism. Prestigious or prominent members of left-wing parties often constitute a milder replica of these sorts of authority, wielded via mediation, influence, or personal and familial authority.

Once a movement has passed its peak, elite politics are apt to deflect the mobilization of subalterns toward the institutional terrain of elections, in other words, the existing state apparatus. At the same time, this is the terrain of legitimization of elite politics and of its bearers as the institutionalized leaders of the subaltern classes and groups, whether leaning on these to bolster their rule or forming an opposition that aspires to replace the ruling group within existing political institutions. It is not, therefore, a matter of new relations of dominance (a new state form) but of modifying the existing relation as the result of subaltern mobilizations.

12 Ibid., p. 4.
13 Ibid., pp. 4–5.

Where do the ideas proceed from, the imaginary, the traditions of these movements of the lowly? According to Guha,

> the ideology operative in this domain, taken as a whole, reflected the diversity of its social composition with the outlook of its leading elements dominating that of the others at any particular time and within any particular event. However, in spite of such diversity one of its invariant features was a notion of resistance to elite domination. This followed from the subalternity common to all the social constituents of this domain.[14]

In the case of subaltern classes, "the experience of exploitation and labor endowed this politics with many idioms, norms, and values which put it in a category apart from elite politics." Guha points out that these distinctive features of the politics of the people do not, of course, always appear in a pure state, nevertheless they help to demarcate the domain of subaltern politics from that of elite politics.

We may find these common features in the most diverse and, at times, apparently incompatible movements of subaltern resistance to the new modernity of capital known as globalization. It is there, perhaps, and not in the movement of capital itself under globalization, that the similarities reside in which those subaltern movements are able to recognize one another, despite their clearly different outward traits.

As ever in history, the available communication technology (successively: printing, telegraph, telephone, radio, video, internet), properly utilized, can *boost* the repercussions of those movements and have a bearing on their outcome, but it can never *replace* their materiality. The real terrain of struggle, organization, and strength in the face of the adversary is what it always was: the social, corporeal, and spiritual reality of human beings, the reality which is created and recreated in the infinite weave of their daily lives and dreams. The uprising of the EZLN and the indigenous Zapatistas has reminded us of this truth once more. The technological, "rational" toolbox of the dominators is much more easily assimilated by an elite stratum of the dominated than are the "hidden" organizational customs of the dominated by the dominant elites.

But without that reality, the internet is a useless tool; or else it will serve, as has happened more than once with other communications

14   Ibid., p. 5.

technologies, the elites of both domains as an instrument for settling their own disputes. Indeed, amid the excitement aroused by the genuine possibility of deploying these new tools in support of mobilizations and rebellions, it should not be forgotten that they are no less newly at the disposal of the dominant, the possessors of money, power, information, communications, and arms. It is not there but in the opposing domain that "the birth of our power," in the words of Victor Serge, will be found.[15]

4.

Early in the twentieth century, at the height of the Belle Époque, Rosa Luxemburg (in *The Accumulation of Capital*, 1913) cast a penetrating eye on what was taking place in plain view of all—theorists, analysts, writers, and researchers: the relentless worldwide struggle of capital against the natural economy (peasant communities, feudal powers, ties of personal dependency, any non-capitalist social spaces), against the simple commodity economy (craftsmen and independent producers), and between the various capitals. Colonial military violence, credit and fiscal pressures, and cheap goods were the weapons in this merciless war waged in the colonies and in those parts of Europe where spaces of natural economy persisted.[16] For the sake of its own valorization and reproduction, capital needed to accelerate the "liberation" of the natural resources and labor power locked up in those hermetic spaces

---

15   Victor Serge, *Birth of Our Power*, trans. Richard Greeman (Oakland: PM Press, [1931] 2014).

16   The movement for enclosure of common lands, by hedging or fencing, began in England in the twelfth century and was virtually complete by the end of the nineteenth, according to the *Encyclopaedia Britannica*. "In the rest of Europe, enclosure made little progress until the nineteenth century. Agreements to enclose were not unknown in Germany in the sixteenth century, but it was not until the second half of the eighteenth century that the government began to issue decrees encouraging enclosure. Even then, little advance was made in western Germany until after 1850. The same policy of encouragement by decree was followed in France and Denmark from the second half of the eighteenth century, in Russia after the emancipation of the serfs (1861), and in Czechoslovakia and Poland after World War I." ("Enclosure," *Encyclopaedia Britannica*, February 25, 2013, britannica.com, accessed 11 March 2022.)

Many regions saw a parallel process of marginalization and suppression of local languages in favor of linguistic unification in the tongue of the dominant nation-state: just as the official language is the vehicle of rule and of commercial and cultural exchanges in the space of the nation-state, so, too, are regional languages often the idiom of conspiracy or of the "hidden discourses" of the oppressed.

and so "prevented" from taking part in the cycle of value. Just like in the centuries-long process of land enclosure, dispossession by actual or potential violence was, and still is, the instrument of choice.

Rosa Luxemburg, seeing the entire twentieth century encapsulated in its first decade, considered that "any hope to restrict the accumulation of capital exclusively to 'peaceful competition,' i.e., to regular commodity exchange such as takes place between capitalist producer-countries," was mere illusion:

> Accumulation, with its spasmodic expansion, can no more wait for, and be content with, a natural internal disintegration of non-capitalist formations and their transition to commodity economy, than it can wait for, and be content with, the natural increase of the working population. Force is the only solution open to capital; the accumulation of capital, seen as an historical process, employs force as a permanent weapon, not only at its genesis, but further on down to the present day. From the point of view of the primitive societies involved, it is a matter of life or death; for them there can be no other attitude than opposition and fight to the finish—complete exhaustion and extinction. Hence permanent occupation of the colonies by the military, native risings, and punitive expeditions are the order of the day for any colonial regime. The method of violence, then, is the immediate consequence of the clash between capitalism and the organisations of a natural economy which would restrict accumulation.[17]

"Indian masses in the second half of the nineteenth century did not die of hunger because they were exploited by Lancashire; they perished in large numbers because the Indian village community had been demolished," wrote Karl Polanyi in 1944.[18] This second half of the nineteenth century, the age of the great colonial expansion in Asia, Africa, and the

---

17   Rosa Luxemburg, *The Accumulation of Capital*, trans. Agnes Schwarzschild (London and New York: Routledge Classics, 2003), p. 351.

18   Karl Polanyi, *The Great Transformation* (Boston: Beacon, 1944), p. 160. Polanyi highlights the process of destruction of a natural economy by the violent imposition of capitalist markets: "The catastrophe of the native community is a direct result of the rapid and violent disruption of the basic institutions of the victim (whether force is used in the process or not does not seem altogether relevant). These institutions are disrupted by the very fact that a market economy is forced upon an entirely differently organized community; labor and land are made into commodities, which, again, is only a short formula for the liquidation of every and any cultural institution in an organic society." (As quoted in Mike Davis, *Late Victorian Holocausts* [London: Verso Books, 2001], p. 10.)

Middle East, of the conquest of the West in the US, and the penetration of modern capitalism in Latin American countries; the cruel age of colonial armies (external and internal), of the massacres of indigenous peoples, of the expansion of rail networks to carry soldiers, goods, and the capitalist market; the age of the enclosure and violent expropriation of communal lands across the ancient, vast swathes of the natural economy—this age inflicted hundreds of millions of deaths by arms and by hunger, as well as ecological and natural disasters on an unfathomable scale.[19]

This unbounded violence whereby capitalism achieves global expansion, while it did not escape the notice of the likes of Georges Sorel, went unremarked by many European socialists and Marxists. This may explain their indifference or remoteness toward a great revolution such as Mexico's—even as it attracted the attention of anarchists in the US, Latin America, and Spain.[20] Jean-Marie Vincent points out a "particularly deficient reflection on the problems of violence" among almost all the socialist tendencies during those years:

> The appearance of normality taken on by capitalist society in Europe has blinded many Marxists to the scope for violence hidden behind the mask. They were unwilling to see that violence against the other is inscribed into social relations and the everyday confrontations between individuals. Nor did they see that the legality to which states adhere in their repressive policies is ambiguous. The rule of law is a step forward compared to the arbitrariness of absolutist policies. At the same time, it provides a means of branding and criminalizing one sector of society in order to reassure the dominant classes and flatter their sense of superiority. Even more astonishingly, scarcely any account is taken of colonization with its numberless massacres and the devastation it causes over great expanses of the planet. A sizable contingent of revisionists was even convinced of the civilizing mission of colonialism and unmoved by the racist conduct of the colonizers. The radical left that rejects colonialism and imperialism has often tended to minimize their importance

---

19   Including at the hands of the dispossessed: In 1880 in Algeria, in the Sétif region, the cradle of the rebellion of May 8, 1945, which prefigured the Algerian revolution, the locals set fire to the woods that had been confiscated by the colonial state and given to French settlers. See Yves Benot, *Massacres coloniaux* (Paris: La Découverte, 2001), p. 19.

20   It is worth recalling here that ever since the late nineteenth century, the artisans' and workers' organizations founded by anarchists and anarcho-syndicalists in Argentina and Uruguay were known as Sociedades de Resistencia, the latter term being of long-standing currency and not a present-day discovery.

(an exception being Rosa Luxemburg). The arms race in Europe and the recurrent international crises among the great imperial powers are, admittedly, a concern for many socialists, but they believe they can avert the danger with pacifist campaigns and appeals to the rulers' good sense with suggestions for compromise. They refuse to even imagine that the world could be plunged into barbarism and an orgy of violence.[21]

And yet that was the terminus of the pomp and glories of the Belle Epoque, its *douceur de vivre* and deluxe train journeys like those extolled in the peerless "Ode" by Valery Larbaud:

> Prête-moi ton grand bruit, ta grande allure si douce,
> Ton glissement nocturne à travers l'Europe illuminée,
> *Ô train de luxe*! Et l'angoissante musique
> Qui bruit le long de tes couloirs de cuir doré,
> Tandis que derrière les portes laquées, aux loquets de cuivre lourd,
> Dorment les millionnaires . . .
>
> J'ai senti pour la première fois toute la douceur de vivre
> Dans une cabine du Nord-Express, entre Wirballen et Pskow.
> On glissait à travers des prairies où des bergers,
> Au pied de groupes de grands arbres pareils à des collines,
> *Étaient vêtus de peaux de mouton crues et sales* . . .
> (Huit heures du matin en automne, et la belle cantatrice
> Aux yeux violets chantait dans la cabine à côté.)[22]

21   Jean-Marie Vincent, *Un autre Marx: Après les marxismes* (Lausanne: Page Deux, 2001), p. 16.

22   "Lend me your great sound, your great and gentle motion, / Your nighttime glide across illuminated Europe, / O deluxe train! and the heartbreaking music / Sounding along your gilt leather corridors, / While behind lacquered doors with latches of heavy brass / Sleep the millionaires [. . .] / For the first time I felt all the sweetness of living / In a Northern Express compartment, between Wirballen and Pskov. / We slipped across meadows where shepherds / Under clumps of big trees that looked like hills / Were dressed in uncured, dirty sheepskins . . . / (Eight o'clock of an autumn morning, and the beautiful soprano / With violet eyes was singing in the next compartment.)" Valery Larbaud, "Ode," in Michel Décaudin, ed., *Anthologie de la poésie française du XXe siècle* (Paris: Gallimard, 1983), pp. 196–97; English trans. Ron Padgett and Bill Zavatsky, *Alligatorzine* 54, 2008, alligatorzine.be (accessed March 11, 2022).

For the opposite camp, these were times of anarchism. One day in 1893, Pietro Rigosi, a stoker from Bologna, hailed in the 1972 song "La loco-motiva" by Francesco Guccini, could not restrain his ire and smashed his locomotive full speed into a high-class train, "a train full of gentlemen." I don't know why he did it, says the Italian singer-songwriter; "perhaps some ancient rage, nameless generations crying for revenge, blinded his heart." The lyrics seem like a distant echo of Walter Benjamin's reasoning. A few years later, Europe's *douceur de vivre* and the two counterposed forms of violence—luxury above, rage below—would all meet their end in a gigantic bonfire.

5.

The modern colonial empires—whose creation is chronicled in texts from Joseph Conrad's *Heart of Darkness* to Mike Davis's *Late Victorian Holocausts*—were founded on slaughters more horrendous than those of World War I and II put together. Those two terrible wars over the carve-up of colonial booty and world markets, in whose preparation and execution further tens of millions perished, including the victims of Nazi extermination camps and Stalinist concentration camps, were in a sense the culmination of those colonial bloodbaths through which the disputed booty was amassed.

Following the first great victorious revolutions of the twentieth century—Mexico in 1910, China in 1911, Russia in 1917—there rose a tide of rural, peasant-based rebellions destined to undermine and sweep away, along with the Belle Epoque, the colonial empires of the nineteenth century. World War II heralded the end of the British, French, Dutch, Belgian, German, Italian, Japanese, Spanish, and Portuguese empires. The tipping point likely occurred between 1948 and 1949, with the British withdrawal from India and the victory of the Chinese Revolution. Through the second half of the twentieth century, the wave of colonial and agrarian revolutions defeated the imperial armies of France, Japan, Portugal, and the United States, and instituted new nation-states. Nation-alist elites in these states were compelled to make pacts with the forces of resistance and rebellion that had lifted them to power, to accept detours to and alter the pace of the centuries-long process of the destruction of natural economies and expansion of monetary relations. However, sub-scribing to the common denominator of ideologies of progress, they did not consider a change of direction, and indeed, it would not have been in their power to do so.

Seen from this viewpoint, the so-called Cold War (1946–91) looks nothing like the official version of a long, defensive struggle by the US against oppressive, dictatorial regimes, which supposedly concluded in the last decade of the twentieth century with the collapse of the Evil Empire and the triumph of democracy. To the contrary, it was a war of the capitalist world—led by its military, industrial, and financial center, the United States—against the social, nationalist, and colonial revolutions of all five continents, aimed at subordinating or toppling their expressions as states. The triumph was that of the empire of exchange value and its quest to invade and conquer the most recondite corners of life.[23] This meant dismantling or fragmenting the pacts that had been imposed on states by popular movements from below—whether in "communist" or Keynesian forms—as dikes, provisional after all, against the tide of exchange value. It must be noted that these states, having embraced the ideology of technical and scientific progress, themselves participated in the dismantling of natural economies. Once a new level of accumulation and subsumption of knowledge to capital had been reached, the way was paved for the next expansive wave of capital that arrived during the 1990s.

Today—backed by a military violence which is sometimes visible, more often invisible, but always present and watchful—it is the violence of money that, with all the speed and ubiquity enabled by contemporary technologies, is pursuing the project, namely: commodification of society's every realm and interstice; incorporation of all concrete labor as abstract labor into the process of the valorization of value; and extermination by destitution or war of any who resist dispossession or fail to become part of the universal valorization of capital, whether as peoples, ethnic groups, cultures, or individuals.

Globalization is nothing other than a fresh exacerbation of this universal despoilment, the latest onslaught by the owners of money, power,

---

23 Bolívar Echeverría summarizes what he calls "the nucleus of Marx's discourse" as follows: "At the basis of modern life is a mechanism acting with tireless repetition to subordinate in systematic fashion the 'logic of use value,' the spontaneous sentiment of concrete life and of human labor and enjoyment, the production and consumption of 'earthly goods,' to the abstract 'logic' of 'value' as a substance that is blind and indifferent to any quality of 'exchange value.' Such is the implacable reality of alienation, the subjection of the realm of human will to the hegemony of the purely 'thingly' 'will' of the world of commodities inhabited by capitalist economic value." (Bolívar Echeverría, *Valor de uso y utopía* [Mexico City: Siglo XXI, 1998], p. 63.)

and knowledge, who are also, therefore, the proprietors of technology and arms, in order to enlist the two sources of all wealth—nature and human labor—into the seemingly limitless world of capital, without exceptions or reservations. (Nevertheless, the limits of this world, as Luxemburg discerned, are implicit in the capital relation itself and in the ceaseless resistance and rebellion of living labor against the tyranny of dead labor, but that is a topic for another time.)

With the restructuring of capitalism that began in the 1970s and accelerated in the 1990s (that is, through the last quarter of the twentieth century), this onslaught broke down the defensive and protective barriers raised by the oppressed, their revolts and their organizations, over the first three-quarters of the century. The tide of 1968 and the defeat of the US in Vietnam—a singular event for the twentieth century and unique in the military annals of the United States—combined with the faltering of the long surge of global economic expansion to step up the offensive against the gains achieved by the workers of Western Europe and the US, on the technological (digital), juridical, political, and social levels.

The military victory of the Vietnamese Revolution, with logistical support from the Soviet Union and China, sounded the final alarm. The subsequent expansion of the US military-industrial complex, with its many ramifications and by-products for science and technology, would supply the torque force required to ensure the exhaustion and fall of the Soviet Union in the global Cold War competition.

In 1975, the Group of Seven (G7) was set up and the process of valorization of capital in these central countries embarked on a new phase, departing from the regulatory framework established at the end of World War II. That offensive on the terrain of the great capitalist powers was the indispensable prologue to the next phase of the deregulated global expansion of capital, now called globalization, and to the consequent "unsustainable poverty of the world" we live in today.[24]

The intoxicated gaze of the financial commanders over this world can only be compared to the drunken binge of the Belle Epoque that succeeded the Paris Commune, amid ongoing colonial looting: the spree that ended with the killing fields of World War I and the ensuing era of wars and revolutions.

24 Richard Poulin and Pierre Salama, eds., *L'insoutenable misère du monde: Économie et sociologie de la pauvreté* (Quebec: Vents d'Ouest, 1998).

6.

Every revolution of the modern age has been assailed by violent pressures and outside interventions because it assumes the modification and recasting of power relations between countries, alongside a threat to the legitimacy and stability of the dominance established inside neighboring countries. Examples would include Mexico (1910), Russia (1917), China (1949), Bolivia (1952), Korea (1953), Vietnam (1954), Algeria (1954), Guatemala (1954), Egypt (1956), Hungary (1956), Cuba (1959), Angola (1961), Guinea-Bissau (1963), Mozambique (1964), Czechoslovakia (1968), Chile (1970), Iran (1979), Nicaragua (1979), El Salvador (1980), and Grenada (1983). The list of external interventions could go on. In this sense, the history of revolutions is also the history of the outside interferences aimed at corralling, disorganizing, and crushing them.

Specific branches of the US military apparatus, such as the CIA, must be counted as part of this external violence, in light of their backing for and sometimes direct intervention in the installation and stabilization of military dictatorships in the Southern Cone (Argentina, Uruguay, Chile, Bolivia), as well as for their wars of extermination on the networks and modes of organization of urban and rural workers, and of any left-wing or democratic culture. In all four countries, such organizations and networks were forcibly eradicated and many of their leaders assassinated during the 1970s and '80s, as were thousands of trade-union organizers and common citizens: tortured, murdered, their bodies disposed of in "death flights" or in mass graves. How can this hideous internal war, supported from outside and encapsulated in "Operation Condor," be excluded from the broader offensive of capitalism in those very years? Similar backing and counsel were on hand, moreover, against the revolutions in Central America during the 1970s and '80s. In Argentina and other countries, French Army officers trained in the colonial wars of Indochina and Algeria lent their services as consultants in torture. They were not the only ones.

In the present era of globalization, this joint deployment of economic and military force (economic pressure, bullying, undercover operations, blockade, and armed intervention) has been institutionalized in practice: see, on the one hand, the steady growth of the North Atlantic Treaty Organization (NATO) and of the military initiatives that go with it; on the other, the role of universal policeman assigned by the UN Security Council to the armed forces of the United States and those of its subordinate powers.

At the end of the year 2000, the Socialist International reaffirmed its support for "the right to 'intervention on humanitarian grounds,' always within the framework of international law, as an integral part of the struggle for democracy and human rights."[25] Who is to define what this right and the "legitimate use of violence" consist of, in order to apply them in every case? The facts show that in the end, whoever holds the firepower decides in which cases and in what ways a military force may exercise that ambiguous "right to intervene." Czechoslovakia in 1968, Afghanistan in 1980, Panama in 1989, and the Gulf War in 1990 are unequivocal examples of this. As for the "monopoly of the legitimate use of physical force" as one of the attributes of a state community, we have come a long way from Max Weber's definition. Rather, an expanding NATO, with or without the blessing of the United Nations, looks the most realistic candidate for holding and legitimating this monopoly on a global scale.

7.

The two great wars of the twentieth century (1914–18 and 1939–45) shattered the existing relations of dominance between nations and rebuilt them along different lines. Globalization does not herald the abolition or dissolution of those relations so much as a new definition of their rules. This new definition rests on the legitimated violence of nations, as embodied in their armies.

In other words, the present form of globalization is unthinkable without the existence of the Pentagon, its military bases, its war industry, its information and communications systems, and its planet-wide arsenal, as the hub of global violence.

The new monopoly, on a global scale, of the exercise of possible physical violence is the ultimate, if not the only, guarantor of the reproduction of the modern "transnational community" of exchange value, whose legitimacy relies on a kind of "community of money" that includes all the participants in the reproduction of value and excludes all the rest as pariahs, barbarians, marginals, surplus to requirements. The classification of certain countries as "rogue states" is the international equivalent of the criminalization of entire sectors of domestic societies (the return of the "dangerous classes").

25 Socialist International Council, "Platform for Global Progress," Maputo, November 10–11, 2000.

At the same time, the relentless, borderless expansion of wage relations, in the conditions imposed by the wholesale devaluation of a workforce that enjoys ever fewer protections on the national level, gives rise to violent and chaotic rehearsals of the inevitable conflict over the value of waged labor set against that of capital.

The current emergence of this kind of society may be classified as an epochal break relative to all preceding ones. As Bolívar Echeverría notes:

> The archaic forms of destructive violence do not disappear, or tend to disappear, in capitalist modernity. On the contrary, they reappear, repurposed, on a doubly propitious terrain: that of a scarcity that no longer has any technical reason to exist and yet, following a "perverse logic," must be reproduced. The history of the proletariat in the eighteenth and nineteenth centuries; of the populations colonized in the nineteenth and twentieth centuries; of the "lumpen" informals or marginals; of "minorities" in terms of race, gender, religion, opinion, etc.; these are tantamount to so many histories of the others/enemies which the "national community," set up by the owners of private property around an accumulation of capital, have "constructed" to assert themselves. "Against the grain"—as Benjamin said that a materialist should narrate history—the dazzling history of capitalist modernity, of its progresses and liberations, would show its darker side; it would have to be related first as a history of oppressions, repressions, and exploitations. A history of the countless holocausts and genocides of all kinds that have proliferated through the centuries of its existence, and most of all in the century which is now about to end.[26]

The violence of capitalist modernity encapsulates and absorbs into itself all preceding manifestations. Concentrating in just one pole the capacity to unleash the power of destruction and extermination, in diffused or focused fashion, it propagates, like a pandemic, through contemporary society—whose natural bonds are increasingly saturated or replaced by the bond of exchange value—an inner violence both verbal and physical, virtual and material, which, like money itself, is gradually becoming the customary and even accepted form of interchange and relation between human beings. It may be that the barbarism of these modern capitalist societies was what Rosa Luxemburg glimpsed—already looming, if still contained—as the possible future when she branded the expansion of capitalist relations into colonial lands as anti-human.

---

26   Echeverría, *Valor de uso y utopía*, p. 116.

8.

The norms governing the relations between nations and between the citizens of one nation-state, enshrined on a formal level after World War II in the Universal Declaration of Human Rights, became obsolete as of 1990.[27] The globalization of the dominance of finance capital meant the imposition and legitimation of new rules for the relations between countries, between capitals, and between capital and labor, applying within each country as much as in the global market, which imposes those norms on national markets.

The predominance of the world market over national markets is nothing new: it has been an intrinsic feature of capital's existence since at least the sixteenth century. What is new is the tearing down of the defensive barriers, always relative and porous, that had been erected against this predominance: for example, the state monopoly on foreign trade that was decreed by the Russian Revolution from the outset, or the various forms of welfare state that arose after World War II.

The globalization in force today recognizes neither barriers, borders, nor limits. One of its great feats is to draw into the market, slowly but surely and for the first time in history, the vast territorial expanses of Russia and the boundless reserves of human labor in China. Another is the ongoing expropriation and commodification of genetic codes and the biological reproduction of the natural world, like some crazed culmination of the centuries-long process of the enclosure of common lands.

We stand before an epochal mutation. On both international and national stages, it is also known as "deregulation." Looking out from this early moment in the new modernity of capital, it is difficult to discern what lies beyond the horizon, although history, theory, and reason allow us to hazard a guess.

The new dominance of capital exacerbates rather than eliminates competition between capitals, especially between the various financial concentrations that rule the capital markets. This competition now spans the whole surface of the planet. In the history of capital, such periodic and recurrent conflicts have been resolved time and again through war.

27   Universal Declaration of Human Rights: "Everyone has the right to a standard of living adequate for the health and well-being of himself and of his family, including food, clothing, housing and medical care and necessary social services" (Article 25); "Everyone, as a member of society, has the right to social security" (Article 22); "Everyone has the right to work . . . and to protection against unemployment" (Article 23); "Everyone has the right to education" (Article 26). (United Nations, "Universal Declaration of Human Rights," December 10, 1948, available at ohchr.org/EN/UDHR.)

There is no reason to think that weapons of mass destruction and new technologies have changed the terms of the relationship between capital, military industry, and war, as is confirmed by the new anti-ballistic space shield created by the United States.

9.

Just as violence is inherent to the competition between the various capitals, resistance is a necessary corollary of the ascendancy of capital over human beings. From the resistance of living work within capital relations, to the resistances of the plentiful enclaves of human societies attached to material and spiritual forms of natural economy, enclaves which still persist beneath the worldwide dominance of capital, forces exist to prevent the abstract logic of self-valorizing value from seizing control of human wills and lives down to the last iota, as would be its vocation.

Now that the organizational materializations of resistance erected over the course of the twentieth century have been smashed or dismantled, it does not follow that the human experience of resisting and organizing has equally vanished—whether to think and imagine another world, or to negotiate time and again the forms of this new domination if it cannot be changed, or to rebel against it when its inevitable future fractures permit. That has been the constant feature of every insurgency of the subaltern and the oppressed, and again, there is no reason to suppose that this way of being and existing as human beings in relation to the domination exercised over them has vanished into thin air. Only dead labor can exist without resisting, and while it does not think, or organize, or instigate revolt, it does not produce surplus value, either.

All resistance to domination on the part of subaltern classes, groups, and communities is a relation that by definition implies violence on both sides, to different degrees but always real. In what organizational forms this ever-present, inevitable resistance will come to be condensed is something that only the experience of the new domination can fully reveal. Whatever those forms turn out to be, the human condition dictates that here, too, no prior experience will go to waste.

Under globalization, new relations are emerging between dominance, resistance, and violence. Hence globalization carries the seed of new wars and revolutions in which violence, as the ultimate reason, will redefine those relations. In the current state of human affairs, any other supposition belongs to the realm of fantasy.

16

Lawless Planet

(2007)

The tradition of the oppressed teaches us that the "state of emergency" in which we live is not the exception but the rule.
Walter Benjamin, "Theses on the Philosophy of History"

How slow life is,
How violent Hope.
Guillaume Apollinaire, "Le pont Mirabeau"

What came to be called "populism" in Latin America following World War II consisted in political alliances between nationalist leaders and popular social movements of peasants and workers. These alliances, resting on various forms of popular organization and mobilization from below, yielded three main results:

a) A new regulation of the relations between capital and labor, a previously nonexistent legal net protecting the rights and incomes of the workers: wages and salaries, health care, vacation time, stable employment, collective bargaining, and worker representation in the workplace. That is, a new generation of workers' rights and the consequent broadening of citizenship.
b) A new relationship between the national state and foreign powers.
c) A tide of organizing by workers, campesinos, and the people, a new

feeling and new practice of solidarity, and an assertion of the respect due to all, which also goes by the name of dignity.

These legal and organizational rights were the material expression of the immaterial inheritance of long decades of struggle on the part of workers, peasants, and peoples, indigenous and Black, during the tough times of the first half of the twentieth century; and not only of those struggles but also and above all of the most hidden and universal experiences of their everyday lives, the realm—invisible from without—of the social and political life proper to subaltern populations.

This world was by no means a paradise. But its novelty brought with it a certain charge of hope for the next generations: it was possible to imagine a secure job, education, health care, housing, and leisure as a social future available to all.

This can be called "populism" if we look at what the ruling nationalist elites were thinking and doing then. But if our gaze and feeling start from what the subaltern groups and classes were doing and undergoing, from the point of view of their experiences and thoughts, then another name is called for.

Now all this lies in the past. A whole world has been destroyed. Today, just as at the end of the nineteenth century, we have embarked once more upon an age of violence and dispossession. This age was inaugurated by a merciless state violence designed to open the way, both material and human, to the "deregulated global market." This was pioneered in Chile and for all Latin America by Pinochet and Kissinger, with the military coup of September 11, 1973. So began the lawless planet of our present day.

Much more than an "economic model," neoliberalism is a form of domination, dispossession, and private seizure of both the social surplus product and the social patrimony, based on a subordination of knowledge to capital that far exceeds anything previously imagined.

What is happening can also be seen as a new historical phase of the worldwide appropriation of common goods, the privatization of what once belonged to everyone, the redistribution of land rents and of the surplus value generated by living labor. To use more abstract terms, we are facing a new and far more concentrated form of the domination of past labor—crystallized in instruments of production and in knowledge subsumed into capital—over present, living labor, over that substance which constitutes the life of us human beings scattered about the world.

This form of dominance is sustained by an unprecedented concentration of violence and of knowledge placed at the disposal of that violence.

In various Latin American societies—Mexico, Brazil, Argentina, Chile, Uruguay, Bolivia, and others—successive generations had built, transmitted, and expanded a social patrimony of public services, national property, public education, and protected natural resources which, however insufficient, belonged to the national community. These national "public savings" and "public investments" that had been passed down from generation to generation were dismantled during the 1990s, their ownership transferred, sold for a song to the old and new owners of wealth and power.

Neoliberal deregulation has, moreover, left helpless those who built up this patrimony, for they are now subject to the competition between the mass of wage earners in the global market and to the devaluation of their labor. At the same time, the number of informal wage earners, with their families, their relationships, their urban or semi-urban environments, has never been so high: more than a billion around the world, according to Mike Davis's estimate in *Planet of Slums*.[1]

The political expression that will emerge from this turbulent social upheaval which is still underway in Latin America cannot be called "populism" nor even "radical populism." Its historical precedents should rather be sought in the traditions of Jacobinism, of revolutionary syndicalism, of the popular urban uprisings and agrarian revolutions that marked the end of the Belle Epoque, or in Mexico, the era of Don Porfirio [Díaz]. But its hazy features will require time, suffering, and fighting before they take a precise form. Any rush to classification will only muddle the issues.

Neoliberalism has given rise to a new breed of impoverished, displaced, and informal workers, alongside men and women in precarious employment and lacking the qualifications to enter the restricted and fast-changing formal job market: they include migrants, itinerants, the underemployed, vendors, scavengers, and odd-job workers, both adults and children.

This violent uprooting and shuffling together of the Latin American workforce and subaltern classes is a brutal and irreversible process unleashed in shanties and villages, in insecure, lawless suburbs

---

1 Mike Davis, *Planet of Slums* (London and New York: Verso, 2006), p. 178.

surrounding urban centers and places of employment across the territory. This is in no sense whatsoever a process of deindustrialization or marginalization. On the contrary, it is the high road of the new industrialization, from Latin America to Eastern Europe, China, India, Indonesia, and South Africa.

People today have been forced to adapt to unemployment, vulnerability, precarity, homelessness, insufficiency of public services and health care, emigration, insecurity, violence, and hunger. With their unique mixture of experiences, both lived and inherited, such populations come up with fresh forms of organization and struggle. They are not only resisting, as they did in the 1990s; they are fighting back, in a host of original ways and on terrains that have only just become apparent.

Where formal politics are concerned, among the first reflections of the restless state of mind that appeared at the turn of the twenty-first century we find the misnamed "populist" governments—those led by Lula in Brazil, Kirchner in Argentina, Correa in Ecuador, and Tabaré Vázquez in Uruguay—as well as the radical trio of Bolivia, Venezuela, and Cuba in overt defiance of the US. At present, the IMF, World Bank, and international financial hubs are forced to acknowledge these leaders (who are quite different from each other) as mediators legitimated by the votes of the citizenry.

Of course, the global neoliberal order is here to stay. These political changes do not disrupt its domination of the world and its essential bases in each country. They are, however, one more proof of how this order, in the twenty-five years and more since it irrupted, has been unable to claim a stable legitimacy—in contrast to the so-called populist regimes that emerged after World War II.

Latin American subalterns have begun to utilize some of the options of representative democracy: organizing in plain view, mobilizing in legal fashion, protesting, and expressing their views without fear of reprisals. They are also attempting to turn the accepted (if not respected) rules of the political game to their advantage: elections, citizens' political rights, individual human rights.

On the other hand, many erstwhile organizational terrains have vanished or been destroyed by the neoliberal order, while others have moved from a productive context to a territorial one. Examples include the neighborhood committees of El Alto, Bolivia; the *piqueteros* [road blockers] and barrio organizations of Argentina; the Movimento dos Trabalhadores Sem Terra [Landless Workers' Movement] of Brazil; in Mexico, the Juntas de Buen Gobierno [Zapatista Good Governance Councils] in

Chiapas and Alianza Popular de los Pueblos [Popular Peoples' Alliance] in Oaxaca; the local and national indigenous movements in Ecuador and over the whole continent, including the organizations of Mexican and Latin American migrants in the United States; and the many forms of organized indigenous insurgency in Mexico, Bolivia, Ecuador, Peru, and Chile.

This is the subtle link that unites such diverse situations, precedents, and outcomes as those of the rebellions against neoliberal governments that have occurred in three faraway Latin American cities: Buenos Aires, Argentina, 2001; El Alto, Bolivia, 2003 and 2005; Oaxaca, Mexico, 2006.

This Latin American social situation has entered the United States with the unprecedented migrant mobilizations of 2006 and, on the other side, with the repressive tasks assigned to the National Guard and the delirium of building a Great Wall on the border with Mexico.

All this forms part of a turbulent process of delineating political rules and relations, a process itself unfolding under pressure, on the one hand, from the world economy and, on the other, from the Pentagon and the global military apparatus of the United States.

In 2005, the Pentagon had 737 military bases spread like a net over the whole planet. This is the basic material structure of the capitalist global market: deregulated, to be sure, but also under close military surveillance and subject to military initiative. Its long-term subsistence is likewise inconceivable without wars, and, ultimately, without a global war. The issue of war is a paramount theme of any democratic and left-wing project in the US. As on other occasions, it is above all from inside that the emergency brake will finally be pulled on the empire's runaway war machine.

With all their different traditions, intensities, and organizations, the peoples of Latin America are on the march for the recovery and expansion, in new, democratic, and autonomous forms, of lost protective and solidarity networks, as well as for new rights, guarantees, and freedoms. The indigenous uprisings in the lands of the originary civilizations, like the mobilization in their own right of people of African descent in Brazil, Venezuela, and Cuba, form part of this emergent reality.

At the same time, we must not forget that the neoliberal order has its own social pillars, minoritarian perhaps but no less solid for all that.

In its economies, a thick web of interests has aggregated, pertaining to capitals old and new, national and foreign, legal and illegal, formal and informal; so, too, has a social sector made up of technicians, professionals, businesspeople, executives, and experts in new technologies, ready to defend their privileges and mobility to the last ditch while clamoring for the criminalization of social protest. A sizable number of the votes consistently obtained by right-wing parties are cast by these aggressive sectors and their clientele. And it is they who bolster the conservative ideology of the corporate media and neoliberal policies of the governments of Colombia, Peru, Mexico, and a few others.

Nothing was easy before, and nothing will be easy in the future. We have just emerged from the great universal disaster of the 1990s, which fortified and made fiercer the world's rich, whether new or old, and ignited fresh anger in the ancient and modern wretched of the Earth.

Let no one try to tell us that now is the time for hope. Now is the time for fury and rage. Hope invites us to be patient; rage exhorts us to organize. That is how revolution broke out in Bolivia at the beginning of the twenty-first century. That is how other futures can dawn in Latin America.

The so-called populism of some of its governments marks a first, moderate—and significant—response on the level of the existing institutions. But the most important, if still undefined, processes of social insurgency are taking shape in this underworld of the neoliberal order, brimming with action and fury, teeming with the modern victims of exploitation, dispossession, racism, and repression.

There is a time for hope and a time for rage. This is the time for rage. After rage will come hope.

17

The Emerging "Threat" of Radical Populism

(2005)

At a House Armed Services Committee meeting in March 2004, the then-commander of the US Southern Command (SOUTHCOM), Gen. James Hill, made the obligatory mentions of terrorism and narco-trafficking as pressing issues of "hemispheric security." But he also added, "These traditional threats are now complemented by an emerging threat best described as radical populism, in which the democratic process is undermined to decrease rather than protect individual rights."[1]

According to the former SOUTHCOM commander, "Some leaders in the region are tapping into deep-seated frustrations at the failure of democratic reforms to deliver expected goods and services. By tapping into these frustrations, which run concurrently with frustrations caused by social and economic inequality, the leaders are at the same time able to reinforce their radical positions by inflaming anti-US sentiment." As examples, he mentioned Venezuela, Bolivia, and Haiti, but he also pointed to the general questioning of "the validity of neoliberal reforms" expressed in the October 2003 Buenos Aires Consensus signed by Brazil's Luiz Inácio Lula da Silva and Argentina's Néstor Kirchner. The declaration, according to Gen. Hill, "stresses 'respect for poor countries.'" "Populism in and of itself is not a threat," said Gen. Hill. "Rather,

---

1 All the quotes from Gen. James Hill in these opening paragraphs are from "Posture Statement of General James T. Hill, United States Army Commander, United State Southern Command, Before the 108th Congress House Armed Services Committee," March 24, 2004, Washington, DC.

the threat emerges when it becomes radicalized by a leader who increasingly uses his position and support from a segment of the population to infringe gradually upon the rights of all citizens."

What Gen. Hill describes, in effect, is not a reappearance of the post–World War II nationalist-popular movements, commonly labeled "populisms." Instead, this is a new trend, stemming from the effects of neoliberal structural reforms throughout the region in recent decades. Indeed, he is alluding to a phenomenon that is difficult to define when compared to the movements led by Juan Perón in Argentina, the Nationalist Revolutionary Movement (MNR) in Bolivia, Jacobo Árbenz in Guatemala, João "Jango" Goulart in Brazil, and, especially, Fidel Castro in Cuba and Salvador Allende in Chile. The repeated recourse against these governments were military coups or invasions sponsored by the US State Department and the Pentagon, for which Gen. Hill, until recently, served as regional representative and spokesperson.

The only survivor among these is the Cuban movement. It has survived for several reasons, among them that it has not played by the rules of the game. It transformed its national revolution into a social revolution, expropriated the land and money of the oligarchy, and directly challenged imperial power. Significantly, a characteristic shared by the new political subjects Gen. Hill calls "radical populists" is that they all maintain close ties to Cuba—Lula, Kirchner, Chávez, Evo Morales, Tabaré Vázquez, and others. It is doubtful that the general has overlooked this detail, which effectively makes Cuba a bridge between the old epoch and the new.

In this way, from their respective positions, the IMF and the Pentagon —guarantors of capital's world dominance and the hegemony of the United States within that system—are seeking to redefine their relationship with Latin America's new reality. For Gen. Hill, this reality is the "emerging threat." It is important then to consider this situation from another vantage point: from within the social realities generating this "threat."

More than an economic model, neoliberalism is first and foremost a mode of domination on a national and global scale. It is a mode of domination that arose from the restructuring and global expansion of capitalist relations beginning in the 1970s after the US defeat in Vietnam.

This global restructuring, also called globalization, culminated in the 1990s with a frenzy of privatizations (the plundering and private appropriation of the national and public commons); labor flexibilization (the weakening or abolition of legal structures protecting workers); financial and commercial deregulation (the absolute power of financial capital in capitalist relations as well as its unrestricted power over governments); and the incorporation of land and labor from Russia, China, Eastern Europe, and Southeast Asia into an unbridled global marketplace.

Deregulation under neoliberalism unleashed the destruction of the hard-won legal, political, and social protections that were gained by the struggles of workers and societies throughout the twentieth century. Successive generations had constructed, inherited, and augmented these benefits of their shared patrimony with public services, public education, and protected lands and resources. These collective "savings" and "investments," passed on from generation to generation, were left in ruins during the 1990s in Argentina, Bolivia, Brazil, Mexico, and the other countries of the region.

At its most abstract, the neoliberal expansion of capital, unfettered by laws or controls, can be understood as a global process that destroys small businesses, continuously makes technology obsolete and, above all, devalues labor power on a planetary scale. It has incorporated hundreds of millions of new entrants into capitalist labor markets at the same time that it has disqualified and expelled millions more from those same markets. Dislocated workers have been made as obsolete and redundant as the machinery with which they once worked. The crowning achievement of neoliberal deregulation is probably the lawless, unregulated competition of wage earners in the global market and the consequent devaluation of their labor compared to the mass of valuable commodities they produce.

The neoliberal regime creates a new mix of dispossessed, displaced, and informal-sector workers, along with men and women with no stable work and no qualifications to enter the new labor markets—migrants, the uprooted, street vendors, trash pickers. In this new mix there are also children pulled from school and thrown into the world of work, panhandling or illegal activities. The mixing and upheaval of the workforce and the subordinated classes is a brutal and permanent process that takes place in neighborhoods newly situated on the margins of workplaces and urban centers. Moreover, it takes place in the bosom of a population that carries within itself an intangible heritage of know-how, histories, and the shared experiences of "unofficial" narratives.

This is a population forced to adapt to the new reality of unemployment, vulnerability, precariousness, and hunger. With its unique blend of inherited, lost and lived experiences, it emerges not with passivity or individual solitude but with new forms of self-management and self-organization. The principal center of organization today is not production-based but territorial: neighborhood committees in El Alto near La Paz, piqueteros and communal organizations in Argentina, Councils of Good Government in Chiapas, or the Landless Rural Workers' Movement in Brazil.

In the cases of Bolivia and Mexico, the heritage of indigenous communities and the experience of campesinos and miners are clearly visible. In Argentina, the organizational knowledge of the piqueteros, the neighborhood assemblies, and the occupied factories are all part of an inheritance from the direct action of revolutionary unionism, as well as the more recent union movement that led the general strikes at the end of the 1960s and beginning of the 1970s.

The researcher or historian, taking a longer view than the reporter, cannot help but acknowledge the reappearance and the extraordinarily diffuse presence of older traditions and experiences in these new movements, even among those participants who are too young to have lived them but who have nonetheless inherited them as their cultural patrimony.

These movements appropriate the open spaces of freedom of action left by the dismantled corporatist controls of "classical populism" (if we may call it that). The movements also appropriate the supposed "rules of the game": democracy, the political rights of citizens, and the human rights of individuals. The political use of repressive forces against popular movements, though never abandoned, has been rendered "illegitimate" by these rules.

This illegitimacy is no minor detail but a real opening in the new framework of the "permitted," and it has been firmly implanted in the collective imagination. This was evidenced by the way the police and military forces were physically confronted and beaten back during the December 2001 mobilizations in Argentina, and again during the February and October 2003 mobilizations in Bolivia. In both cases, the presidents tried to assert their rule through military force by declaring a state of siege but were nonetheless forced to resign, albeit at the cost of dozens of lives in Argentina and over a hundred in Bolivia. Those spaces of freedom of action exist and persist, above all, because popular and subordinated classes have appropriated them for self-organization.

It is in moments like these that the nearly always invisible politics of the lower classes dispute the dominant institutional politics of representative democracy. They challenge legislators, presidents, judges, leaders, television hosts, "opinion-makers," and the other usual actors of the theater of dominant politics where they are most visible: in public spaces and in the headlines. Lower-class politics is rudimentary and dense; it takes place in the neighborhood, in the community, in places of production. Rarely is it granted the "honor" of being called "politics" by the canonical texts; instead, it is called daily life, conversation, gossip, rumor, local squabbles.

These moments of insurrection are also carriers of the fluid processes inherent in the formation of new legitimacies. Programs and organizations float like skiffs on an unquiet sea, pushed and pulled by opposing and newly discovered currents that are not registered on existing charts. It is a condition that has no fixed and recognizable representation in the public politics of republics. It exists at the intersection of neoliberalism's dismantling of protective structures and the insurrection against this dismantling. In the language of Gen. James Hill, it is an explosion of "deep-seated frustrations."

To borrow a metaphor from the Argentine sociologist Maristella Svampa: now, at the beginning of the twenty-first century, the plazas are again beginning to fill up. What she calls the "emptying of the plaza" describes the profound change under neoliberalism that vacated the symbolic place of encounter between the protector-state and the people; that is, the geographic heart of the nationalist-populism of previous decades: the plaza.[2] Today, the plaza is filled with new protagonists and different social and political subjects still in the process of formation. These multitudes have their own reasons and symbols for mobilizing, but they have no single leader, nor are they in search of one.

In a situation marked by uncertainty and turbulence without clearly set definitions, symbolic actions take on enormous importance for both the privileged and the unprivileged, the rulers and the ruled: removing portraits of repressive Argentine rulers from the halls of power and sending them to the Museum of Memory, challenging the IMF, or maintaining cordial relations with Havana. These are measures that don't alter the substantive dependent relationship of a country with the IMF and its dictates. But they do mark early and provisional attempts to construct a new reality with elements and points of equilibrium that have yet to be specified (and that cannot be specified until they pass through the processes and conflicts of their societies). Nevertheless, the symbolic

2   Maristella Svampa and Sebastián Pereyra, *Entre la ruta y el barrio: La experiencia de las organizaciones piqueteras* (Buenos Aires: Biblos, 2003), p. 202. Also see Maristella Svampa, "Las dimensiones de las nuevas protestas sociales," *El Rodaballo* (Buenos Aires), no. 14, Winter 2002, pp. 26–33.

dimension has an initial importance: it organizes feelings and thoughts, it blocks returns to the past, and it disrupts the trivial terrain of television and the media.

These conflicts and redefinitions will eventually pass into the realm of practice. Then, in one form or another, the hard questions posed by reality will have to be restated and resolved: the fate of natural resources; the fate of privatized common goods and public services; rural issues and agrarian reform. Practical definitions of the forms of societies' organization and the relationship of these organizational forms with state powers will also have to be confronted. This includes the now-inescapable question of broadening and consolidating the rights, guarantees, and ownership inherent in citizenship. The framework and content of negotiations with global capital and its institutions—such as the IMF and the World Bank—will also have to be confronted, as will the configurations of investment and regional trade, like the FTAA, NAFTA, and Mercosur. A redefinition of sovereignty and of each republic's control of its territory will be necessary, given the global power of the United States.

All this is part of a turbulent process of definition and is subject to the inflexible constraints posed by a world economic cycle in contraction. However, the subordinated are no longer caught off-guard by the neoliberal assault, and their fight now focuses on mending or restoring the protective networks woven in difficult struggles that were so quickly destroyed. Although an idealized longing for the past remains alive, many are looking for something else: new rights, guarantees and protections, and new liberties. This intersection is far from having left the stage of politics. In all probability, we are living in an interregnum in which, as always, members of the subordinated classes are putting their bodies and lives at risk to regain and expand their rights, their land, their material and symbolic patrimony.

It is in this interregnum that what I call "unidentified political objects and subjects" appear, or, in the words of the general-cum-sociologist, the "emerging threat of radical populism." But the threat he perceives as coming from the leaders is really the uprising of the subordinated. With their own style of organizing and engaging in politics, with their own imaginations and subjectivities, with their demands, and with their transitory and permanent organizations, their insurrections are once again filling the plazas, the neighborhoods, the streets, and towns. These groups are struggling from the outside, facing in; and from below, facing up.

As Charles Tilly once wrote about popular protest in France, and Javier Auyero echoed with regard to Argentina: "We shall know a new era has begun not when a new elite holds power or a new constitution appears, but when ordinary people begin contending for their interests in new ways."[3]

3   Charles Tilly, *The Contentious French* (Cambridge: Cambridge University Press, 1986), cited in Javier Auyero, *La protesta: Relatos de la beligerancia popular en la Argentina democrática* (Buenos Aires: Libros del Rojas, 2002), p. 11.

Part IV

Politics and Letters

18

Star and Spiral: Octavio Paz, André Breton, and Surrealism

(2014)

> It is impossible to write about André Breton in any other language than that of passion. To him, the powers of the word were no different from the powers of passion, and passion, in its highest and most intense form, was nothing less than language in its wildest, purest state: poetry.[1]

So wrote Octavio Paz in New Delhi on October 5, 1966. On September 28, Breton had died in Paris, aged seventy. This text, memoir or tribute —"André Breton or the Quest of the Beginning"—was also a farewell to the man whose writing and worldview had influenced him more than any others, like an unseen river flowing constantly beneath his poetic oeuvre; as his childhood flowed, too, father Octavio absent but grandfather Irineo present in the old house in Mixcoac. That house was the source of one of the most "Éluardean" of his poems, "Epitaph for No Stone":

---

1 Octavio Paz, "André Breton o la búsqueda del comienzo," *Estrella de tres puntas: André Breton y el surrealismo* (Mexico City: Editorial Vuelta, 1996), pp. 61–77. [Throughout this essay, Gilly cites several Paz texts collected in this volume; where English translations of these essays exist, they are cited in square brackets, as here: Octavio Paz, "André Breton or the Quest of the Beginning," in *Alternating Current*, trans. Helen Lane (New York: Viking Press, 1973), p. 47.]

Mixcoac was my village: three nocturnal syllables,
a half-mask of shadow across a face of sun.
Our Lady, Mother Dustcloud, came,
came and ate it. I went out in the world.
My words were my house, air my tomb.[2]

Ⓡ

Estrella de tres puntas: André Breton y el surrealismo (Three-Pointed Star: André Breton and Surrealism), a slim 130-page volume, was Paz's last book, the end of the spiral of his life and work. This farewell occupies a precise point of equilibrium between, on the one hand, pages devoted to the French poet, the Surrealist, the man of *la tour Saint-Jacques chancelante* [the tottering Saint-Jacques Tower] and the café in Place Blanche, and on the other, his own discovery of love and of poetry. Thinking about Breton, Paz is reminded of his own life:

His affection and generosity always amazed me, from the beginning of our relationship till the very end of his life. I have never known why he was so kind to me. Was it, perhaps, because I was from Mexico, a country he loved all his life? Apart from these personal reasons, I must confess that many times I write as though I were having a silent conversation with Breton: objections, answers, agreement, disagreement, homage, all these things at once. I am experiencing that sensation at this very moment.

In my adolescence, in a period of isolation and great elation, I happened to read a few pages that I found out later are Chapter V of *L'amour fou* [*Mad Love*]. In them, he tells of climbing the volcanic peak of Teide, on Tenerife in the Canary Islands. This text, which I read at almost the same time as *The Marriage of Heaven and Hell*, opened the doors of modern poetry to me. It was an "art of loving," not in the trivial manner of Ovid's *Ars Amatoria* but an initiation to something that my later life and the East have given me further proof of: the analogy, or, rather, the identity between [the loved person] and nature.[3]

(A story I shouldn't be telling now but later will be too late and it will have passed: at much the same period of my own life, around 1946, the

---

2   Octavio Paz, "Epitafio sobre ninguna piedra" / "Epitaph for No Stone," in *The Collected Poems of Octavio Paz, 1957–1987*, ed. and trans. Eliot Weinberger (New York: New Directions, 1987), pp. 550–1.
3   [Paz, "André Breton or the Quest of the Beginning," p. 53.]

young socialist that I was also came across both those books and likewise almost simultaneously: *L'amour fou* by André Breton and *The Marriage of Heaven and Hell* by William Blake. The latter had been published in Mexico by Octavio Paz—I could not know this—in a small, meticulous collection, *El Clavo Ardiendo* [The Burning Nail]. I can still remember the bookstore where I found each book.)

Octavio Paz continued this farewell on two tracks, his voice present in it, the other's absent but still there:

> Is water feminine, or is a woman a succession of waves, a river at night, a beach at dawn tattooed by the wind? If we are a metaphor of the universe, the human couple is the metaphor par excellence, the point of intersection of all forces and the seed of all forms. The couple is time recaptured, the return to the time before time. Against wind and tide, I have endeavored to be faithful to that revelation: the powers the word *love* has over me have remained intact.[4]

◌

Paz reminisces about being taken by Benjamin Péret to meet Breton in that mythic café in Place Blanche:

> I saw Breton frequently over a long period of time. Although spending a great deal of time together sometimes interferes with the interchange of ideas and feelings, I was often aware of that sort of free-flowing current that really unites two people talking together, even if their views are not identical. Among all these conversations, I shall never forget one we had in the summer of 1964, just before I returned to India. I remember it not because it was the last one we ever had but because of the atmosphere surrounding it. This is not the proper place to tell about this meeting. (I have promised myself that someday I will write about it.)[5]

I don't know if he ever did. But I do know, as another clue, that his time in India had opened a new sightline for him on André Breton and his version of Surrealism; and from New Delhi, three years later, he would write his farewell to the poet. That conversation, Paz recalls, "was an *encounter*, in Breton's meaning of the word: predestination and election":

4   [Ibid.]
5   [Ibid., p. 54.]

That night, as the two of us strolled through Les Halles together, the conversation turned to a subject that was worrying him: the future of the Surrealist movement. I remember what I told him, more or less: that to me Surrealism was the sacred malady of our world, like leprosy in the Middle Ages or the state of possession of the Spanish Illuminati in the sixteenth century; since it was a necessary negation in the West, it would remain alive as long as modern civilization remained alive, whatever political systems and ideologies might prevail in the future.[6]

"I have no idea what the future of the Surrealist group will be; I am certain, however, that the current that has flowed from German Romanticism and Blake to Surrealism will not disappear. It will live a life apart; it will be the *other* voice," Paz continued on that October day in 1967, writing down his thoughts on his poet friend, now gone, and on that poet's school of letters and life. Almost exactly one year later, the Tlatelolco massacre of October 2, 1968, would make Paz resign his diplomatic post, return to Mexico, and embark on a tour of the universities of Austin, Pittsburgh, Pennsylvania, and Harvard.

And so, he was really writing about himself and his destiny—which, of course, he could not know—when he posited the predestination of Surrealism: "I have no idea what the future of Ambassador Octavio Paz will be," he might have said, with truth and poetry.

Talking about Breton in this 1966 essay, reprinted in 1996—thirty years later—in *Three-Pointed Star*, Octavio Paz introduces personal memories of the kind that are seldom committed to paper:

[Breton] was one of the centers of gravity of our time. He not only believed that we humans are governed by laws of attraction and repulsion; he himself was the personal incarnation of those forces. I confess that for a long time the thought that I would say or do something that might provoke his reprobation kept me awake nights. I believe that many of his friends felt the same way. A few years ago, Buñuel invited me to a private showing of one of his films. When it was over, he asked me: "Would Breton think it within the Surrealist tradition?" I mention Buñuel not only because he is a great artist but also because he is a man possessed of great moral integrity and freedom of spirit. These feelings have nothing to do with fear or respect for a superior (although I believe that if there is such a thing as superior men, Breton was one of them). I

---

6   [Ibid.]

never considered him a leader, much less a Pope, to repeat the ignoble epithet popularized by certain swine. Despite the fact that we were personal friends, my activities within the Surrealist group were quite tangential.[7]

Paz could well have given to the fervor of those memories the title of a piece by Breton, published in 1924 in *The Lost Steps*: "The Disdainful Confession." This was a key text in the configuration of Surrealism, as Paz said in his lecture at the Museo Tamayo in January 1996 to mark the centenary of the French poet's birth.

"*The other voice*": the romantic enigma of inspiration always preoccupied both Paz and the Surrealists. In *The Bow and the Lyre*, his personal treatise on poetry, Paz had written:

> We know that the "other voice" filters through the holes that the vigilance of attention leaves unattended, but—where does it come from and why does it leave us as suddenly as it comes? Despite the experimental work of surrealism, Breton confessed that "we continue to be as little informed as ever about the origin of this voice." . . .
>
> Here is the poet before the paper. It does not matter whether or not he has a plan, if he has meditated for a long time about what he is going to write, or if his consciousness is as empty and blank as the immaculate paper that alternately attracts and repels him. The act of writing involves, as the first movement, a separating oneself from the world, something like throwing oneself into the void. Now the poet is alone. All that was his everyday world and his usual preoccupations a moment ago, disappears. If the poet truly wishes to write and not to perform a vague literary ceremony, his act leads him to break away from the world and to interdict everything—not excluding himself.[8]

During those same years, another master goldsmith of the poetry trade, the Polish-Lithuanian Czesław Miłosz, in his novel *The Seizure of Power* (1955), gave to the enigma of the writer and his guardian angels an answer between myth and history, in a secret and unwitting dialogue with the answer given by Octavio Paz in *The Bow and the Lyre* (1956):

---

7   [Ibid., p. 53.]
8   [Octavio Paz, *The Bow and the Lyre: The Poem, The Poetic Revelation, Poetry and History*, trans. Ruth Sims (Austin: University of Texas Press, 1973), pp. 156, 159.]

The summer sky was blue, with white clouds, and the darting flight of swallows. In the distance the sound of a brass band mixed with the rattling of streetcars. Gil put the finished pages in order. He straightened them and squared the pile with the palms of his hands. In spite of everything, a man was given a chance to get a little peace. He allotted himself a task and, while performing it, realized that it was meaningless, that it was lost among a mass of human endeavours and strivings. But when a pen hung in air and there was a problem of interpretation or syntax to solve, all those who once, long ago, had applied thought and used language were near us. You touched the delicate tracings warmed by their breath, and communion with them brought peace. Who could be so conceited as to be quite sure that he knew which actions were linked up and complementary; and which would recede into futility and be forgotten, forming no part of the common heritage? But was it not better, instead, to ponder the only important question: how a man could preserve himself from the taint of sadness and indifference.[9]

Objective chance?

In 1991 Paz wrote a prologue to Breton's *Je vois, j'imagine: Poèmes-objets* (I See, I Imagine: Object-Poems), whose first lines seem to express Paz's own attitude to the experience of literature and of life:

There are two, opposite images of André Breton that are nonetheless equally true. One is the intransigent man of negation, the indomitable rebel, *le forçat intraitable* [the intractable convict]; the other is the man of effusion and hugs, alive to the hidden pull of congeniality, a believer in collective action and still more in inspiration as a universal faculty, common to all. His life was a series of separations and breaks but also of encounters and loyalties. Surrealism was a violent movement of severance from the mainstream of Western tradition; it was also a search for other values and other civilizations. The myth of a lost golden age, a paradise once open to everyone, illuminates some of Breton's greatest writings.[10]

9   Czesław Miłosz, *The Seizure of Power*, trans. Celina Wieniewska (London: Abacus, [1955] 1985), pp. 243–4.
10   Octavio Paz, "Poemas mudos y objetos parlantes," in *Estrella de tres puntas*, pp. 90–101.

Might that myth not equally and insistently illuminate some of Paz's greatest writings, from *The Labyrinth of Solitude*, *The Violent Season*, and *Children of the Mire* to *Itinerary* and *Three-Pointed Star*?

"A violent movement of severance from the mainstream of Western tradition": that is how Paz describes Surrealism. But in "The Morning Star" he seems to assert the contrary:

> In Breton, the duality of Surrealism once again manifests itself: it was a subversion, a rupture, yet at the same time it continued the central tradition of the West, that current which periodically seeks to unite poetry and thought, criticism and inspiration, theory and action. In the days of the great moral and political disintegration that preceded World War II, it was exemplary of Breton to proclaim the cardinal place occupied by exclusive love in our lives. No other poetic movement of this century has done so, and therein lies the superiority of Surrealism—not as aesthetic superiority, a spiritual one. [. . .] To lend his support to the idea of exclusive love in the very days of the great erotic liberation that followed World War I was to expose himself to the derision of many; but with courage and intelligence, Breton dared to defy avant-garde opinion. He was not an enemy of the new erotic freedom, but he refused to confuse it with love.[11]

ca

How did Octavio Paz, writer, moralist, and poet, wash up on the shores of the Surrealist movement? Why did he persist to the end in both claiming it for his own and observing it as an alien object? In 1956, he wrote in *The Bow and the Lyre*:

> The most desperate and total attempt to break the siege and make of poetry a common property occurred in the place where objective conditions had become critical: in Europe, after the First World War. Of all the adventures of that period, the most lucid and ambitious was surrealism. To examine it will be to give an account of the pretensions of contemporary poetry, in its most extreme and radical form.[12]

---

11   [Octavio Paz, "The Morning Star," in *The Double Flame: Love and Eroticism*, trans. Helen Lane (New York: Harcourt Brace and Co., 1995), pp. 171–2.]
12   [Paz, *The Bow and the Lyre*, p. 225.]

And in 1954, he affirmed in a lecture at the National Autonomous University of Mexico:

> Thrown back on its own resources, Surrealism continues to insist that the liberation of mankind should be total. In the heart of a society in which masters have truly disappeared, a poetry will arise which will be a collection creation, like the myths of the past. Mankind will then witness the reconciliation of thought and action, of desire and its fruition, of word and thing. Automatic writing will cease to be an aspiration: to speak will be to create.[13]

Paz came back to this idea time and time again, over and over, from the dazzling *Children of the Mire* to the last lecture he ever gave, under the title "André Breton: Fog and Lightning," in which he said:

> My friendship with the Surrealists and especially with Breton and Péret began when the movement had already ceased to be a burning flame. But it was still a cinder that could light up the imagination and warm the spirit in the barren years of the Cold War. Once, in conversation with Luis Buñuel, we asked each other about the motives that had driven us to join the Surrealist movement at different periods: he at its high noon, me at its twilight. We agreed: beyond the aesthetic revolution and Breton's magnetism, it was the moral aspect that had been decisive. For Buñuel, the morality of Surrealism was synonymous with purity and rebellion, each blurring into one another in his continual struggle—a real *agony*, in the original sense of the Greek word—against the Christian faith of his youth. For me, the attraction was condensed in a passionate triangle, a three-pointed star, as Breton himself used to say: poetry, love, freedom. Aesthetic theories pass but works remain. In Breton's case, the figure, the person also remains. He was not only the author of several books that have marked, or rather *tattooed*, our century, books which it would be no exaggeration to call electric—they jolt and illuminate—but he also always lived in harmony with his writings. He was never unfaithful to himself, not even in his contradictions or passing deviations. He was accused of being intolerant and rigorous; it is often forgotten that he exercised that rigor above all on himself.[14]

---

13 Octavio Paz, "Estrella de tres puntas: El surrealismo," in *Estrella de tres puntas*, pp. 25–6.

14 Octavio Paz, "André Breton: La niebla y el relámpago," in *Estrella de tres puntas*, pp. 124–5.

I attended that 1996 lecture, having just arrived in Mexico City after a long drive down from the University of Maryland, where Saúl Sosnowski had had the kindness to invite me as a visiting professor. My reading for the road was *Perspective cavalière*, a last compilation of Breton's writings edited by Marguerite Bonnet, continuing and concluding the collections he had himself compiled in life: *Les pas perdus* (*The Lost Steps*, 1924), *Point du jour* (*Break of Day*, 1934), and *La clé des champs* (*Free Rein*, 1953).

On my final stopover, at San Juan del Río, I read in *La Jornada*—the first copy I'd bought on coming back—that the next day Octavio Paz would be speaking in the Tamayo Museum about André Breton on the centenary of his birth. I decided to go. Another text in my suitcase was "André Breton, la brume et l'éclair" [André Breton: Fog and Lightning], printed days earlier in *Le Monde*. I went to the Tamayo, I heard Octavio speak, and afterward I managed to wave at him through the heavy glass door his protective friends were closing behind him. I still remember the surprise and affection in his voice as he exclaimed, "Adolfo . . ."

Objective chance?

I first read Octavio Paz in the most unlikely place: the penitentiary of Lecumberri. Poetry and the Surrealists had always accompanied me; with me came André Breton and Paul Éluard and Benjamin Péret and Guillaume Apollinaire and Max Ernst and the Peruvian César Moro and the Martiniquan Aimé Césaire, and the fantasy worlds of Paul Delvaux, Giorgio de Chirico, René Magritte, and Leonora Carrington.

In Lecumberri I discovered *The Labyrinth of Solitude*. I quoted one of its lines on the first page of the book I wrote during my six years in jail, *La revolución interrumpida*, knowing that this would anger many of my friends.[15] But it fit perfectly. In prison I read and reread *The Violent Season*, which opens with a line of Apollinaire's that had always been with me: *Ô Soleil c'est le temps de la Raison ardente* (O Sun now is the time of burning Reason). I was stunned by *Sunstone*, that litany of love and desire.

On January 1, 1970, when Lecumberri was packed with hundreds of political prisoners from the student movement of 1968 or those who had been swept up in earlier raids (remember, the student movement began by demanding the release of the political prisoners who, like me, were

15 [Adolfo Gilly, *La revolución interrumpida* (Mexico City: El Caballito, 1971); published in English as *The Mexican Revolution* (London: New Left Books, 1983, rev. ed. New York: New Press, 2005).]

already in that jail), we had to take shifts guarding our corridor at night. The unbalanced Mexican president, Gustavo Díaz Ordaz, had arranged for the common prisoners to attack the three corridors—C, M, and N— housing political inmates. Corridor N, where I was, inaugurated under Porfirio Díaz, is a circular construction around a handsome central two-story tower of red brick, crowned by battlements made of stone that had been imported from France. There, we managed to resist; the assailants did not get in, and we kept watch from then on.[16]

At the foot of this red tower—today an emblem of the General National Archive, housed in Lecumberri thanks to the happy brainwave of [the historian] Alejandra Moreno Toscano when Jesús Reyes Heroles was secretary of the interior—we used to take turns on guard in case we needed to raise the alarm. A memory remains of those nights: whenever it was my shift, from three to six in the morning, I used to take *The Violent Season* with me to reread. When I was released and deported, bundled straight from Lecumberri onto a plane headed for Paris, I took with me a single book: *The Violent Season*. In France, I gave it to a person who loved me.

Something I haven't forgotten from those nocturnal sessions are the following four lines from "Masks of Dawn," perhaps because I had seen Venice before, when I was free:

> The bronze horses of San Marco
> pass wavering architecture,
> go down in their green darkness to the water
> and throw themselves into the sea, toward Byzantium.[17]

⚭

I was still in Lecumberri when, one February morning in 1972, an issue of *Plural* reached us. This was the magazine directed at the time by Octavio Paz, and the cover announced a piece of his: "Letter to Adolfo Gilly," dated Cambridge, January 19, 1972.[18] It consists of a long and amicable

---

16   On January 2, we issued a communiqué to the press describing the aggression. The original, transcribed by a Federal Security Directorate officer, is now stored in Mexico's National Archive: in other words, back where it started, in the former Lecumberri Prison building—a spiral trajectory, Octavio Paz would have said.

17   "Masks of Dawn," in *The Poems of Octavio Paz*, ed. and trans. Eliot Weinberger (New York: New Directions, [1948] 2018), p. 109.

18   [The text was included, under the title "Burocracias celestes y terrestres," in Paz's essay collection *El ogro filantrópico: Historia y política, 1971–1978* (Mexico City: J. Mortiz, 1979). It appeared in English as a postscript to Octavio Paz, *The Other Mexico: Critique of the Pyramid* (New York: Grove Press, 1972), pp. 115–48.]

discussion of my book, *The Mexican Revolution*. It presaged the way that doors would soon begin to open for me; it was also an unforced and generous gesture—one soon repeated by Rafael Galván and Rodolfo Peña in their magazine *Solidaridad*, the organ of the democratic electricians of the STERM union. Paz's letter ended with these words:

> History is diachronic: variation, change. It is the world of the unpredictable and the unique, the region in which the historic day *par excellence* is "the one we least expect." Hence it gives rise to the feeling (or perhaps the delusion) that it is the realm of freedom: history presents itself to us as the possibility of choice. You chose socialism—and that is why you are in prison. This fact leads me to make a choice, too: to condemn the society that has put you behind bars. Thus, at certain moments at least, our philosophies and political differences dissolve and can be reconciled in a single statement: it is necessary to fight against a society that jails dissidents.
>
> It is time to bring this letter to a close. I hope that when I return to Mexico, we may continue this conversation, out in the fresh, open air. If that is not possible, I will come visit you in your cell in Lecumberri—that prison that Jack Womack says is turning into our Institute of Political Sciences.[19]
>
> Cordially,[20]

On March 4, two Trotskyist prisoners were given their freedom: Oscar Fernández Bruno and Adolfo Gilly. We were taken under strict security to the airport, where a few friends were waiting to see us off from afar, as they were not allowed to come near us: Víctor Rico Galán, his wife Ingeborg Diener, Francisco Colmenares, and other comrades of those hard years.[21] Stubborn as ever, in 1976 I sought a way back to Mexico. I was helped by Carlos Fuentes, then ambassador to France, and by Javier Wimer.[22] And here, a Mexican, I stayed.

◌⃝

19   [John Womack, Jr. (1937–): US historian of Mexico, especially known for his classic 1968 study *Zapata and the Mexican Revolution* (New York: Vintage Books, 1968).]

20   [Paz, *The Other Mexico*, pp. 147–8.]

21   [Víctor Rico Galán (1928–74): Spanish-born Mexican leftist journalist; Ingeborg Diener (1929–2014): born in Mexico to German parents, taught German at UNAM; they and the historian Francisco Colmenares were all imprisoned in Lecumberri at the same time as Gilly.]

22   [Javier Wimer Zambrano (1933–2009): Mexican diplomat and writer, founder of the Trotsky Museum in Mexico City.]

My long journey toward the poet had begun with William Blake and André Breton, in a different time and a different city that now feel remote. I came to see, like the reverse of the fabulous "Garden of Forking Paths" by Jorge Luis Borges, a kind of immense garden of paths that cross at last, roamed by characters like those of the Montevidean Felisberto Hernández in his *No One Had Lit a Lamp* (1947), or the figures that move through the paintings of Remedios Varo and Paul Delvaux.

And so, whenever I am asked the irrelevant political question: Was Octavio Paz a man of the right or of the left? I recall his motto: poetry, love, freedom. I glance at the questioner with faint, distant surprise, and think of Paul Valéry telling the twenty-year-old Breton: "It's your turn to speak, young seer of things." And then, if the questioner persists, I merely say that the answer lies in "The Spiral," that long essay about his life, his beliefs, and his death, written in Mexico City and dated January 2, 1993, when he was sixty years old. It is the opening piece of *Itinerary*.[23]

In his last book, *Three-Pointed Star: André Breton and Surrealism*, paying homage to the Parisian poet on the centenary of his birth, Paz wrote the following words as a prologue:

> André Breton did not like commemorations. They struck him, rightly, as ceremonies that were almost always vain and even ridiculous. Yet commemoration can have another meaning: it is a way of telling ourselves that an author who has left us is still alive, and that the best way of remembering them is to converse with them, by reading their works. That is why I have ventured to gather into this small volume the poems and essays I have written about him and about Surrealism.[24]

Let those words now close this minimal commemoration of Octavio Paz in March 2014, on the centenary of his birth.

23   [Octavio Paz, *Itinerary: An Intellectual Journey*, trans. and intro. Jason Williams (London: Menard Press, 1999).]
24   Octavio Paz, *Estrella de tres puntas*, p. 7.

19

Deep Rivers: José María Arguedas, Mario Vargas Llosa, and Papacha Oblitas

(1999)

*The foreigner permits you to be yourself
by making a foreigner of you.*

Edmond Jabès, "Un étranger avec, sous
le bras, un livre de petit format"

1.

Nationalism is a system of ideas and beliefs based on the distinction between one's own national community and the rest—the foreigners who people the wide world—and on the assumption of the specificity—real—and the essential superiority—imagined—of one's community with regard to all others. Hence the proliferation in Latin America of terms denoting this specific difference and implying pride in that essential superiority: *mexicanidad, bolivianidad, peruanidad, argentinidad, colombianidad*. The idea that to each of these national essences there corresponds a literature (narrative, essays, poetry) and a historiography seems to be a corollary already contained in the word, as obvious as the fact of the corresponding national territories.

This foreigner, however, rejects any such corollary.

Nationalism supposes a pride in one's own nation, that invention of recent centuries; a shared language, that distillation of ancient eras; and a feeling of belonging and safety, that timeless need of humanity. What ends up as the national language has displaced, relegated, and crushed those that once coexisted in the same territory, in order to affirm itself as the sole language of rule and of exchange. The nation, one and indivisible, and the state that embodies it, abhor diversity. In Latin America, this operation of displacement and obliteration of the various languages spoken across the territory was chiefly carried out by the Conquest and the nineteenth-century republics. The enforced loss of indigenous languages and their worlds of images and meanings went hand in hand with the theft of territories and lands or followed only a short way behind.

The two constitutive dimensions of the space of the nation-state—the relation of command–obedience and the relation of mercantile trade (power and money, the sovereign and the merchant), both enshrined in law—require a common language as the vehicle for command and exchange along with an army for the first and a currency for the second. The national-state community is a historical product in that it is founded on a common past, like all human communities, and imagines a common destiny. It has been called "a national historic enterprise." Nationalism is the ideology that exalts those values. To this end, it requires, as well as a corpus of laws, a literature that unifies the sense of belonging to this community and a historiography that imagines and recreates the common past, turning it into the mythical heritage of all. The "national language" and "national history" are subjects taught at every level of elementary education. This requirement has sparked or nourished endless historiographical and literary disputes, which are as familiar as they are repetitive.

Nationalism supposes the existence, or incipience, of a state community; that is, a community of rulers and ruled in political terms, of dominators and dominated in social terms, and of proprietors and non-proprietors in economic terms. In this double, internally split community (which explains the need for a state relation, for the sake not of administration but of cohesion), nationalism is the ensemble of beliefs and ideas every citizen harbors about the common past, the common enterprise, and the common destiny—the destiny of the nation in which everyone recognizes themselves and to which everyone belongs.

Nationalism is the ideology that unites in some imaginary community the disparate, conflicting components—they the rich, we the poor—even if in real life everyone knows exactly where the dividing line falls in each case, shifting and unstable as it is by its nature. Nationalism is not concerned with the human being as such but rather with a shared identity enclosed by a frontier. It is one of the modern forms of the immemorial "yearning for community," for protection, for belonging. Like religion and blood ties in the societies of the ancien régime, nationalism is a boundary that defines us, separating and protecting us from Them, the Foreigners, the Jews, the Muslims, the Outsiders, bearers of evil one and all.

The nation desperately needs to order literature according to its unity and relations of command. A nationalistic use of the writings of national authors contributes to creating the imaginary territory of the community in which superior and inferior people are identified, people governed by the unwritten pact of command and obedience. The literary imagination forms part of the connective tissue of the imaginary community, and since it occupies this zone of connection, there, too, it finds material to work with.

Nationalism is intensely real within national communities. At the same time, it is an imaginary construct used to veil or mitigate real wounds, internal borders, different timescales, asymmetrical and unequal relationships, and to prevent these from shattering the imagined national community, of which one anthem says: "In the heavens your eternal destiny by God's own finger writ."[1] Like any other product of spirit and hard work, literature can, and often does, serve nationalism, and a writer can make that mission his own. Nevertheless, in its origin and its finality, literature is not about the nation but about human beings (one of whose attributes is nationality), with their lives, their words.

2.

Literature is an open artifact made of words and ideas, sustained by the commonality of a language and a past. It is possible, I submit, to place literature at the service of nationalism (or communism, or any other system of ideas and beliefs), but that would be an unnecessary operation, foreign to its nature. Literature feeds on a human past distilled in a language. It feeds, as has been said often enough, on things lived and read. "The child dictates, the man writes," said Julien Green, not necessarily in the literal sense.[2] Man writes a language whose words contain a "dark,

---

1 [The lines are from the first stanza of the Mexican national anthem.]
2 [Julien Green, *Personal Record, 1928–1939* (London: Harper and Bros., 1939), p. 176.]

unrevealed depth," in [Wilhelm von] Humboldt's phrase.[3] The time that charges words, their sounds, and their combinations with meaning is, as Fernand Braudel said, the time of the "particularly slow-paced history of civilizations . . . of their depths, of the characteristics of their structure and layout," a history which precedes the nation and contains it.[4]

To be sure, words also change over the short term. But underneath, a long-term history continues to govern them, and the meanings and senses that change the least may be those that organize those shifting from below: passions, gestures, or agrarian and funerary rites. This buried humus nourishes the language and, with it, the writer.

Is this substructure linked to the time of nationalisms, that is, to the time of the nation-state's institutions and imaginaries? Yes, it is, but it orders that time secretly, from below, and this oceanic duration of history remains unperturbed by the choppy surface of daily events recorded in the nation's chronicles. Notwithstanding the inconstancy of discourses, the weight of words is almost always a creature of the deep.

Writer and language are fed by a common history. But this is not so much the story of everyday events, though they may be the subject matter of the writing; instead, it is that of the vicissitudes and ways of being in the world—and in those everyday events—of human beings in whom, as individuals and as communities, the massive, cumulative weight of preceding history is condensed.

Braudel's motionless history, the *longue durée*, that which barely changes while everything changes, acts upon literature and upon the writer. When the writer speaks of human beings, even if his narrative seems like a fictional piece of the history of immediate events and even if he regards it that way himself, he is in reality speaking of men and women whose gestures, words, reactions, relationships, and dreams were formed in the *longue durée*, in motionless time, and have become incarnate in the events of their lives.

The historian performs something similar, in keeping with his own methods and tests. The relationship of the nation and its institutions to historiography testifies to similar pressures. The nation needs a history that has been instituted in its own likeness, whereas history, as a knowledge and an art, does not need the nation; it needs humans, in all the

---

3 [Wilhelm von Humboldt, *On Language* (Cambridge: Cambridge University Press, [1836] 1999), p. 162.]

4 [Fernand Braudel, *On History*, trans. Sarah Matthews (Chicago: University of Chicago Press, [1969] 1980), p. 12.

diversity of their changeable relationships through time. What enthralls the writer of the deep is not the quarrels of nationalism—though he is familiar with them and may even take them for his subject—but the tongue and the life of the human community that is now a nation.

3.

The writer remains, notoriously, a craftsman. Although he may be producing for the market, he attempts every time to achieve a unique work, he tweaks and polishes, he "caresses" it to feel the texture or the smoothness.

He is not only an artisan in his working method and singular relationship with the object. The writer sets out first and foremost to produce something with use value. He cares above all that it be well crafted, and less about how widely it circulates. When a writer starts caring chiefly about circulation, and sacrifices words or paragraphs to ensure it; when his prime concern is with exchange value, thus treating use value as a mere support, then he will continue writing, more or less well, but he will have swapped his craft for a career.

I am not denying the possibility, indeed, the existence of masterpieces produced under contract. Far from it. In the realm of painting, architecture, music, or craft, works through which the spirit freely blows have at various times been commissioned, under strict and specific orders. But a commission is obviously not the market of today, and to produce for the one or the other are different matters. To be a musician or a writer is still to ply a trade whose chief purpose is personal effort and reward: these are artisanal trades. And artisans have been with us since long before nations, and, God willing, they will outlive them.

Skilled artisans. I shall say here, using their words, how two writers work with lived experience and with the language. Being cosmopolitans by vocation and by trade, they have a language, a history, and a past, but no nationalism that I can discern.

One is Sergio Pitol, whom I do not yet know well but shall dare to quote. In "The Dark Twin," a kind of story-cum-essay-cum-divertimento included in *The Art of Flight*, Pitol quotes Justo Navarro: "Being a writer is to become a stranger, a foreigner: you have to start to translate yourself. Writing is a case of impersonation, forging an identity: writing is passing yourself off as someone else." And he goes on to say:

I cannot imagine a novelist who does not use elements of his personal experience, a vision, a memory from childhood or the immediate past, a tone of voice captured in a meeting, a furtive gesture glimpsed by chance, only to incorporate them later into one or more characters. The narrator–writer delves deeper and deeper into his life as his novel progresses. It is not a mere autobiographical exercise; writing a novel solely about one's own life, in most cases, is a vulgarity, a lack of imagination.[5]

The text takes straight off into a story that mixes the incident, the novelist, and the characters of his subsequent novel. It docks with these penultimate lines:

> The last novel by José Donoso, *Donde van a morir los elefantes* (Where Elephants Go to Die), carries an epigraph from William Faulkner that illuminates a novelist's relationship with his work in progress: "A novel is a writer's secret life, the dark twin of a man." A novelist is someone who hears voices through the voices.[6]

Here comes the Double. We had better pause and turn the corner.

The other is E. M. Cioran. *History and Utopia* contains a letter he wrote in 1957 from Paris "to a faraway friend" who, "from that country which was ours and now is no one's," Romania, wonders whether he plans to "return to our own language" or remain faithful to his hard-won French:

> It would be the narrative of a nightmare, were I to give you a detailed account of the history of my relations with this borrowed idiom, with all these words so often weighed, worked over, refined, subtle to the point of non-existence, bowed beneath the exactions of nuance, inexpressive from having expressed everything, alarming in their precision, burdened with fatigue and modesty, discreet even in vulgarity. How should a Scyth come to terms with such terms, grasp their true meaning, and wield them with scruple, with probity? There is not one among them whose exhausted elegance fails to dizzy me: no longer a trace of earth, of blood, of soul in such words. A syntax of severe, of cadaverous dignity encompasses them and assigns them a place from which God Himself

---

5   Sergio Pitol, *The Art of Flight*, trans. George Henson (Dallas: Deep Vellum Books, 2015), p. 156.
6   Ibid., p. 170.

could not dislodge them. What consumption of coffee, of cigarettes, and of dictionaries merely to write one halfway decent sentence in this inapproachable language, too noble and too distinguished for my taste? I realized as much, unfortunately, only after the fact, when it was too late to change my course; otherwise, I should never have abandoned our own, whose odor of growth and corruption I occasionally regret, that mixture of sun and dung with all its nostalgic ugliness, its splendid squalor. Return to it, I cannot; the tongue I was obliged to adopt pinions and subjugates me by the very pains it has cost me. Am I a "renegade," as you insinuate? "A man's country is but a camp in the desert," says a Tibetan text. I do not go so far and would give all the landscapes of the world for that of my childhood.[7]

And here comes the Wandering Foreigner. Let us pause once more, turn back altogether. Too many extraneous characters cropping up.

4.

In 1996, Mario Vargas Llosa published *La utopía arcaica: José María Arguedas y las ficciones del indigenismo* (Archaic Utopia: José María Arguedas and the Fictions of *Indigenismo*), a study of the work and life of the Peruvian writer who killed himself on November 28, 1969.[8] It was clearly written in a hurry, as if pressured by a deadline, as well as being inadequately revised, short on sources, reductive, and repetitive. The same allegations and conclusions are reiterated from chapter to chapter, whole sentences appear more than once, and the quotations seem random. The book is moreover freighted with ideology, from the title on down, taking as a given what it purports to demonstrate.

Vargas Llosa analyzes all these years after Arguedas's death, the political and ideological content he ascribes to the oeuvre, largely overlooking the writing and the use of language. He regards Arguedas as an "indigenist" author (though Arguedas denies this in his essays) and decides that his work exemplifies "a view of literature in which the social outweighed the artistic and to some extent determined it." To this imputed view Vargas Llosa opposes his own: "To be a writer means first,

---

7   E. M. Cioran, *History and Utopia*, trans. Richard Howard (London: Quartet Books, 1996), pp. 1–2.

8   Mario Varga Llosa, *La utopía arcaica: José María Arguedas y las ficciones del indigenismo* (Mexico City: Fondo de Cultura Económica, 1996).

or exclusively, to assume a personal responsibility: responsibility for an oeuvre that, if it possesses artistic value, will enrich the language and culture of its native country."

"Its native country." The nationalism of Vargas Llosa is a modern one, proposing and depicting what he sees before him—a "de-Indianized" Peru comprised of millions of rural migrants to the cities, a "hodge-podge," a "mishmash," where not pure Castilian but a "strange hybrid" is spoken: "the rudimentary Spanish or criollo argot that serve to communicate are accompanied by certain tastes, a particular sensibility, an idiosyncrasy, even some aesthetic values, which are virtually new and define chicha culture." Chicha music, for example, crosses Andean huaynos with rock and Caribbean rhythms.

In "this new, informal Peru," thanks to the informal economy created by the migrants, "popular capitalism and a free market have emerged in Peru for the first time," Vargas Llosa writes. "There is no doubt that developments in Peru over recent years have dealt a death blow to the archaic utopia." "That traditional Andean society, communitarian, magico-religious, and Quechua-speaking, conservatively attached to collectivist values and atavistic customs, which fueled indigenist fiction in ideological and literary terms, has ceased to exist." Regardless of the political stamp and economic policies of future governments, he concludes, "Peru is on track to be a society that definitively rejects archaism, and indeed utopia."

Yes, he may be right. His Peruvian proclamation cannot but remind us of the program for a dynamic, modernizing nationalism launched in Mexico by Plutarco Elías Calles in his day, and even more strongly of that promoted by Carlos Salinas de Gortari and his ilk in our own time.

Yes, he may be right. Except that Arguedas never proposed the utopia of a return to the Incan Empire, the Tahuantinsuyo; and he was not an indigenist writer, if we take *indigenismo* to mean that strain of nationalism (widespread following the Mexican Revolution, in Mexico, Peru, Ecuador, and Bolivia) that commits to respect, absorb, and integrate native cultures into the single current of national culture and language —in contrast to the nineteenth-century liberal policy of ignoring and erasing it in the name of progress, the republic, and the unity of the modern nation.

Arguedas's imagination followed a different path. In "La novela y el problema de la expresión literaria en Perú" [The novel and the problem of literary expression in Peru], a 1950 essay he revised in 1968 to form the prologue of the Chilean edition of *Yawar Fiesta* [1941], he writes: "But the two worlds into which these countries descended from Tahuantinsuyo are divided, the Quechua and the Castilian worlds, will either merge or part ways for good one day. In the meantime, the heroic and beautiful Via Crucis of the bilingual artist will continue. With regard to this serious problem of our destiny, I outline in this essay the reasons for my vote in favor of Castilian."[9]

In *Los ríos profundos* (*Deep Rivers*), the literary peak around which his work and life revolved, Arguedas set out to do two things: to recount the enchanted world of the Peruvian Andes through the eyes of his own transfigured childhood, and to find in his Castilian Spanish an idiom for channeling a world that names itself in Quechua; Quechua being a tongue in whose structure both the enchantment of the world and the indigenous thought that is one with it live on. He would speak up, he, José María Arguedas, the bilingual son of an itinerant lawyer from Cuzco and a mother who died when he was three years old, born in 1911 in Andahuaylas province (where in 1940, of a total population of 90,195, just 265 spoke no Quechua and 80,611 spoke nothing but), raised by Indians and taught in childhood by Don Felipe Maywa and Don Víctor Pusa, community leaders. He would speak in a language that would carry their voices and the voices, for these also speak, of deep rivers, hills, and stones.

To judge from his book, Vargas Llosa lacks a handle on the very idea of such a world. At most, he interprets it as "animate nature" or an "animist conception"; a suitable source of inspiration, he allows, for the "so-called ecologist movements . . . the newest political phenomenon of the past few years." Indeed "the activist youth of this crusade may claim José María Arguedas for their own, since the utopia of the author of *Deep Rivers* is also theirs."

As for childhood, Vargas Llosa is simplistic enough to look for direct correspondences between the stories of Arguedas's life as a boy and the episodes related in the novels. Positivism and its writers know nothing of the "dark twin," nor do they hear "voices through the voices." They tend instead to transpose their own lives into novels, in a species of realist fiction, and to hunt for the same propensity in the work of others. It is not unlike the way the nationalism of literary critics scans every writer for his relation to national issues.

Arguedas is pursuing something quite different when he recreates the

9   J. M. Arguedas, "La novela y el problema de la expresión literaria en Perú," in *Un mundo de monstruos y de fuego*, selected and introduced by Abelardo Oquendo (Mexico City: Fondo de Cultura Económica, 1993).

indigenous world with the dark materials of his childhood, and makes it speak in an "almost foreign" tongue:

> Self-realization, self-translation; how to convert the seemingly alien language into a diaphanous and legitimate torrent; how to imbue the almost foreign tongue with the matter of our spirit. That is the hard, the difficult question. The universality of this rare balance of content and form, a balance reached through intense nights of unbelievable labor, is something that will come as a function of such human perfection as may be achieved in the course of so outlandish an effort. Does the true face of human beings and their abode exist in the depths of this work? . . . But even as a language thus charged with unaccustomed essences affords a glimpse of the profundity of the heart, even as it conveys the story of humanity's passage on earth, universality may yet lag far behind. All the same it will come, because we well know that mankind owes its preeminence and kingship to the fact of being one, a single uniqueness.[10]

To achieve this goal, it was necessary to find what subtle disruptions would turn Spanish into the right mold, the fitting instrument. And these discoveries being aesthetic, they were reached like discoveries are in dreams—imprecisely.

Did he succeed? Arguedas says that he did, that he got there in his story titled "Water," and to dispel any doubts he puts it as follows:

> This was the world! The small village ablaze with the fires of love and of hate, of the great sun and of silence; alive with the song of thrushes hidden in the trees; open to the towering, miserly sky, beautiful but cruel. Could this world be conveyed to others? Would they feel the extreme passions of the human beings who dwelled there? Their great weeping and the incredible, transparent joy with which they used to sing in the quiet hours? It would seem so.[11]

5.

In *Deep Rivers*, the enchanted world of Indian time converses with the enchanted world of childhood, but this is not to say that they are two happy or ideal worlds, far from it. Violence, passion, meanness, exaltation,

10 Ibid.
11 Ibid.

and humiliation coexist in them without cease. The lyricism of Argue-das's text springs from the constant tension between both worlds, as well as from his working material: a Castilian that is constructed and uttered with a Quechua timbre, a peasant-indigenous imagery that becomes one with the forms of its telling.

Young Ernesto goes into a *picantería*, where men drink chicha and eat very spicy snacks. The waitress says to him: "So you'll be listening to Papacha Oblitas," and points at the harpist. The itinerant musician, "a maestro . . . famous in hundreds of towns" begins to play a huayno, talking to the river, verse after verse, in the soft Quechua tongue: "River Paraisancos, strong-flowing stream, you must not fork until I return." The boy recalls:

> The high voice fell upon my already heavy heart like an icy river. Enthu-siastically, Papacha Oblitas repeated the chorus, playing it like a native of Paraisancos. The harp sweetened the song; it didn't have in it the steely sorrow of the man's voice. Why, in the deep riverbeds, in those abysses of rocks, bushes, and sun, did the songs have such a sweet tone, when the powerful torrent of the waters was so wild and the precipices looked so terrifying? Perhaps because on those rocks the most delicate of tiny flowers frolicked with the wind, and because the thundering current of the great river flows through flowers and vines, where the birds are for-tunate and joyous, more so than in any other part of the world.

The harpist continues playing and talking to the river: "When it is the traveler who returns to you, you will fork, you will branch out." The cus-tomers stop drinking and chatting. They listen. So does the boy:

> Who is capable of setting the bounds between the heroism and the iciness of a great sorrow? With music such as this a man could weep until he was completely consumed, until he vanished, or he could just as easily do battle with a legion of condors and pumas, or with the monsters that are said to inhabit the depths of the highland lakes and the shadowy mountain slopes. I felt myself more disposed to fight the devil as I lis-tened to this song. If he should appear wearing a puma- or condor-skin mask, waving immense plumes, or baring his fangs, I would take him on, certain of victory.[12]

12   José María Arguedas, *Deep Rivers*, trans. Frances Horning Barraclough (Long Grove, IL: Waveland Press, [1958] 1978, pp. 169–72.

I arrived in Peru in 1959, after three years of being a foreigner in Bolivia. A friend gave me lodging and a book that had just been published, *Deep Rivers*. As I began to read, I was overcome by the same inner ferment as the boy feels before the playing and singing of the harpist. It was the same Spanish with Quechua undertones that I'd heard in Bolivia, spoken by Nina, a miner from La Paz, by Constantino, a miner from Oruro, and by Amadeo Vargas, a student from Cochabamba. It was those scents, it was those slow, vast landscapes of the altiplano below the glassy blue vault of the highland skies.

"Could this world be conveyed to others? Would they feel the extreme passions of the human beings who dwelled there?" wondered Arguedas. "It would seem so," he answered himself. I went to live in Europe the following year. I only took two books with me, *Deep Rivers* and [César Vallejo's] *Human Poems*, as well as a translation task to while away the long sea voyage: a French edition of Trotsky's writings. The ship was new, the *Maipú*, plying between Buenos Aires and Hamburg; a few crossings later, it sank.

6.

In my view, Vargas Llosa's book constitutes a progressivist, positivist, national exorcism designed to scare away the old ghosts that still haunt the Peruvian Andes, "informal Peru," and what he describes as "this new country made up of millions of beings of rural origin, brutally urbanized by political and economic vicissitudes": humiliation, hatred, violence.

The criollo and mestizo custom of humiliating the Indian is old indeed, as old as the customs of hatred. Its deepest roots lie in the worlds recreated by Arguedas, and the author sees these roots as such, much more than his critics do. These customs live on, persisting in the fracture between the two communities—them and us—into which each imagined national community in Latin America is divided. Nationalism fails to register this fracture. The humiliated register it. I cannot say whether there is a single literature in these lands that does not brush at times along its edge.

On November 14, 1969, Hugo Blanco—imprisoned since 1963 on the penal island of El Frontón, off the port of Callao—wrote a letter to Arguedas in Quechua, after receiving via Sybila, Arguedas's wife, Arguedas's novel *Todas las sangres* (All the Bloodlines): "I can't tell what it is that pervades me when I read you, that's why I don't read your writing the way I read ordinary things, nor with such constancy: my heart might break. My *punas* [high grasslands] begin to come to me in all their silence, their dry-eyed grief, clenching my chest, clenching it tight." Then he recalls the indigenous movement that landed him in jail: "How happy you'd have been to see us come down from all the punas and enter Cuzco with our heads high, not cringing, and shouting from street to street: Death to all the *gamonales* [landlords]! Long live the men who work!" They came down from the punas and entered the city "heads high, not cringing": that was the unprecedented feat. "We made them hear every single thing, the truth itself . . . We told it to them in Quechua . . . And those *maqtas* [young men] in their ponchos, they nearly made the Plaza de Armas explode."[13]

The letter in Quechua from the prisoner of El Frontón kindled in Arguedas an intense spiritual agitation. He replied, also in Quechua: "I received your letter yesterday: I spent the whole night, walking at first, then in a turmoil, so powerful was my sense of joy and revelation."

Undated but written on November 24, four days before his suicide, this letter from Arguedas begins, "Brother Hugo, beloved, heart of stone and dove," and goes on—perhaps intuiting that it may be the last—to speak of *Deep Rivers*:

> You may have read my novel *Deep Rivers*. Remember, my strongest of all brothers, remember. In that book I do not speak only of how I wept burning tears; with more tears and greater fervor I speak of the *pongos* [indigenous servants], of the *colonos* [hacienda laborers], of their hidden and immense strength, of the rage that smolders in the kernel of their hearts, a fire that will not go out. Those flea-ridden wretches, flogged every day, forced to lick the earth with their tongues, despised even by their communities, those are the men who in the novel invade the city of Abancay, without fearing machine guns or bullets, defeating them. And that's how they force the big preacher of the city, the priest who looked down on them as lice; defeating bullets, the serfs force the priest to say mass, to sing in the church: they impose their strength on him.

Later, Arguedas says that he imagined this invasion "like a premonition" so that "those who understand about social struggles and politics . . . may grasp the significance of this capture of a city that I imagined":

---

13   The correspondence between Hugo Blanco and José María Arguedas was first published in the journal *Amaru*, no. 11, December 1969, in Lima.

How, with what boiling blood, would these men rise up if they were not merely seeking the death of the mother of plagues, typhus, but that of the gamonales, on the day when they manage to vanquish their fear, their horror of them! Who will help them overcome this terror formed and nurtured over centuries, who? This man who could illuminate and save them, is he anywhere on earth? Does he exist or not, goddam and blast it, saying, *I like you was weeping fire, waiting, all alone.*

"I am afraid this dawn will cost blood, so much blood," Arguedas continues. "You know it and that's why you admonish, you cry out from prison." And then he returns to hatred, the hatred of the humiliated:

> Just as there was in the hearts of the *runas* [people] who cared for me as a child and raised me, there is hatred and fire in you against the gamonales of every stripe; and toward those who suffer, who have no home or land, the *wakchas*, you have the mockingbird's warm heart and a fortifying love, pure as the water of certain springs, to the delight of the heavens.[14] And all of your blood has wept, my brother. He who cannot weep, the more so in our times, knows nothing of love, he does not know what it is.

After this, a return to childhood, the voices that speak through other voices, and the announcement of his impending death, like a farewell:

> Your blood is already mingled with mine, like the blood of Don Víctor Pusa and Don Felipe Maywa. Don Víctor and Don Felipe speak to me day and night, they cry ceaselessly within my soul, they call to me in their tongue, with their great wisdom, with their sorrow that pierces distances beyond measure, farther than the light of the sun. Listen Hugo, they brought me up, loving me very much, because, though I was the son of a *misti* [member of the mestizo ruling class], they saw me being treated with contempt, like an Indian. It is in their name, remembering them in my very flesh, that I wrote what I have written and learned everything that I have learned and done, overcoming barriers that sometimes seemed impassable. I discovered the world. And you, too, in the name, I think, of runas very like those two, have been a brother to he who knows of brotherhood, a likeness of your likeness, he who knows how to love.

---

14   [Arguedas's words here, "*tienes pecho de calandria*," literally mean "you have the breast of a mockingbird." In this context, the expression signifies a continued capacity to express positive emotion—to sing—amid harsh surroundings. Thanks to Odi Gonzales for elucidating this point.]

How much longer, how much farther should I write you? You will not forget me now even if death should take me, listen, Peruvian strong as our mountains where the snow never melts, strengthened by prison as it strengthens the stone and the dove.

So, now, I have written to you, joyfully in the midst of the great shadow of my mortal afflictions. We are not touched by the sadness of the *mistis*, the egoists; the powerful sadness of the people touches us, the sadness of the world, of those who know and sense the dawn. And therefore, death and sorrow mean neither to die nor to suffer. Isn't it true, brother? Receive my heart.

I say that the "dark twin" accompanied the writer down to that moment. Through the voices, he heard voices in his two languages: the "soft and palpitating Quechua," the inherited and literary Castilian, and the "subtle disruptions" in which the two are crossed. Is this nationalism? Nationalism mitigates this conflict, but for this foreigner in his Peru, the conflict became untenable: humiliation, hatred, and tenderness, as evoked in his last letter, could no longer be assuaged or find an outlet in his great skill as a writer.

There are those who will discern a political writer in that letter. I see it differently. I see it for what it is: the writer's farewell to a world, his world, where he no longer has a place, looking back with anger, with hatred, and with tenderness. I see the shadow of Walter Benjamin, a Jew and a foreigner, who wrote in 1940 on the eve of his suicide that "the main sinews" of the strength of the working class—hatred and the will to sacrifice—are nourished by "the image of enslaved ancestors rather than that of liberated grandchildren."[15]

People who study, people who know, and people who simply look at life all concur that, in this fin de siècle, poverty is rising vertiginously year on year across the globe. It is not a transitory situation but a stable, necessary relation for the reproduction of this world we live in. With the rise of poverty comes that of destitution, humiliation, and hatred, while nations split and fragment, and nationalities grow apart. If it is perhaps not announcing better futures, then this explosion of inequality, rage, and disparity is surely incubating powerful ideas and great literary works, for times such as these are fruitful for them.

---

15   Walter Benjamin, "Theses on the Philosophy of History," in *Illuminations: Essays and Reflections*, ed. and with an introduction by Hannah Arendt, trans. Harry Zohn (New York: Schocken Books, 1969), p. 260.

7.

In the early hours of January 1, 1994, an army of Chiapanecan Indians in revolt, with and without weapons, wearing ski masks and talking among themselves in their various languages, took the city of San Cristóbal de las Casas, once the colonial Ciudad Real, the landowners' capital, and the next day they withdrew to the forest in the same orderly fashion in which they had come. Perhaps not everyone understood the immensity of that gesture at the time, but Arguedas certainly would have.

20

"Whiteness," Modernity, Humiliation

(2011)

1.

The scene unfolds in Austria in 1938, during the German military occupation:

> In the house at No. 67, Obere Donaustrasse in Vienna, a seventy-two-year-old Jew was forced to climb a fireman's ladder, the hose in his left hand, the right on the guard rail. The men of the SA called this a "baptism of fire." When the caretaker of the building announced to the executioners that he was prepared to take the Jew's place, he was threatened with arrest and ordered back into the basement.

Joseph Roth, the Austrian author of *The Radetzky March* and other memorable works, who died in Paris in 1939, aged forty-five, consumed by nostalgia, horror, and alcohol, relates this incident in a piece from 1938 titled "The Inexpressible."[1]

Set beside the tragedy of World War II, the Holocaust, and the limitless atrocities committed by all sides, the humiliation of an elderly Jew seems a minor anecdote. Like countless similar events, it prefigured the final tragedy, whose essence it already contained. The episode also

---

1   Joseph Roth, *On the End of the World*, trans. Will Stone (Hesperus, London 2019), p. 47.

enacted, and no less intensely, the collective humiliation of its spectators, whether or not they agreed with what they were seeing. That is why the doorman who attempted to break the spell with a simple gesture was immediately threatened and banished.

Less ferocious perhaps than the scenes of Viennese Jews made to clean the sidewalk with their bare hands, watched with curiosity by their "Aryan" neighbors, the story is a distillation of what was to come. In it we see the whole infernal chain of naked domination, without law or impediment. This chain comprises five links: domination, subordination, humiliation, submission, extermination.

Where human law vanishes, in this sequence, is not in the initial relation between domination and subordination—or between command and obedience—for there is always a shifting frontier between the two terms, an invisible line of resistance, negotiation, and consensus of which all are aware, regardless of the specific form taken by this relation in each case.

Lawfulness vanishes at that point which no law enshrines: that burning, painful and extralegal point we call *humiliation*, the central link in the chain, the quintessence of a lawless world where the relation does not hang on the other's obedience but on his submission, and, at the extreme, in his annihilation, ensuring that a submissive, accepted humiliation is the rule of life for those who survive.

2.

Humiliation is the component in which domination becomes depoliticized, exits the realm of political law, whatever this may be, and becomes naturalized, becomes *nature*. The humiliated are the *natives*, the "*naturales*" [in Spanish], the colonized, objects of domination by their nature not as the result of accords or pacts between human beings. In her study of the thinking and writing of Jesuit missionaries in northern New Spain, Ivonne del Valle notes: "In order to create Indians apt to play the role of subordinates assigned to them since the sixteenth century, they had to be made to fit into a static mold of devaluation through the reiteration of old paradigms."[2] She goes on to cite the precepts of the Jesuit Juan Nentuig in his *Rudo ensayo* (Rough Essay) of 1764:

---

2   Ivonne del Valle, *Escribiendo desde los márgenes: Colonialismo y jesuitas en el siglo XVIII* (Mexico City: Siglo XXI, 2009), p. 153.

It does not benefit religion because no matter how good the Indian, before he becomes esteemed and improved by any allotted privilege, his humble demeanor turns to pride; his diligence to laziness and negligence because it seems to him there is no more to aspire to; his obedience and docility to a stubborn, headstrong willfulness . . . I warn all who must treat with Indians that none can be praised to his face without spoiling him because for an Indian to hear himself praised or to be treated as a gentleman, as many imprudent Spaniards do, is poison of the most violent order.[3]

To *create* Indians: the colonial enterprise set out to transform the Seri, the Pima, the Nayar [Cora], the Opata into Indians, and in this way to establish *humiliation*—a hateful human relation but a transitory and reversible one—as the status, condition, and destiny of these *Indians* forevermore. It was not a question of *subordination*, though this, too, was demanded and expected, but of *submission*, imposed for life and for all successive lives to come.

As we know, this racism proper to the colonial project was a foundational relation of capitalist modernity, ever since it made its first appearance following the Conquest. Racism constituted a biological padlock attached to this particular form of domination. Nazism was a cruel, extreme distillation of this, carried into European metropoles. This metropolitan racism, a frenzy of extermination symbolized by Auschwitz, is the ultimate image of the serpent that bites its tail and devours itself.

The racism proper to capitalist modernity, in all its variants, is Bolívar Echeverría's object of study in "Images of 'Whiteness.'" He writes:

In the preliminary note to his *Sociology of Religion*, Weber suggests that the ability to correspond to the ethical request of capitalist modernity, the capacity to assume the ethical practice of Puritan Protestantism, may have had an *ethnic foundation* and been connected to certain racial characteristics. The following reflections attempt to problematize Weber's approach to this topic by describing a kind of "racism" constitutive of capitalist modernity, a "racism" that demands the presence of ethical or

---

3   Juan Nentuig, *El rudo ensayo: Descripción geográfica, natural y curiosa de la provincia de Sonora. 1764* (Mexico City: SEP/INAH, 1977). As quoted in del Valle, *Escribiendo desde los márgenes*, pp. 153–4. It is worth pointing out that the same changes overtake many who are not indigenous when occupying positions of command or receiving honors.

civilizational "*whiteness*" [*blanquitud*] as a condition of modern humanity but that in extreme cases, such as the one of Nazi Germany, further
demands the presence of ethnic, biological, and "cultural" whiteness
[*blancura*].[4]

Echeverría's use of the term "whiteness" [in Spanish, *blanquitud*] does
not refer to a biological trait but rather to the distillation, in terms of
attitude, behavior, and corporeal expression, of what he calls "ethical
capitalist identity," which becomes visible in people's demeanor, a "com-
posure that denotes 'whiteness,' and not racial whiteness." In this way,

> the condition of whiteness for modern identity happened to become a
> condition of "*whiteness*," that is, its ethnic order became subordinated
> to the identitarian order imposed by capitalist modernity . . . This is the
> reason why, in principle, in capitalist modernity, individuals of colour
> can obtain modern identity without having to completely "become" white
> [*blanquearse*]; it is enough for them to demonstrate their "whiteness."[5]

The photographs included in the [original Spanish-language] book of
various figures "of color" who have made it in show business or politics
illustrate this aspect of what Echeverría means by "whiteness." The relevant essay, "Images of 'Whiteness,'" was written in 2007. Today Bolívar
would be treated to a highly refined product of this kind of "ethical
capitalist identity" in the shape of President Barack Obama.

How many of those who voted for him, placing their hopes in his
outward appearance and seeing his electoral victory as a requital for
old humiliations, do not feel bitterly deceived by the revelation of this
ruler's "whiteness"? But how many genuine WASPs, on the other hand,
do not feel outraged by having to accept a man of color as president
of the United States, no matter how thorough the show of "whiteness"
made by this dark-skinned fellow in both his manners and his policies?
A Black man, with a Black wife and two Black daughters, president of the
USA—even one who plays golf and exhibits the demeanor, education,
and politics of the white elite?

The weakening of an imperial power is always a space and time of
ambiguity, negotiation, and uncertainty. Symptoms emerge that seem
to contradict the persistence and appearance of health. At such time,

---

4   Bolívar Echeverría, "Images of 'Whiteness,'" in *Modernity and "Whiteness,"* trans.
Rodrigo Ferreira (Oxford: Polity, 2010), p. 39.
5   Ibid., pp. 41–2.

as a minimal symptom, the formerly irreducible requirement of *whiteness* is transmuted and negotiated into "whiteness." This is the process described by Bolívar Echeverría.

3.

Back in 1935, when Nazism was on the rise in Europe and the savagery of European empires ran rampant in the colonies, Aimé Césaire—the surrealist Martiniquan poet then studying in Paris—coined the term *Négritude* in the third issue of *L'Étudiant noir*, the journal of French colonial students. "Negritude" emerged as an affirmation of anticolonial Black identity, deliberately recuperating the word *negro* and its cognate *negritude* as a badge of pride, since in colonial French the word *nègre* was a derogatory term, as *indio* was in Latin America.

Aimé Césaire defined it as follows: "Negritude is the simple recognition of the fact of being Black, which implies the acceptance of this fact, of our destiny as Black people, and of our history and culture."[6] Negritude was thus the human content of an existence, a genealogy, a history, and an experience, all inherited and shared down the generations.

Negritude developed into a broad, anticolonial literary and political movement whose influence reached well beyond those who identified with the term. Léopold Sédar Senghor, who became the first president of Senegal, was quick to link his name to the movement.

Just as "whiteness" in Bolívar Echeverría's definition is a term that conveys ideas of negotiation of one's status and adaptation to the mode of domination of capitalist modernity, so Negritude is a term of defiance, of affirmation of one's identity along with proud rejection of the word's pejorative sense—much like the expression "*somos raza*" in the mouths of those Mexicans whom the *catrines* [posh dandies] despise as riffraff.[7]

The word Negritude thus sprang up as a rebellion of language against European colonial domination and its prolongation in the white settlers in the US and their descendants, slavers or not. Aimé Césaire tells us that the first insurrectional irruption of Negritude was the revolt of Black slaves in Saint-Domingue (Haiti) against their masters in August 1791, fanned by the winds of the French Revolution of 1789 and its motto,

---

6 Interview with Césaire in Lilyan Kesteloot, *Les écrivains noirs de langue français: naissance d'une littérature* (Brussels: Université Libre de Bruxelles, 1963), pp. 113–14.

7 [*Somos raza*: literally, "We are the race," but the phrase could also be translated as, "We are the people."]

"Liberty, Equality, Fraternity," which the colonial slaves embraced word for word. A month later they were joined by Toussaint L'Ouverture, who would become their leader and emblematic figure. The classic, if not the only, account of this revolution is *The Black Jacobins* by C. L. R. James.

Negritude was a word of revolt, then, and at the same time an affirmation of identity on the part of the most dispossessed of the dispossessed, the Black slaves hauled from Africa to the Americas, stripped of their lands, their gods, their history, and even their human condition, taken to a different continent as merchandise and property: human bodies—and souls—turned into an exchange value whose use value depended on their becoming beasts of labor.

To affirm one's Negritude or blackness, then, recuperated and celebrated a historic heritage of culture and civilization. A heritage preserved and transmitted by persistence and resistance, kept alive by a person's secret or overt pride in their being and their customs, and finally illuminated by the lightning flash of insurrection. It is the same as the claim to the myths, customs, and rituals past and present of the originary peoples, their languages and their living worlds, made by the indigenous insurrection in Chiapas at the end of the twentieth century, or by the Bolivian revolution at the start of the twenty-first. It is the cry of "*¡Ya Basta!*"—"Enough!"—uttered by the Zapatistas of the Mexican southeast.

4.

When Bolívar Echeverría presents "whiteness" as a constitutive trait of capitalist modernity, he is defining it as the quintessence of domination in that globalized modernity:

> The intolerance that characterizes "identitarian-civilizational racism" is much more elaborate than that of ethnic racism: it focuses its attention on more subtle indications than whiteness of skin, such as evidence of internalization of the capitalist historical ethos. These are the features that serve as criteria for the inclusion or exclusion of singular or collective individuals in modern society. Unlike the ethnic fanaticism found in pursuing whiteness, such forms of racism represent an intolerance that easily strikes against even humans of impeccable racial whiteness but whose behavior, gestures, or appearance indicate that they have been rejected by the "spirit of capitalism." The "racism" of "whiteness" only demands that the internalization of the capitalist ethos be made manifest

in some way, with some sign, in external or corporal appearance. The biological traits related to racial whiteness are a necessary but not sufficient expression of that internalization.[8]

The refined racism of "whiteness," Echeverría tells us, is not confined to a handful of perverse characters. It is the final distillation of a mode of domination, the terminal point—to date—of a history of crimes, aberrations, and disasters mixed with an unprecedented deployment of human ingenuity. It is an unending story that, unless we can put an end to it in this mode, will spell the end of us, carried along by what Echeverría calls "the demands of the current social order and . . . its deaf, yet relentless, will to catastrophe."[9]

As Echeverría reminds us, one extreme form of the exercise of "whiteness" was the Holocaust—the murderous ethnic cleansing of Jews and Gypsies and the disabled in Nazi extermination camps, where death was scheduled for some on arrival and for others when they had grown too starved to yield one more gram of work.

5.

Halfway through that twentieth century that was ours, in 1955, the publishers Présence Africaine released a memorable text by Aimé Césaire, *Discourse on Colonialism*. It begins like this:

A civilization that proves incapable of solving the problems it creates is a decadent civilization.

A civilization that chooses to close its eyes to its most crucial problems is a stricken civilization.

A civilization that uses its principles for trickery and deceit is a dying civilization. . . .

First, we must study how colonization works to *decivilize* the colonizer, to *brutalize* him in the true sense of the word, to degrade him, to awaken him to buried instincts, to covetousness, violence, race hatred, and moral relativism.[10]

---

8   Echeverría, "Images of 'Whiteness,'" p. 43.
9   Echeverría, *Modernity and "Whiteness,"* p. xxi.
10   Aimé Césaire, *Discourse on Colonialism*, trans. Joan Pinkham (New York: Monthly Review Press, 2000), pp. 31, 35.

At the end of this "decivilization," Césaire finds its refined product, which is Nazism. It would be worthwhile, he says, "to reveal to the very distinguished, very humanistic, very Christian bourgeois of the twentieth century that without his being aware of it, he has a Hitler inside him, that Hitler *inhabits* him." Even when his ignorance leads this gentleman to rail against Nazism, at bottom, says Césaire,

> what he cannot forgive Hitler for is not *the crime* in itself, *the crime against man*, it is not *the humiliation of man as such*, it is the crime against the white man, the humiliation of the white man, and the fact that he applied to Europe colonialist procedures which until then had been reserved exclusively for the Arabs of Algeria, the "coolies" of India, and the "niggers" of Africa. . . .
>
> Colonization: bridgehead in a campaign to civilize barbarism, from which there may emerge at any moment the negation of civilization, pure and simple.[11]

On reaching this end point, embodied in a statement that, for Césaire, "plants us squarely in the middle of howling savagery," he touches the key word of all rebellions, that last resort that, when it is pressed to the extreme by an inhumane form of domination, blows up and blows everything up with it: *humiliation inflicted, humiliation lived, humiliation suffered.*

This eruption tends to begin with low voices and small gestures: for example, the voice and gestures of a man whose son was recently killed in Cuernavaca, one among the 50,000 men and women who have been killed in this country over the last five years, at a rate of 10,000 a year, and on that day he said, "We've had it up to here," and set off walking, collecting wounds and sorrows along the roads of Mexico.[12]

Perhaps the time has come for this great university, the UNAM, and others too, to set off walking in our own fashion against humiliation, against fear, against indifference, against the war inflicted on us from this side and that by people identically immersed in the glacial waters of selfish calculation and in the grotesque world—devoid of pity, law, and honor—of finance and its politicos and scribblers of all colors and stripes.

---

11   Ibid., pp. 36, 40.

12   [A reference to the Mexican poet Javier Sicilia, whose son was murdered by organized crime in 2011. Sicilia was among the most prominent organizers of the subsequent wave of nationwide protests against the violence and impunity of Mexico's "war on drugs."]

21

The Art of Storytelling

(2005)

Historians often speak of themselves as craftsmen. They are linked to craft by their flair for following traces, finding clues, gathering evidence, and subjecting these to a form of critique similar to that practiced by the carpenter on his wood and the weaver on his yarns. Marc Bloch called himself an artisan, close to his working materials and resistant to the speculative generalization that characterizes other fields of knowledge. "Among the specters which a wrong understanding of the past raises along our path, and which a more precise knowledge exorcises, I would give first place to false analogies."[1] One of these simple exorcisms lies in the artisan's respect for the material with which he works.

The theses in *On the Concept of History* went through lengthy maturation in Walter Benjamin's earlier work. Ideas in those theses, even entire paragraphs, appeared in his writings of the 1930s, including "The Story-teller: Reflections on the Works of Nikolai Leskov" (1936) and "Eduard Fuchs: Collector and Historian" (1937).[2] In what follows, I will attempt to tease out some of the strands that intertwine in the theses.

---

1 Marc Bloch, *Histoire et historiens*, texts gathered by Étienne Bloch (Paris: Armand Colin, 1995), pp. 36, 33. The resources the researcher mobilizes in this artisanal aspect of his work are addressed in Carlo Ginzburg's classic study "Clues: Roots of an Evidential Paradigm," in *Clues, Myths, and the Historical Method*, trans. John and Anne Tedeschi (Baltimore: Johns Hopkins University Press, 1989), pp. 87–113.

2 Walter Benjamin, "The Storyteller," in *Illuminations*, trans. Harry Zohn (London: Fontana, 1973), pp. 83–109, and Benjamin, "Eduard Fuchs: Collector and Historian," in *One-Way Street and Other Writings,* trans. Edmund Jephcott and Kingsley Shorter (London and New York: Verso, [1979] 1997), pp. 349–86.

Cℛ

Building on a lapidary paragraph by Paul Valéry, Benjamin asserts in "The Storyteller" that in the craftsman, "soul, eye, and hand are brought into connection . . . That old coordination of the soul, the eye, and the hand . . . is that of the artisan which we encounter wherever the art of storytelling is at home." We may even wonder, he continues, "whether the relationship of the storyteller to his material, human life, is not in itself a craftsman's relationship, whether it is not his very task to fashion the raw material of experience, his own and that of others."[3]

In his posthumous work of 1942, *Apologie pour l'histoire* [translated as *The Historian's Craft*], Marc Bloch claimed for historical knowledge the same primacy of experience and wisdom proper to working hands: "one may feel with words as well as with fingers."[4]

The historian, a craftsman as he sees himself, both is and is not a storyteller. He is not a storyteller in so far as the latter, telling stories by the fire, does not have to offer proof for anything he says; he needs only to claim that he knows a thing firsthand or through the experiences relayed to him by others. Such points of reference are very different from those that the historian must adduce. But the historian is nevertheless a craftsman, insofar as he, too, transmits and recounts in the present ("the present is our closest fragment of the past," said Bloch) a bygone human experience that he has reconstructed by means of another artisanal art, that of the tracker or sleuth, uncovering those scant or plentiful traces of the past that can still be found if you know how to look. The researcher is a man whose task still requires that old coordination of soul, eye, and

---

3 Benjamin, "The Storyteller," p. 108.
4 There is no less beauty in a precise equation than in a felicitous phrase, but each science has its appropriate aesthetics of language. Human actions are essentially very delicate phenomena, many aspects of which elude mathematical measurement. Properly to translate them into words and, hence, to fathom them rightly (for can one perfectly understand what he does not know how to express?), great delicacy of language and precise shadings of verbal tone are necessary. Where calculation is impossible we are obliged to employ suggestion. Between the suggestion of physical and of human realities, there is as much difference as between the task of a drill operator and of a lutemaker: both work down to the last millimetre, but the driller uses precision tools, while the lutemaker is guided primarily by his sensitivity to sound and touch. It would be unwise either for the driller to adopt the empirical methods of the lutemaker or for the lutemaker to imitate the driller. Will anyone deny that one may feel with words as well as with fingers?

(Marc Bloch, *The Historian's Craft*, trans. Peter Putnam
[Manchester: Manchester University Press, 1992], pp. 22–3.)

hand. And once he has found the fragments and, through them, an image of that past, he has no option but to tell its story.

This is where he becomes a storyteller, one of the most ancient trades on earth.

"Experience which is passed on from mouth to mouth is the source from which all storytellers have drawn. And among those who have written down the tales, it is the great ones whose written version differs least from the speech of the many nameless storytellers," writes Benjamin.[5] And among those anonymous narrators, he continues, two groups constantly overlap. One is the sedentary tiller of the soil, who has lived and heard much. The other is the trading seaman, who has traveled much. One knows the tales and traditions of his parish, the other brings news of far-flung lands. These archetypes give rise to two kinds of storytellers.

And yet the art of storytelling

in its full historical breadth is inconceivable without the most intimate interpenetration of these two archaic types . . . If peasants and seamen were past masters of storytelling, the artisan class was its university. In it was combined the lore of faraway places, such as a much-traveled man brings home, with the lore of the past, as it best reveals itself to natives of a place.[6]

In this way, the art of storytelling found its first masters in those who work with their hands.

The historical researcher, for his part, is faced with a specific exigency of his trade, a trade not solely concerned with storytelling. Benjamin demands a spiritual commitment from him: to "renounce a calm, contemplative attitude toward its subject to become aware of the critical constellation in which precisely this fragment of the past is found with precisely this present." In other words, he asks him to bring about "an engagement with history original for every present." Historical materialism, he writes, "has recourse to a consciousness of the present that shatters the continuum of history. [It] conceives historical understanding as an afterlife of that which is understood, whose pulse can still be felt in the present."[7]

---

5 Benjamin, "The Storyteller," p. 84.
6 Ibid., p. 85.
7 Benjamin, "Eduard Fuchs," pp. 351, 352.

An afterlife of the past in the present: if that is so, Benjamin explains, the object of future historical knowledge is not "a tangle of purely factual details but . . . the numbered group of threads that represent the weft of the past as it feeds into the warp of the present." It would be a mistake, he argues, to "equate this weft with the mere nexus of causation. Rather, it is thoroughly dialectical, and threads may have been lost for centuries that the present course of history erratically, inconspicuously picks up again."[8]

During the thirties of the last century, that course had taken an appalling turn. A shrewd and subtle adept of the writings of Marx, the inhuman logic of capital, and the ascent in Europe of a barbarism dressed up as technical progress, Benjamin noted the following:

> The questions which mankind asks of nature are determined among other things by its level of production. This is the point where positivism breaks down. In the development of technology, it saw only the progress of science, not the retrogression of society. It overlooked the fact that capitalism has decisively conditioned that development.

Thus was consummated in the nineteenth century a fact that would define the future: "the defective reception of technology." This reception took place via a series of conceptions that all strove "to get round the fact that technology serves this society solely for the production of commodities."[9]

Benjamin continues his pitiless diagnosis of his century, the twentieth, which once was ours:

> It may fairly be wondered whether the *Gemütlichkeit* [cheerful coziness] in which the [nineteenth] century's bourgeoisie rejoiced may not stem from a vague satisfaction at never having to experience at first hand the development of the forces of production. That experience was really reserved for the following century. It is discovering that traffic speeds, like the capacity to duplicate both the spoken and the written word, have outstripped human needs. The energies that technology develops beyond their threshold are destructive. They serve primarily to foster the technology of warfare, and of the means used to prepare public opinion for war.[10]

---

8   Ibid., p. 362.
9   Ibid., pp. 357–8.
10 Ibid., p. 358.

That lucid historical reason was to nourish his writing throughout the tragic decade that encompassed the crisis of 1929, the parallel rise of Fascism, Nazism and Stalinism, the defeat of the Spanish Revolution in which all three converged, and the start of World War II in 1939. On the threshold of this catastrophe, between 1938 and 1939, his writing was animated by what he called "the courage of desperation": "the knowledge that tomorrow could bring destruction on such a scale that yesterday's texts and creations might seem as distant from us as centuries-old artifacts."[11]

In 1940, that consciousness flashed through the last two gestures of his soul and hand: his theses in *On the Concept of History* and his death in Port Bou; dark lightning flashes that seem to illuminate the violent times that would follow in the century to come.

The unmatched violence of the twentieth century did more than incubate that of these times we are entering upon. It also instilled creativity and brought a wealth of experience as regards resistance, organization, and thought. It brought experience in imagining and practically realizing life's meaning and significance in ways different or contrary to the reified barbarity of the universal kingdom of merchandise, to the "dependence on objects" as the raison d'être and founding moral principle of existence.

Experience means having confidence in one's strength. "In the long run, without self-confidence, no class can engage in political action with any success," Benjamin wrote.[12] In our time, this means the boundless class of those oppressed, dispossessed, exploited, and humiliated by the present inhuman configuration of the world. However, he added, to trust one's own capacity for action is one thing, another is optimism about the conditions in which the action will take place: confidence in the lived vs. confidence in the instituted, we might say. The latter optimism is the most groundless and problematic: "the prospects of incipient barbarism, which had dawned on Engels in his *Condition of the Working Class in England* and on Marx in his predictions of the course of capitalist development," continues Benjamin, was unimaginable for social-democratic minds of the late nineteenth and early twentieth centuries.[13] Since they had not seen from their lofty metropoles the barbarity of colonialism,

11   Walter Benjamin, "Commentary on Poems by Brecht," in *Selected Writings, Vol. 4: 1938–1940*, trans. Edmund Jephcott et al. (Cambridge, MA: Belknap Press, 2003), pp. 215–16.

12   Benjamin, "Eduard Fuchs," p. 371.

13   Ibid.

World War I and everything that followed came crashing down on their calm and unsuspecting heads.

Barbarism and senselessness do not threaten the current city of capital from outside its walls, and its emblem and coat of arms are not the skyscrapers of Wall Street but the five ramparts of the Pentagon. The barbarism comes from within those ramparts and their financial out- skirts and is spilling out across the whole world.

From the other side, no institution contains it. What opposes it instead, diffuse and borderless, is human experience, that "critical constellation in which precisely this fragment of the past is found with precisely this present," that exact group of threads of the past woven into the fabric of the present. It is here that the self-confidence of the subaltern classes is revealed and, in times of violence, becomes a material force; for it is a confidence handed down through the events of multiple histories in the voices of their chroniclers, trackers, travelers, troubadours, and storytellers.

Note on the Text and Acknowledgments

The translation of these essays was made possible by grants from the Center for Latin American and Caribbean Studies (CLACS) at New York University and the Program in Latin American Studies (PLAS) at Princeton, and by the generous support, via the Toledo Translation Fund, of the following individuals: Sinclair Thomson, John Coatsworth, Samuel Farber and Selma Marks, Gilbert Joseph, and Michelle Chase. The editor is extremely grateful to all the above for their crucial contributions, in particular to Sinclair Thomson for his invaluable advice and support throughout this project. This book would also not have been possible without the skilled and patient work of its translator, Lorna Scott Fox, and the editorial team at Verso.

The essays in this volume were selected from across Adolfo Gilly's remarkable oeuvre; almost all of them are being published in English for the first time. Details of the original publication venues for each chapter are given below.

PART I. WITNESSING REVOLUTION

1. Cuba in October: published as "Inside the Cuban Revolution" in *Monthly Review*, vol. 16, no. 6, October 1964; extracts reprinted here with the kind permission of *Monthly Review*.

2. Chile: A Day with Allende: translated from "Una jornada con Allende," in Adolfo Gilly, *Por todos los caminos: Escritos sobre América Latina, 1956–1982*, vol. 1 (Mexico City: Editorial Nueva Imagen, 1983).

3. The Guerrilla Movement in Guatemala: published in *Monthly Review*, vol. 17, no. 1, May 1956 and vol. 17, no. 2, June 1965; extracts reprinted here with the kind permission of *Monthly Review*.

4. Camilo Torres, The Forerunner: translated from "Camilo Torres, el precursor," originally published in *La Jornada*, February 15, 2016.

5. A Political Defense: translated from "Defensa política," in Gilly, *Por todos los caminos*.

6. Nicaragua and Bolivia: Two Paths: translated from "Nicaragua y Bolivia: dos caminos," in Gilly, *Por todos los caminos*.

PART II. CLANDESTINE HISTORIES

7. Mexico: Subaltern Civilization: translated from "México: la civilización subalterna," in Adolfo Gilly, *Historia a contrapelo: Una constelación* (Mexico City: Ediciones Era, 2006).

8. A Certain Idea of Mexico: delivered at the seminar "Lázaro Cárdenas: A Model, a Legacy" at the Instituto Nacional de Estudios Históricos de la Revolución Mexicana, Mexico City, in June 2002; originally published as "Una cierta idea de México," in Adolfo Gilly, *Historias clandestinas* (Mexico City: La Jornada Ediciones, 2009).

9. The Indigenous Army and the Mexican State: lecture delivered at the conference "State, Class, Ethnicity, and Gender in Latin America," at the Universidad Mayor de San Simón, Cochabamba, Bolivia, June 4–5, 1999; epilogue written in August 2002. First published as "El ejército indígena y el Estado mexicano," in María L. Lagos and Pamela Calla, eds., *Antropología del Estado: Dominación y prácticas contestatarias en América Latina* (La Paz: INDH/PNUD, 2007).

10. A Twenty-First-Century Revolution: originally published as "Bolivia, una revolución del siglo XXI," in Gilly, *Historias clandestinas*.

11. Intermittent Insurrections: presented on January 3, 2009 at the Festival de la Digna Rabia (Festival of Dignity in Rage), San Cristóbal de las Casas, Chiapas, convened by the EZLN; published as "Las insurrecciones intermitentes," in Gilly, *Historias clandestinas*.

PART III. BETWEEN PAST AND FUTURE

12. Bolivia Fifty Years On: edited transcript of an interview conducted in New York City in May 2003 by Sinclair Thomson and Seemin Qayum; originally published as "Ahora que lo pienso, cincuenta años después …" in Gilly, *Historias clandestinas*.

13. Destinies of a Revolution: first published in Adolfo Gilly, *El Siglo del relámpago: Siete ensayos sobre el siglo XX* (Mexico City: Editorial Itaca, 1992); this text is translated from a revised version, "Los destinos de una revolución," published in a special supplement to *La Jornada*, October 17, 2017.

14. Ernest Mandel: Memories of Oblivion: published as "Ernest Mandel: recuerdos del olvido," in Adolfo Gilly, *Pasiones cardinales* (Mexico City: Cal y Arena, 2001).

15. Globalization, Violence, Revolutions: published as "Globalización, violencia, revoluciones," in Gilly, *El Siglo del relámpago*.

16. Lawless Planet: text delivered at the opening plenary session of Left Forum at Cooper Union in New York City in March 2007; published as "Planeta sin ley," in Gilly, *Historias clandestinas*.

17. The Emerging "Threat" of Radical Populism: first published in *NACLA Report on the Americas*, vol. 39, no. 2, Sept–Oct 2005; reprinted here with the permission of Taylor and Francis.

PART IV. POLITICS AND LETTERS

18. Star and Spiral: Octavio Paz, André Breton, and Surrealism: first published as "Estrella y espiral: Octavio Paz, André Breton y el surrealismo," in José Antonio Aguilar Rivera, ed., *Aire en libertad: Octavio Paz y la crítica* (Mexico City: Fondo de Cultura Económica – Centro de Investigación y Docencia Económicas, 2015).

19. Deep Rivers: José María Arguedas, Mario Vargas Llosa, and Papacha Oblitas: presented at the conference "Literature and Nationalism in Latin America at the End of the Twentieth Century," at Georgetown University, Washington, DC, April 6, 1999; originally published as "José María Arguedas, Mario Vargas Llosa y el Papacha Oblitas," in *Argumentos*, no. 50, Universidad Autónoma Metropolitana–Xochimilco (Jan–Apr 2006), pp. 99–114.

20. **"Whiteness," Modernity, Humiliation**: delivered at the international colloquium on "Modernity and Resistances," Homage to Bolívar Echeverría, at the Faculty of Philosophy and Letters, National Autonomous University of Mexico, September 2011; first published as *"Blanquitud, modernidad, humillación,"* in Adolfo Gilly and Rhina Roux, *El tiempo del despojo: Siete ensayos sobre un cambio de época* (Mexico City: Editorial Itaca, 2015).

21. **The Art of Storytelling**: originally published as "El arte de narrar," in Gilly, *Historia a contrapelo.*

Index